The sceptical realism of David Hume

When we question whether the underlying object is such as it appears, we grant the fact that it appears, and our doubt does not concern the appearance itself but the account given of that appearance – and that is a different thing from questioning the appearance itself.

– Sextus Empiricus, *Outlines of Pyrrhonism*

If I examine the PTOLOMAIC and COPERNICAN systems, I endeavour only, by my enquiries, to know the real situation of the planets; that is, in other words, I endeavour to give them, in my conception, the same relations, that they bear towards each other in the heavens. To this operation of the mind, therefore, there seems to be always a real, though often an unknown standard, in the nature of things; nor is truth or falsehood variable by the various apprehensions of mankind. Though all human race should for ever conclude, that the sun moves, and the earth remains at rest, the sun stirs not an inch from his place for all these reasonings; and such conclusions are eternally false and erroneous.

– Hume, 'The Sceptic'

We of the Academy are not people who will accept *nothing* as true. But we do hold that every true perception has in it an admixture of falsehood so similar to the truth that we have no certain criterion of judgement and assent. It follows that we can attain only to a number of probable truths, which although they cannot be proved as certainties, yet may appear so clear and convincing that a wise man may well adopt them as a rule of life.

– Cicero, *The Nature of the Gods*

We are so much persuaded of the truth of this our Hypothesis, that we have employ'd one of our Members, a great Virtuoso at Nuremberg, to make a sort of an Hydraulic Engine, in which a chemical liquor resembling Blood, is driven through elastic chanels resembling arteries and veins, by the force of an Embolus like the heart, and wrought by a pneumatic Machine of the nature of the lungs, with ropes and pullies, like the nerves, tendons and muscles: And we are persuaded that this our artificial Man will not only walk, and speak, and perform most of the outward actions of the animal life, but (being wound up once a week) will perhaps reason as well as most of your Country Parsons.

– Arbuthnot & Pope, *The Memoirs of Martinus Scriblerus*

John P. Wright

The sceptical realism
of David Hume

University of Minnesota Press
Minneapolis

Copyright © 1983 by John P. Wright

Published by the University of Minnesota Press,
2037 University Avenue Southeast, Minneapolis MN 55414

Printed in Great Britain

ISBN 0-8166-1223-4
       0-8166-1224-2 paperback

Contents

Preface

A consideration of the main headings and sub-headings listed in my Table of Contents and of the summaries in the introductions to each chapter should make clear the overall structure of the argument. Throughout the book my central aim has been to explain and develop my interpretation of Hume's philosophy as clearly and simply as possible: for this reason I have been compelled to relegate much of the historical background and subsidiary argument to the notes which appear at the end of each chapter. At the same time, these notes contain material which is required to evaluate that interpretation properly. I hope that the reader will freely consult the notes on specific issues.

A study like this cannot be carried out without the support of others. Above all, this book would not have existed without the constant intellectual encouragement and criticism, over many years, of John Yolton and Rena Wright. I must also thank Michael Ayers, George Davie, Roger Emerson, Tom Lennon, Patrick Maynard, Robert McRae, Patrick Nowell-Smith, Douglas Patey, Terence Penelhum, and David Raynor – each of whom has contributed in a particular way to my work on Hume. Special thanks go to M. A. Stewart and the press readers who have made valuable suggestions which have improved the final product.

A first draft of this book was written in Edinburgh in 1973–4, during which time I held a British Council Research Grant. Since that time I have held postdoctoral fellowships from the Canada Council Killam Foundation, the Hannah Foundation for the History of Medicine, and the William Andrews Clark Memorial Library in Los Angeles: these have given me the opportunity to rewrite the whole at the same time as I worked on a related project in the history of seventeenth- and eighteenth-century medical psychology. I must thank the Department of the History of Medicine and Science at the University of Western Ontario which has provided a congenial base of operation over the past three and a half years while I completed my work.

Unless otherwise indicated all translations from the French in this book are my own.

Piscataway, New Jersey

Abbreviations

Works by other authors

Dictionary	*The Dictionary Historical and Critical of Mr Peter Bayle*, translated and edited by P. Des Maizeaux. References are given by volume and page number.
Popkin, *Selections*	Pierre Bayle, *Historical and Critical Dictionary: Selections*, translated and edited by R. H. Popkin and C. Brush.
Principles	George Berkeley, *A Treatise concerning the Principles of Human Knowledge*. References are given by part and section number in the collected edition by A. A. Luce and T. E. Jessop.
A.T.	*Oeuvres de Descartes*, edited by C. Adam and P. Tannery (new edition). References are given by volume and page number.
H.R.	*The Philosophical Works of Descartes*, translated by E. S. Haldane and G. R. T. Ross. References are given by volume and page number.
Essay	John Locke, *An Essay concerning Human Understanding*. References are given by book, chapter and section number to the edition by P. H. Nidditch.
R./*Recherche*	Nicolas Malebranche, *De la Recherche de la Vérité*. References are given by volume and page number to the edition by G. Rodis-Lewis in the collected edition of *Oeuvres de Malebranche*.

Introduction

A brief look at the competing present-day interpretations of
Hume's philosophy will leave the uninitiated reader completely
baffled. On the one hand, Hume is seen as a philosopher who
attempted to analyse concepts with something of the spirit of
twentieth-century writers of analytic philosophy.[1] On the other
hand, he is regarded as a philosopher whose importance lay in
the fact that he recommended 'an empirically based description
and explanation of human actions, thoughts and feelings'.[2] On
the first view Hume presumes that 'people are, as it were,
bodiless collocations of experiences'.[3] On the second, Hume's
theory regards 'every aspect of human life as naturalistically
explicable. It places man squarely within the scientifically
intelligible world of nature, and thus conflicts with the traditional
conception of a detached rational subject'.[4] On the first
interpretation Hume reduces objective causation to a constant
conjunction of experiences and our belief in necessity to a
subjective feeling of expectation.[5] On the second view it is said
that he never attempted to justify a 'uniformity view of
causation': rather, in Hume's discussions objective 'causal
agency – power, efficacy, determination – is presupposed
throughout'.[6] The examples may be multiplied: the main
competing interpretations of his philosophy appear to be entirely
incompatible.

We may dub these two interpretations 'sceptical' and 'realist'.
On the sceptical interpretation Hume's aim is to show what
conceptions of man and the world can be constructed out of ideas
based entirely on our sense-data. Many who have interpreted

Hume in this way have seen him as a self-defeating sceptic who has shown the impossibility of arriving at our ordinary conception of reality by such methods.[7] Others have thought that Hume *was* partially successful in showing how our ordinary conceptions can be derived from the data of the senses, and these writers merge his scepticism with a view called 'phenomenalism'.[8] On the realist interpretation, Hume's major aim is to discredit a 'rationalistic' conception of man as a being who is independent of the rest of nature. While Hume accepted something called the 'theory of ideas' from his predecessors, he 'concentrates on what must be added to it' in order to explain human belief and behaviour.[9] On this view Hume's *scepticism* appears only in those parts of his work where he shows an inadequate attachment to a *scientific* conception of man and reality.

There is no question but that both competing interpretations have some basis in Hume's own philosophical writings. This is apparent from the comments of some of Hume's own contemporaries who, while they considered the negative sceptical strain to be dominant in his philosophical writings, were nevertheless quick to acknowledge his realism. In his *Essays on the Principles of Morality and Natural Religion* (first edition, 1751) Henry Home, Lord Kames, criticised his claim that we have no idea of power. Kames quoted passages from both the *Treatise of Human Nature* and the *Philosophical Essays Concerning Human Understanding* (the work we now know as the *Enquiry Concerning Human Understanding*) in which Hume made the paradoxical claim that necessity is only a subjective feeling in the mind. Yet, Kames argued, Hume gives clear evidence against this view in a number of passages of the *Philosophical Essays* in which he talks of the *unknown powers* in objects.[10] The same point was made a few years later by John Leland in his *A View of the Principal Deistical Writers of the Last and Present Century* (second edition, 1755). In support of the claim that Hume often assumed an unknown power in the nature of things Leland, like Kames, cited a number of passages from the *Philosophical Essays*: but he also claimed that Hume presupposed the existence of causal powers in the *Treatise* when he argued against the Cartesian theory of occasional causes.[11] Moreover, Leland recognised that Hume attempted to ground the belief in causation in 'an *instinct*, or *mechanical tendency'*, and represented it as 'a necessary *act of the mind'*, which is *'infallible in its operations'*. However, Leland thought that Hume's scepticism predominated when he claimed that 'like *other instincts'*, this one *'may be fallacious and deceitful'* (p. 7).

Some interpreters of Hume's philosophy have thrown up their hands in despair and declared that there is absolutely no consistency in his philosophical writings. This seems to have been the intention of those writers of Hume's day who spoke of the frequent *paradoxes* in his writing.[12] In our own day John Passmore has declared that Hume was a philosopher who, unlike Berkeley, had no 'real concern for consistency': he 'was a philosophical puppy-dog, picking up and worrying one problem after another, always leaving his teeth-marks in it, but casting it aside when it threatened to become wearisome'.[13] However it is difficult to accept this solution. Hume himself clearly intended to write a 'System of Philosophy'[14] and had many opportunities – in the nine or so editions of the *Enquiry* which he prepared in his own lifetime – to make his philosophy more consistent. He did make a number of alterations in his text, but none of these suggests that he saw any incompatibility between the sceptical and realist sides of his philosophy. As the passages pointed out by Kames and Leland make clear, Hume's realist assumptions about the existence of unknown powers are more pronounced in the *Enquiry* than in the earlier *Treatise*.[15] However, in the later book, as well as the earlier, Hume clearly indicated his belief that we have no idea of the causal power in objects and that the idea which we have in its place is purely subjective.

In an attempt to provide a more sympathetic unified interpretation of Hume's philosophy many writers have seen their task as one of rescuing him from the negative sceptical consequences of his theory of ideas. I have already noted that many who see Hume's central problem as one of showing how we can construct our normal conceptions of reality out of our sense-derived ideas believe that he achieved some partial success. However these commentators tend to reconstruct Hume's text in order to show that he did not mean what he clearly said he did mean.[16] Hume is unequivocal in his claim that the analysis of our ideas will not lead us to form the belief in the existence of a substantial self, of objects which exist independently of knowers, of causation in objects. Writers of the realist school of interpretation claim that Hume's aim was merely to *supplement* his theory of ideas with a theory of natural beliefs. But this, too, is to fly in the face of textual evidence. Hume clearly believes that certain of his analyses of ideas (most obviously that of matter) would, if they could govern our practice, lead us to *reject* both our natural and our scientific beliefs. In general, a sympathetic understanding of Hume's own philosophy requires that one appreciate the fundamental opposition which he discovers between the results of the analysis of ideas on the one hand, and our instinctive or natural judgements on the other.

It is important to understand that scepticism is a philosophical attitude which is self-consciously adopted by Hume. In this book I attempt to throw new light on Hume's sceptical arguments by placing them in the context of the philosophy of his own day. I argue that Hume's own analyses of the ideas of space and time, matter, and causality become more intelligible when they are seen against the background of the analyses of these ideas presented by Bale, Descartes, Berkeley and Malebranche – writers to whom Hume was indebted for his *metaphysical reasonings*. [17] We find that there is an important sense in which Hume did develop the negative consequences of a 'theory of ideas' which he inherited from his predecessors. [18] It is on this basis that he argues that we have no ideas of absolute space and time, [19] matter, and causal powers. We have no ideas connected with the fundamental principles which underlie experimental science.

At the same time it is important to recognise that Hume himself never adopted the Cartesian principle that our ideas must form the basis of our beliefs about external existence. John Leland noted that, in his discussion of the Cartesian theory of occasional causes, Hume 'seems to censure it as a wrong way of arguing, to deny that a thing is, because we cannot distinctly conceive the manner how it is; or to make our ignorance of any thing a sufficient reason for rejecting it'. [20] I argue that the principle which Leland has identified is a general one which lies at the root of Hume's own philosophical system. Hume's principle allows one to retain a substantial notion of reality in spite of the contrary evidence of ideas. We shall see that an essential part of his own mitigated or academical scepticism lies in the claim that our ideas are *inadequate* representations of reality.

I argue that a central aim of Hume's philosophy of the understanding is to show that we retain commerce with a world of independent objects through a species of *natural judgements*, which involve a systematic confusion of ideas. These natural judgements lie at the root of all perception and experience, and cause us to ascribe properties to objects which do not belong to the sense-derived ideas which represent them.[21] Hume's attempt to ground such judgements in the faculty which he calls *imagination* is bound up with his acceptance of current theories concerning their neurological and biological basis. I argue that it is in the context of these theories that we must understand the project announced in the Introduction to Hume's *Treatise of Human Nature* – that of founding the other sciences on the science of human nature.

In order to appreciate the nature of Hume's realism we must practise that willing suspension of disbelief which stands at the root of all genuine philosophical understanding. We must not approach his text with a set of preconceptions about what constitutes a philosophical problem, and slough off the rest as outdated science. In the following pages I have attempted to discover Hume's own philosophical views through a careful examination of the scientific paradigm within which he himself operated. I have tried to dispense with the preconceptions which often go with the words 'empiricism' and 'rationalism' – preconceptions which, it seems to me, hamper our genuine philosophical understanding of the past.[22] When I examine Hume's writings against the views of his predecessors I attempt to determine just what he accepted and what he rejected in their thought.

I argue that while Hume rejected the Cartesian methods of reaching conclusions about the nature of reality – at least in so far as they were used to support the theodicies of Malebranche and Berkeley – his own science of human nature should be understood in the context of the Cartesian conception of man. Unfortunately that conception has become distorted in contemporary philosophy through a rather selective reading of Descartes' own texts.[23] A popular eighteenth-century understanding of that conception is vividly portrayed in the following excerpt from a play called *Three Hours After Marriage* written by John Gay, Alexander Pope, and John Arbuthnot. The opening speech is given by Dr Fossile, who intends to test the virginity of the women surrounding his supposedly chaste wife:

Foss.: Give ear, all ye virgins: We make proclamation in the name of the chaste Diana, being resolv'd to make a solemn essay of the virtue, virginity, and chastity of all within our walls. We therefore advise, warn and precaution all spinsters, who know themselves blemish'd, not on any pretence whatsoever to taste these our drops, which will manifest their shame to the world by visible tokens.
. . .
1st Wom.: I never take physick.
Foss.: That's one. Stand there. My niece professes herself a Platonick. You are rather a Cartesian.
Clink: Ah dear uncle! How do the Platonicks and Cartesians differ?
Foss.: The Platonicks are for idea's, the Cartesians for matter and motion.[24]

The view that the Cartesians had presented a conception of man as consisting of 'matter and motion' is an accurate one. I have argued elsewhere that Cartesian psychology was conceived almost entirely in mechanistic terms.[25] In the present study I argue that the whole role of *imagination* in Hume's own philosophy of human nature suggests his attachment to a number of details of the Cartesian mechanist conception of psychological processes.

However, I have been forced to conclude that some of those writers who interpret Hume as a realist are entirely mistaken when they suggest that he rejects *reason* as a faculty which is autonomous from the *imagination*.[26] In this respect, too, it is useful to consider Hume as a philosopher who adopted a modified Cartesian conception of man. It is true that he sought to show that the roots of our beliefs about the real world lie in the automatic responses of the imagination. At the same time, he clearly believed that these responses are not *sufficient* to establish the reasoning processes which underlie experimental science. Kant was right when he described Hume's concept of causality as a 'bastard of imagination, impregnated by experience'.[27] However, Hume also believed that, in spite of these rather questionable origins, the causal inferences of experimental science are adopted and respectably nurtured by Reason herself. We shall see that throughout his writings on the understanding Hume contrasts the automatic processes of the imagination with the reflective processes of reason. Moreover, as we have already suggested, *reason* plays a fundamental role in the whole sceptical side of Hume's philosophy.

A great deal has been written, much of it not very profound, about the relationship of Hume's ideas to the Newtonian philosophy of his day. I argue that Hume began seriously to consider that relationship only in the mid-1740s after he had completed his *Treatise of Human Nature*. In order to make that relationship clear I have focused on the central issues which underlie Hume's dispute with John Stewart who was the Newtonian professor of Natural Philosophy at the University of Edinburgh in the early 1750s. I also show how Hume's posthumously published *Dialogues Concerning Natural Religion* can throw light on his position on some major issues which were of central concern to British natural philosophers in the eighteenth century.

My central aim throughout is to understand the epistemology and metaphysics espoused by Hume himself. I try to show how scepticism and realism combine to form a unified philosophical system which, whatever its limitations, presents a coherent and fascinating picture of man and nature and the relations between them.

Notes

1 See, for example, A. Flew, *Hume's Philosophy of Belief*, p. 12 and p. 16.
2 B. Stroud, *Hume*, p. 245. On pp. 6–7 of his book, Stroud states his clear objections to the view that Hume can be approached as if he were an analytic philosopher.
3 A. Flew, *Hume's Philosophy of Belief*, p. 5.
4 B. Stroud, *Hume*, p. 13.
5 See §13 below for a discussion of this interpretation of Hume's views on causality.
6 N. Kemp Smith, *The Philosophy of David Hume*, p. 393. B. Stroud rejects this aspect of Kemp Smith's naturalist (i.e. realist) interpretation of Hume: see *Hume*, p. 146, lines 22–4, for a clear statement of Stroud's own view. I do not understand why Stroud

sees an asymmetry between Hume's discussion of the cause of belief in an external world (where he clearly presupposes external existence throughout) and his discussion of the cause of belief in necessity.

7   H. A. Prichard, *Knowledge and Perception*, pp. 174ff. Prichard's view is essentially that expressed in T. H. Green's massive 'General Introduction' to his edition of Hume's *Philosophical Works*.

8   H. H. Price, *Hume's Theory of the External World*.

9   B. Stroud, *Hume*, esp. p. 9.

10   Henry Home, Lord Kames, *Essays on the Principles of Morality and Natural Religion*, second edition, pp. 230–2.

11   John Leland, *A View of the Principal Deistical Writers that have appeared in England in the Last and Present Century*, volume 2, pp. 10–11. The passages from *Philosophical Essays* which Leland cites include many of those which I have discussed in §§1 and 2.

12   See, for example, the review of the *Treatise* in the *Bibliothèque Raisonnée*, April-May-June 1740, quoted in E. C. Mossner, *The Life of David Hume*: 'His paradoxes favour Pyrrhonism and lead to consequences that the author appears to disown' (p. 128). This review was probably written by Pierre Desmaizeaux.

13   J. Passmore, *Hume's Intentions*, pp. 87–8.

14   Letter to Pierre Desmaizeaux, 6 April, 1739, H.L. I, 29. Cf. T. 455 and R. F. Anderson, *Hume's First Principles*, pp. xi-xii.

15   In general, I do not believe there are any essential differences between the philosophy presented in the *Treatise* and that in the *Enquiry*. Hume officially disowned the *Treatise* in favour of the *Enquiry* in an Advertisement which he had prefaced to the latter work in the last year of his life (see E. 3 and E. C. Mossner, *The Life of David Hume*, Chapter 38). In the Advertisement Hume says that 'some negligences in his former reasoning and more in the expression' are corrected in the *Enquiry*. The Advertisement was intended as 'a compleat Answer to Dr Reid and to that bigotted, silly Fellow Beattie' (Letter to William Strahan, 26 October 1775, H.L. II, 301). Since Reid and Beattie had claimed that Hume's scepticism led to a complete subjectivism, it would make sense, for the reasons I have suggested, that Hume would want the *Enquiry* to speak for him. But I shall argue that realist assumptions are implicit throughout the *Treatise* itself. The advantage of the *Treatise*, for our purposes, is that it gives a clear indication of the nature of doctrines which are only described in an abstract way in the *Enquiry*. See also §8, below.

16   Cf. M. R. Ayers, 'Analytical philosophy and the history of philosophy', in Jonathan Rée, Michael Ayers, and Adam Westoby, *Philosophy and its Past*, pp. 47ff.

17   See the beginning of Chapter 3. Hume speaks of his own 'metaphysical reasonings' in his letter to Henry Home, 13 February 1739 (H.L. I, 26), where he says that if his principles were adopted, 'they would produce almost a total alteration in philosophy'.

18 However this is *not* the sense given to this claim by Hume's contemporary Thomas Reid (*Inquiry into the Human Mind*, Chapter 1, in *The Works of Thomas Reid, D.D.*, volume 1, pp. 97ff.; cf. my Chapter 2, n. 16 and Chapter 5, n. 31). Reid entirely distorted the theory of ideas by tying it to the claim that ideas are intermediate entities which stand between knowers and external objects. The essence of the theory lies in the claim that knowledge of reality must be based on the analysis of our idea-contents. *Hume* claimed that these contents cannot give us any idea of independency: but this is *not* the view of Descartes or Locke. See §§5 and 6.

19 When I speak of *absolute* space and time in the following study I refer to the view that space and time can exist apart from matter or things which change.

20 John Leland, *A View of the Principal Deistical Writers . . .*, volume 2, p. 11. Leland says that Hume's argument is against 'Malebranche, and the modern Cartesians, who deny all power and activity in second causes and ascribe all to God'; his analysis of Hume's argument is in accord with the one I present in §14. However, Leland thinks that Hume has not consistently adhered to the principle he adopts in opposition to the Cartesians.

21 This sentence describes the function of natural judgements from the external standpoint of a dualist ontology – the one which, I argue, is consistently adopted by Hume himself.

22 Consider a recent characterisation of empiricism: 'empiricism requires theories only to give a true account *of what is observable*, counting further postulated structure as a means to that end. In addition, empiricists have always eshewed the reification of possibility (or its dual necessity)' (B. Van Fraassen, *The Scientific Image*, p. 3). If I were to accept this definition of 'empiricism' I would be forced to conclude that Hume is *not* an empiricist in two essential respects.

23 For a good discussion of the eighteenth-century legacy of Cartesianism, see Aram Vartanian, *Diderot and Descartes*. In a letter in which Hume advises his friend Michael Ramsay to read Descartes' *Meditations* as well as other metaphysical books, he adds that he doesn't know if Ramsay will easily find a copy (see the letter I discuss at the beginning of Chapter 3). There is good reason to think that eighteenth-century English intellectuals did not interpret Cartesian philosophy through the abstruse metaphysics of the *Meditations*.

24 John Gay, Alexander Pope, John Arbuthnot, *Three Hours After Marriage*, pp. 179–80.

25 'Hysteria and mechanical man', *Journal of the History of Ideas*, 41 (1980), pp. 239ff.

26 It is this which most clearly distinguishes Hume's philosophy from that of Reid. See n. 78 to Chapter 5.

27 I. Kant, *Prolegomena to any Future Metaphysics*, pp. 5–6.

ONE

Hume's philosophy of scepticism

§1

It must certainly be allowed, that nature has kept us at a great distance from all her secrets, and has afforded us only the knowledge of a few superficial qualities of objects; while she conceals from us those powers and principles on which the influence of those objects entirely depends.

– Hume, *Enquiry*, pp. 32–3

§2

From circumstances and relations, known or supposed, [reason] leads us to the discovery of the concealed and unknown . . . [Its] standard . . . , being founded on the nature of things, is eternal and inflexible, even by the will of the Supreme Being.

– Hume, *Enquiry Concerning the Principles of Morals*, p. 294

§3

Nature, by an absolute and uncontroulable necessity has determin'd us to judge as well as to breathe and feel.

– Hume, *Treatise*, p. 183

§4

And it seems unreasonable to judge of the measures, embraced during one period, by the maxims which prevail in another.

– Hume, *History*: Charles I, chap. 3

Scepticism is generally identified as a thesis about the impossibility of human knowledge. However, the significance of this identification depends upon one's understanding of the term 'knowledge'. Many recent discussions in epistemology, particularly among North American writers, have centred on a definition of knowledge as justified true belief.[1] The sceptical denial of knowledge, as thus conceived, can be identified in three different ways: with the denial that certain beliefs can be justified, *1* with the denial that certain beliefs can be true, or with the denial *2* (or suspension) of certain beliefs as such. In order to reach an *3* understanding of the problem of scepticism as it appears in the philosophy of Hume we shall look at the sense in which he himself can be considered a sceptic in each of these ways. In each case we shall find it helpful to compare the major present-day concerns which fall under each of these conceptions with the concerns which troubled Hume. In each case we shall find that we have to make an important shift in our perspective in order to understand the problem of scepticism as it appears in the works of the eighteenth-century thinker.

§1   *Justification*

Questions of justification have played a central role in twentieth-century philosophical discussions of the theory of knowledge. The question of whether we can have knowledge in general, or knowledge of this or that kind, is commonly reduced to a question of whether we are *justified* in holding certain beliefs. To say that a man is justified in having a belief is to grant to him the *right* to be sure. This right is granted if his belief is up to *certain standards*. The 'sceptic' is thought of as a philosopher who denies that one can have knowledge, because he demands higher standards than most philosophers and ordinary people. For many, the legal and ethical terminology in these discussions suggests a certain arbitrariness. Thus the 'sceptic' appears to have no real dispute with the person who claims knowledge; he merely questions what standards to apply before someone is granted the right to believe.[2]

It is in this light that Hume has often been regarded as the paradigm of a philosophical sceptic. Like others of this sect Hume is supposed to be denying that certain beliefs can be justified. He is supposed to be denying our right to be sure about such matters as inductive inference, causal efficacy, and belief in an external world independent of our mind and its contents. At the same time Hume is interpreted as holding that our ordinary grounds of belief are the only possible ones, and as arguing that there is really nothing we do not know. Thus H. H. Price writes:

When the plain man insists that there are objective causal sequences which go on regardless of people's feelings and habits, he really only means that there are objective *constant conjunctions*; and here (Hume would say) I thoroughly agree with him.[3]

According to such accounts Hume 'reduces' causal connections to experienced conjunctions of events, causal efficacy to a subjective feeling of constraint, the external objects themselves to collections of experiences of a certain kind. D. G. C. Macnabb asserts that if anyone claims that there is something more we *do not know*, Hume aims to *persuade* him 'that he is asking for he knows not what, and induces him to be content with what he has already got'.[4] According to contemporary concepts and standards, then, it is an entirely arbitrary matter whether one conceives of Hume as a sceptic or not. There is nothing which, for him, is unknown.

This is wrong. In order to understand Hume's philosophy one must understand the exact basis of his sceptical denial of knowledge. An important place to begin is with the reminder that Hume is not interested in raising the question of the justification of ordinary persons' beliefs at all. Hume thinks that common-sense beliefs are *false* and are shown to be false by scientific investigation. For example, he thinks that ordinary people hold that there is chance in the universe. But for Hume, as well as many other eighteenth-century philosophers, 'what the vulgar call chance is nothing but a secret and conceal'd cause' (T.130). Moreover, according to him, men naturally believe that they directly perceive something which is external – that is, something which continues to exist while unperceived. This is a view that twentieth-century philosophers call direct or naïve realism. But Hume maintains that this view is false and can be shown to be false by a few simple experiments.[5] Thus for Hume the question of the *justification* of common-sense belief does not arise.

If Hume is denying the possibility of *justification* at all, it is primarily in relation to what he conceives to be the inferring procedures and fundamental beliefs of science itself. But here we must take a great deal of care over the term 'justification'. It is not at all clear that Hume denies our *right* to carry on with our scientific inferring procedures. His own words suggest that he did not. In the *Treatise* Hume writes that the relation of cause and effect is the only relation 'on which we can found a *just* inference from one object to another' (T.89). And in the *Enquiry* he says that he is willing to allow that propositions about future observations 'may *justly* be inferred' from those of past experience (E.34: in both quotations the italics are mine). Even a cursory reading of Hume's works indicates that he certainly advocates and employs the experimental method in science – at least as he understood that method. Yet it is obviously central to his philosophy to show that there is something lacking in our experimental or inductive inferences. Likewise, while it is seldom recognised by his commentators, Hume advocates and operates in terms of a belief in real physical causation and a representative theory of perception. He thinks that these are important ontological beliefs underlying science. Nevertheless, a central aim of his writings on the 'understanding' is to show that there is something lacking in these beliefs. It is tempting to say that Hume denies that they are justified. But again such a claim must be considered carefully, since Hume does not appear to be denying our *right* to hold such beliefs.

An important part of Hume's philosophical message is that science itself is not a completely self-justifying activity. What this means is that we cannot, merely through investigation of nature, come to establish the inferring procedures and the metaphysical beliefs which underlie science. But we must be careful not to confuse Hume's claims regarding the foundations of science with his beliefs about the nature of the activity of science itself. Generally Hume has been interpreted as holding of science itself what he holds of the foundations of science. Science for Hume is a reflective activity founded directly upon the reflective rules of the understanding. Hume's scepticism enters when he considers that such principles cannot themselves be entirely established by (what he thought of as) scientific method.

Hume thinks of science as more than a collecting of 'natural histories' of phenomena – as involving more than the discovery of 'what goes with what'. He thinks of science as a predictive activity – as telling what will go with what in the future. Hume holds that 'philosophers' or scientists (he frequently uses the term 'philosophy' where we should use the term 'science')[6] operate on the basis of the principle that '*like objects, plac'd in like circumstances, will always produce like effects*' (T.105). In fact, Hume maintains that by operating on this principle 'we may attain the knowledge of a particular cause merely by one experiment, provided it be made with judgment, and after a careful removal of all foreign and superfluous circumstances'.[7] He is even willing to admit that we have 'many millions' of experiments 'to convince us of this principle' (T.105). But Hume wants to stress that there is an aspect of this principle that is not the result of any investigation of nature, namely, the transition of the mind from the memory of past conjunctions to a belief in resembling future ones. He believes that the foundation for prediction is itself never discovered by empirical science. It is this belief which underlies what is commonly called Hume's inductive scepticism – the claim that no number of similar instances will provide a rational basis for predictions about the future. Hume bases this scepticism on the observation that there is no 'process of reasoning which, from one instance, draws a conclusion, so different from that which it infers from a hundred instances that are nowise different from that single one' (E.36). It will become clear that Hume retains the belief that any valid reasoning about the future would have to be based upon a genuine insight into the relation of cause and effect in at least one given case.[8] For Hume the problem of induction arises because 'we are ignorant of those powers and forces, on which this regular course and succession of objects totally depends' (E.55).

Hume conceives of science as more than a predictive activity based upon observation of past regularities. Science involves an active search for physical causes. Such a search begins precisely at the point where one discovers that a past regularity ceases to hold. We have observed that A has constantly been conjoined to B; then one day we find that A seems to occur and B does not occur. As we have noted, in such a case Hume thinks an ordinary unscientific person will attribute the change to an 'uncertainty in the causes' – that is, to chance. This is really where empirical science begins. Hume thinks of the scientist as operating according to certain principles which lead him to 'farther observation' (T.132, E.86–7). The scientist operates according to his belief that the cause may be hidden, but can be discovered. He searches for the differences in resembling antecedent events on the basis of the observation that 'almost in every part of nature there is contain'd a vast variety of springs and principles, which are hid, by reason of their minuteness or remoteness' (T.132, E.87). In doing so, the scientist assumes that *'whatever begins to exist, must have a cause of existence'* (T.78); and, even more specifically, that 'the difference in the effects of two resembling objects must proceed from that particular, in which they differ' (Rule 6, T.174). The scientifically-minded person shows the falsity of the common man's belief in chance by partially discovering the hidden causes. Hume even seems to have thought that natural philosophers reach the level of 'certainty' about the principle that every event has a cause:[9] this *certainty* is based upon the discovery that 'upon an exact scrutiny, a contrariety of effects always betrays a contrariety of causes, and proceeds from their mutual hindrance and opposition' (T.132, E.87).

The importance which Hume gives to *physical* explanations in science is seldom noted by his commentators.[10] Hume conceives the scientist's discovery on analogy with that of a clockmaker who, upon opening up the back of a clock which 'fails of its usual effect', finds 'a grain of dust, which puts a stop to the whole movement' (T.132, E.87). This analogy, which is common among many seventeenth- and eighteenth-century writers, indicates something important about their conception of just what the scientist is discovering. Throughout his writings Hume indicates that the search for something like mechanical explanations is an important part of the process of resolving 'the many particular effects into a few general causes' (E.30). In an important footnote to his *Enquiry* Hume praises Newton for putting forward a *physical hypothesis*, that of 'an etherial active fluid', to explain the phenomena of universal attraction; he chastens those who have attempted to establish a spiritual explanation on Newton's authority.[11] But it is not only in *natural* philosophy that Hume thinks physical explanation important. He seems to have thought that the search for something like the physical causes described in Cartesian psychophysiology[12] was directly relevant to his own activities as a *moral* philosopher. In his account 'Of the causes of belief' in the *Treatise*, the 'vigour and vivacity' of the action of the mind is bound up with the degree to which 'the spirits are more or less elevated' (T.98). Here he is making reference to a physical change in the *animal spirits*, the nervous fluids which were generally considered to be the immediate cause of most thinking and action. The causal explanation of the association of ideas is bound up with the way 'the animal spirits run into all the contiguous traces, and rouze up the other ideas, that are related to it'.[13] Of course Hume is careful to label all these accounts as speculative; it is fundamental to his method to reject at the outset 'any hypothesis, that pretends to discover the ultimate original qualities of human nature' (T.xvii). Nevertheless, these speculations give us an idea of just what underlies Hume's conception of human nature. Central Humean concepts like 'impression', 'propensity', or 'transition of the mind', have psychophysiological overtones that cannot be neglected in his accounts of the origins of our natural beliefs. In spite of his failure to discover any general causes in the *Treatise*, Hume still hoped that moral philosophers would be able to pursue their researches beyond a general distinction of mental faculties and 'discover, at least in some degree, the secret springs and principles, by which the human mind is actuated in its operations' (E.14). And in fact Hume held that the most probable explanations of the phenomena of human life have to do with 'the particular fabric and structure of the minute parts of [our] bodies and of external objects'.[14]

Despite these claims about physical causation Hume denied that he or his contemporaries had any adequate idea of such causation. They had no idea of the connection by which the cause produces the effect. Hume wanted to stress that our beliefs in causes are not derived from any *discoveries* we make about the causal process itself: he never tires of telling us that the 'ultimate springs and principles are totally shut up from human curiosity and enquiry' (E.30), that 'nature has kept us at a great distance from all her secrets, and has afforded us only the knowledge of a few superficial qualities of objects' (E.32–3), that 'the ultimate force and efficacy of nature is perfectly unknown to us' (T.159). Our ideas about 'what causes what' are not derived from an understanding of the causal process itself. At the same time it must be recognised that some accounts are closer to accounts of ultimate causation than others: 'Elasticity, gravity, cohesion of parts, communication of motion by impulse; these are probably the ultimate causes and principles which we shall ever discover in nature' (E.30). It is important to note that Hume holds that there is something there which is in principle discoverable and which, at the same time, we probably never will be able to discover. What ‖ is in question is not the existence of the hidden properties: 'We must certainly allow, that the cohesion of the parts of matter arises from natural and necessary principles, whatever difficulty we may find in explaining them' (T.401). What is in question is the exact nature of the ultimate causal principles and our degree of awareness of them.

In the light of such evidence it is difficult to understand why numerous commentators claim that Hume denies not only that we can have knowledge of ultimate causation but that there is any such thing as ultimate causation. For example, John Passmore writes that according to Hume 'it is not our incapacity which prevents us from discovering ultimate causes, but the fact that there are no such causes to discover'.[15] Perhaps part of the problem is the difficulty we have in accepting Hume's criterion for determining when we have reached the ultimate level of causation. Yet Hume is quite explicit about what knowledge of causation would be like. If we had such knowledge we would be able 'from a survey of these particular objects', that is, from a consideration of the particular objects which we consider cause and effect, to penetrate 'into their essences' and this would reveal 'the dependance of the one upon the other' (T.86). As we shall see in Chapter 4 Hume clearly attributes our lack of knowledge to a deficiency in our ideas. He assumes that knowledge has to be conceptual: it 'wou'd imply the absolute contradiction and impossibility of conceiving any thing different' (T.87). At the same time it is not trivial. Such knowledge would give us insight into a necessary connection which Hume identifies with the power or force of the cause: 'Were the power or energy of any cause discoverable by the mind, we could foresee the effect, even without experience' (E.63). Such knowledge would involve insight into the causal process itself. Clearly Hume thinks that there is something here that has not been revealed, and that probably never will be revealed.

A great deal of confusion arises because Hume is so often seen through the eyes of his successor and critic, Immanuel Kant. Where Hume denied that we have *knowledge*, Kant rejected the whole *ideal* of knowledge. The notions of reason and knowledge underwent an important shift in Kant's philosophy. He denied the ideal of *a priori* conceptual knowledge of reality: the idea that 'mere concepts' should embody knowledge of the world seemed wrong to him. In fact, Kant attacked Hume precisely on this point: that he did not provide a critique of reason itself. Kant asserted that Hume only considered the 'present bounds' of reason, not its necessary limits. He regarded Hume's employment of reason as *merely* sceptical.[16] It is true that Hume did have some important things to say about the limits of reason and philosophy. But he did not want to say these things, as Kant did, from the point of view of an examination of reason itself. He was concerned with consolidating what some of his important predecessors like Locke and Newton had been saying about the limits of knowledge.[17] But I think it is wrong to say, as do the many commentators who see him from a Kantian point of view, that Hume began a critique of *knowing* itself. Hume was concerned to state that there are many things of which we do not have knowledge. But this task presupposes that he did not set out to *change* what knowing is. Saying that you cannot discover something is very different from saying that you have misunderstood what discovering is. To understand this is to understand the difference between Hume's philosophy of scepticism and the phenomenalist philosophy of Kant.

In fact Kant seems to have been the first modern philosopher to have stressed questions of justification in talking about knowledge. Kant distinguished questions of the justification for applying or right to apply a certain concept to experience from questions concerning the *de facto* origination of the concept.[18] Kant thought that concepts like the concept of cause require a special sort of justification, because they have a kind of rule-like character which can lead beyond the bounds of any possible experience. He thought he could characterise the legitimate employment of such concepts by showing that they are a necessary condition for our having such a thing as experience of an objective world, a world distinguished from the subjective data of sense. Kant sharply distinguished this justificatory account of the concept from the account of the genesis of ideas which he found in authors like Hume. But from Hume's point of view it is important to recognise that Kant's account of the distinction between subjective data and external objects is made on a reflective conceptual level. The assumption that reflection alone can provide the basis for such a distinction was questioned by Hume.

Hume did believe that the scientific distinction between subjective and objective is made on a reflective level:

No man, who reflects, ever doubted, that the existences, which we consider, when we say, *this house* and *that tree*, are nothing but perceptions in the mind, and fleeting copies or representations of other existences, which remain uniform and independent. (E.152)

However, Hume claimed that this theory must have its origins in a non-reflective instinctive belief. He conceives the representative theory of perception as an important part of the foundations of science.[19] But Hume's stress is on the fact that this philosophic system of a double existence of perceptions and external objects cannot be established merely by reason, and that there is no way of independently showing that the perceptions supply us with information about the external objects. He argues that any discovery of the relation would depend upon our being able to compare the perceptions with the external objects; and since we can never be aware of anything but perceptions, no such comparison can be made (T.212). Thus once again we find Hume stressing the aspect of a scientific assumption that cannot itself be discovered. Nevertheless, he certainly seems to hold that perception does sometimes give information about external reality, and distinguishes those aspects of the world where we have adequate ideas (e.g., mathematics) from those in which we do not (e.g., causation). The formal distinction between 'perceptions' and independent objects is fundamental for an understanding of Hume's claim that we have no strict knowledge of causal relations (see pp. 86–90 and 155–6 below).

Thus it is too simple to say that Hume denied the justifiability of the inferring procedures and metaphysical beliefs which underlie science. He certainly *did* want to maintain that they cannot themselves be established entirely by means of reason and science. But he did not deny that they have a partial basis in scientific investigation; and he did not deny that we have a right to accept them. According to Hume, we lack real knowledge and insight into an objective world; but this claim is established quite independently of questions of justification. Questions of justification as they appear in Hume's own philosophy arise after the conclusion that we lack knowledge has been settled. As we shall see in §§8 and 20, Hume's attempts to provide a justification for our fundamental beliefs arise within the context of his own project of founding them on a science of human nature.

§2   *Truth*

There is a kind of scepticism, characteristic of ages such as our own, which involves us denying the possibility of objective truth. In fact this view may more justly be called 'relativism' rather than 'scepticism'. Relativism is the view that the world and our values are such that nothing both positive and universally true can be said about them. In this sort of scepticism the responsibility for the impossibility of truth is placed squarely on the shoulders of reality itself. Protagoras said that man is the measure of all things, implying that the standard of truth lies solely in man. Plato argued that this view led to the ontological thesis of Heracleitus and Empedocles that 'there is no being at all, but only perpetual becoming'.[20] Protagoras' view, as Plato understood it, combines the denial that there is any objective truth with the affirmation that all the standards of what we call truth are to be found in fluctuating and arbitrary cultural patterns.

One twentieth-century philosopher who frequently appears to express this form of scepticism is Ludwig Wittgenstein. In his later writings he stresses that any claim of truth and falsehood is meaningful only within the framework of a 'language game', and that language games themselves only express agreement in form of life:

'So you are saying that human agreement decides what is true and what is false?' – It is what human beings *say* that is true and false; and they agree in the *language* they use. This is not agreement in opinions but in form of life.[21]

Thus it seems that what underlies any claim concerning truth and falsehood is some concept formed within the context of a certain set of human activities. This has the result that the adoption of our scientific world-view can only be by a kind of persuasion:

I can imagine a man who had grown up in quite special circumstances and been taught that the earth came into being 50 years ago, and therefore believed this. We might instruct him: the earth has long . . . etc. – We should be trying to give him our picture of the world.
    This would happen through a kind of *persuasion*.[22]

This view seems to be an extension of a more widespread view of early twentieth-century positivist philosophers that it is wrong to think of a scientific explanation as telling us about a world more *real* than that of common sense.

I have found no evidence that relativism was ever adopted by Hume's contemporaries; he himself does not seriously entertain it. In his *Enquiry Concerning the Principles of Morals*, Hume writes that the operations of reason have a standard which 'being founded on the nature of things, is eternal and inflexible, even by the will of the Supreme Being' (E.M.294). In his essay, 'The Sceptic', Hume confidently *denies* that truth and falsehood are 'variable by the various apprehensions of mankind'. He continues:

Though all human race should for ever conclude, that the sun moves, and the earth remains at rest, the sun stirs not an inch from his place for all these reasonings; and such conclusions are eternally false and erroneous. (G.G. III, 218)

One could hardly find a clearer statement of scientific realism. In a similar spirit, on the opening page of his *Enquiry Concerning the Principles of Morals* Hume rejects out of hand those 'disingenuous disputants' who deny 'the reality of moral distinctions' (E.M.169). As we shall see in a moment, Hume's moral theory presupposes a set of moral standards which are universal for all human beings.

Hume's own stress upon the limited role of reason in founding our scientific activities can be easily misunderstood by twentieth-century philosophers, for his views certainly have a superficial similarity to those of important contemporary thinkers. We have already considered Hume's view that reason cannot form the foundation of our belief that our future experience of constant conjunction will resemble our past experience. On the positive side, however, Hume wants to stress that what leads us to make the inference is *custom*. In apparently similar tones Wittgenstein writes that while one can speak of something justifying our belief in so far as it comes up to 'a particular standard of good grounds', nevertheless, 'the standard has no grounds'. Presumably it is in accordance with a standard like that which states that objects frequently conjoined in the past will also be conjoined in the future that we are justified in thinking that the occurrence of a certain event after the occurrence of another is probable. Wittgenstein, like Hume, stresses that 'justification by experience comes to an end'. Further, Wittgenstein frequently makes the point that following a standard or principle involves following a custom. To obey a rule, he claims, *is* a custom. However, it is precisely in the different meanings that each philosopher assigns to the word 'custom' that we can mark the sharp divergence in their philosophies. For, by 'custom', Wittgenstein means 'uses, institutions' – something relative to the social practices of a given society.[23] In the passages I have been citing on probability, Wittgenstein stresses that justification exists only within the web of social life. Hume, on the other hand, conceives of custom as a principle of the human being as a natural organism. For Hume, custom is a cause, a cause whose nature is determined by his conception of the mechanical operations of the imagination. Custom is that which given 'the repetition of any particular act or operation' produces 'a propensity to renew the same act or operation, without being impelled by any reasoning' (E. 43). Strange as it may sound to us, Hume speaks of custom as 'a certain *instinct* of our nature' (E. 159; italics mine). Elsewhere, it is itself an 'instinct or *mechanical tendency*' which carries us along in our thinking and acting (E. 55; italics added). Similarly he speaks of 'the experimental reasoning itself, which we possess in common with beasts' as 'nothing but a species of instinct or mechanical power, that acts in us unknown to ourselves' (E. 108). (Hume contrasts this unreflective reasoning with reflective scientific experimental thinking. However, as we shall see, he holds that the criteria for reflective scientific thinking about causality have their roots in the natural mechanical principles of the human imagination. In §19 I shall consider the origin and significance of Hume's notion of custom as a mechanical power; in §20 I shall explain Hume's analysis of custom as an instinct.)

Now this distinction in the kind of account which these two thinkers give of causal inference makes their agreements regarding the limits of reason or justification look paltry indeed. Hume believes that while our inferences are not founded in reason, they do have a foundation in the natural organism. He puts forward a theory that our connections with reality are formed at a non-rational instinctive level. Wittgenstein, on the other hand, seems to want to say something about the grounding of inferences and beliefs in our social lives and activities, and our inability to put ourselves logically outside of this framework. *Meaning*, even scientific meaning, is bound up with social action for Wittgenstein. For Hume the world has an intrinsic intelligibility even though we have little access to it.

Again let us briefly consider Hume's stress upon the limits of the role of reason in moral action. Much stress has been laid by contemporary writers on Hume's comment that 'the distinction of vice and virtue is not founded merely on the relations of objects, nor is perceiv'd by reason' (T.470). Hume is often held to be the originator of the concept of the 'naturalistic fallacy', the claim that it is a logical mistake to pass from factual claims to claims about value. But in the hands of many important contemporary thinkers this principle is used to stress the voluntary nature of moral judgement – that any system of moral beliefs rests upon an arbitrary decision. A moral decision, it is argued, must fulfil certain formal criteria such as that of 'universalisability', but its content is determined by an absolute decision on the part of the agent. Now the point in Hume's ethical writings is very different. When he asks himself what, in the last analysis, is the basis upon which we attribute goodness or badness to people, or rightness or wrongness to action, his answer is always 'that this final sentence depends on some internal sense or feeling, which nature has made universal in the whole species' (E.M.173). The value which we attribute to things is not something personal – a result of arbitrary decision. Rather it lies in the natural organism itself. For example, speaking of the love of a parent for its helpless offspring, Hume writes that 'passion alone, arising from the original structure and formation of human nature, bestows a value on the most insignificant object'.[24]

That Hume conceives of both moral evaluation and experimental inference as having their origin in human nature should not disguise the fact that (according to him) the latter can overcome its parentage, while the former cannot. The moral sentiment which we feel in approving of some actions and disapproving of others lies only in the eye, or rather the mind, of the perceiver. Virtue is *'whatever mental action or quality gives to a spectator the pleasing sentiment of approbation;* and vice the contrary' (E.M.289). When we observe a situation which we morally approve, we feel a sentiment which has no objective reality apart from its universality in *human beings*. On the other hand, Hume considers custom as a principle by which a 'correspondence has been effected' between 'the course of nature and the succession of our ideas' (E.54–5). Observed constant conjunction of similar perceptual objects is the stimulus which brings about a union of ideas in our minds. But this union corresponds, at least in some degree, to the connections of cause and effect in reality. It is in the *correspondence* of our ideas to reality that this approximation to *truth* consists. Hume thinks of the kind of truth which concerns us here as lying in the 'conformity of our ideas of objects to their real existence'.[25] Thus custom is, as it were, a natural cause of truth, effecting a correspondence between the connections of our ideas and the real natures of things.

Hume speaks here of a 'pre-established harmony between the course of nature and the succession of our ideas' (E.54). To appreciate Hume's point it is important to understand that for him it is a merely contingent matter that the same causes are constantly operating in our experience. If they did not do so, we would simply have no belief in causation:

It seems evident that, if all the scenes of nature were continually shifted in such a manner that no two events bore any resemblance to each other, but every object was entirely new, without any similitude to whatever had been seen before, we should never, in that case, have attained the least idea of necessity, or of a connexion among these objects. (E.82)

Things would not cease to make one another happen on such a supposition; but we would not have any (subjective) idea or way of telling that they do.[26] Our belief in particular causes depends upon two factors: subjective affinity between ideas, brought about by the human organism when it has repeated experience of a conjunction of similar perceptual objects; and an objective (contingent) repetition of stimuli. But neither of these factors constitutes causation itself according to Hume. Our *belief* in causes is dependent upon contingent facts about the actual course of nature in the region of space-time which we inhabit, and corresponding facts about the human organism which make it associate ideas upon repeated experience.

Hume hypothesises that the natural processes of the human mind, when adhered to in a systematic way, bring us to a limited awareness of objective truth.[27] This hypothesis lies at the basis of his philosophy. He comes to think of natural and moral philosophy as involving 'the reflections of common life, methodized and corrected' (E.162). That is to say that he thinks of experimental science as deriving from the systematic and reflective application of natural principles. Natural principles even obtain thereby some sort of rational status.

Originally the constant conjunction of two events within our experience is not a *reason* for the belief in causation: it is an occasional cause of that belief. Constant conjunction is the stimulus which 'upon the appearance of one event' makes us 'expect its usual attendant' and 'believe that it will exist'. It also occasions a feeling of expectation and it is this feeling which is 'the sentiment or impression from which we form the idea of power or necessary connexion' (E.75). The constant conjunction does not give us any insight into the necessary connection; nor does the feeling of expectation amount to anything more than a natural sign of a process which is cognitively and semantically opaque to our limited understandings. We must form our definition of cause from 'something extraneous and foreign to it' (E.76). Thus the most objective definition we can obtain is drawn from a reflection upon the natural principles of the human understanding: 'We may define a cause to be *an object, followed by another, and where all the objects similar to the first are followed by objects similar to the second*' (E.76). A cause is defined according to objects quite distinct from itself and its effect; namely, those objects whose observation stimulates the human organism to form the belief that it is a cause.

However, this definition can come to be seen as also embodying a normative rule which states the criteria on the basis of which we are justified in asserting a causal connection. Hume thought of normative rules as being derived from reflection upon natural principles of the understanding and their application to experience. Thus constant conjunction, succession and contiguity in space obtain the status of *reasons* for asserting causal connection. But the ultimate justification for this claim must lie in a *theory* like that of Hume's pre-established harmony. There is no contradiction in the claim that A and B have been conjoined in our past experience, that A precedes B, and that A is not the cause of B. 'This happens sometimes, and with regard to some objects: Why may it not happen always, and with regard to all objects?' (E.38). It is not logic but something like Hume's 'pre-established harmony' between the course of nature and the (natural) course of human ideas which secures us against such a supposition.

These reflections show how mistaken is the common view that Hume *reduced* the ontological meaning of causality to succession and constant conjunction. Serious confusion has arisen from the fact that philosophers like Ernst Mach have attributed their own positivistic views to Hume. Hume 'rejects causality and recognizes only a wonted succession in time', writes Mach.[28] But for Hume experience of a repeated succession of events must only do in lieu of a cognitive insight into the objective causal process. Meaning and truth, for Hume, lie outside of man; and human ideas are generally inadequate to their natural objects. This view alone shows the distance between his philosophy and modern positivism.

Hume's views may also be contrasted with the views of those who wish to tie up meaning and truth with conventional rules. In the contemporary philosophy deriving from Wittgenstein, rules based on practice provide the connection between criteria and claims made on the basis of them. That a certain form of behaviour indicates the existence of an emotion, for example, depends upon the existence of a certain rule which connects behaviour with the appropriate circumstances. The existence of culturally embedded rules (in this philosophy) is also a formal condition for the existence of such items as causes. For Hume, on the other hand, the connection between external circumstances and human emotions depends upon instinctive processes. Similarly he considers criteria such as constant conjunction to be natural signs of causality, and believes that it is this which accounts for the success of empirical science. For Hume, the means of scientific discovery can be obtained by reflection on the natural processes of human understanding: 'these rules are form'd on the nature of our understanding, and on our experience of its operations in the judgments we form concerning objects' (T.149). In fact what Hume calls 'the understanding' in this context is nothing but the reflective application of 'the general and more establish'd properties of the imagination'

(T.267). A central aim of Book I of his *Treatise* is to show that the operations of the understanding, our scientific inferring procedures, have their roots in the natural organism. 'Rules' are always a secondary product derived from reflection upon the natural processes of human thinking and their application to the data of experience.[29] Hume believes that these rules, while they are not derived from insight into external nature itself, will lead us toward truth. But this belief, according to his philosophy, rests ultimately on a kind of faith which is itself derived from human nature.

§3 *Belief*

Hume himself conceives of the problem of scepticism in terms of a concern with denial or suspension of belief as such. Belief in this context must be understood as a state of mind, and its denial leads to a contrary state of mind, that of doubt or *scepticism*. Hume uses the notions of belief and scepticism this way in the *Dialogues Concerning Natural Religion* when he says through the mouth of his Cleanthes that while

it seems certain, that though a man, in a flush of humour, after intense reflection on the many contradictions and imperfections of human reason, may entirely renounce all belief and opinion; it is impossible for him to persevere in this total scepticism, or make it appear in his conduct for a few hours. (D.132)

Such a view perfectly reflects Hume's famous statement of scepticism in the conclusion to Book I of the *Treatise*. Scepticism is treated as a state of mind which is brought about by reflection upon what Hume calls the 'contradictions and imperfections in human reason' (T.268). Hume always insists that this state is impossible for any man to continue in for any length of time: 'External objects press in upon him' and 'his philosophical melancholy dissipates' (D.132). A man cannot help believing, whether his beliefs or opinions concern 'action or speculation' (E.149). Hume thinks there are certain instinctive and natural beliefs that no human being can keep in abeyance for any prolonged period.

If, as Hume suggests, *scepticism* is taken *as a state of mind* which is identical to suspension of belief, then the *sceptic* might be taken as a man who claims to be able to suspend some or even all beliefs. But if total scepticism is, as Hume thought, impossible, then the (Pyrrhonian) sceptic may be 'refuted' merely by asking him to be honest with himself. This is the sort of refutation which the authors of an important seventeenth-century logic book propose to those Pyrrhonists and New Academicians who think that they can deny clear and certain knowledge. In *La Logique ou L'Art de Penser*, Arnauld and Nicole claim that

the best means of convincing these philosophers is to restore them to . . . good faith, by asking them whether – after all these arguments by which they attempt to show that one is not able to distinguish sleep from waking, nor madness from good sense – they are not fully persuaded (in spite of their reasons) that they are not asleep and that they are of sound mind.[30]

According to this view no one can really *be* a sceptic because no one can really suspend beliefs like the belief that he is not now dreaming. Hume himself adopts this view in *A Letter from a Gentleman to his Friend in Edinburgh* (1745), in which he defends his own work against the charge of negative scepticism:

I must observe, that the Doctrine[s] of the *Pyrrhonians* or *Scepticks* have been regarded in all Ages as Principles of mere Curiosity, or a Kind of *Jeux d'esprit*, without any Influence on a Man's steady Principles or Conduct in Life. In Reality, a Philosopher who affects to doubt of the Maxims of *common Reason*, and even of his *Senses*, declares sufficiently that he is not in earnest, and that he intends not to advance an Opinion which he would recommend as Standards of Judgment and Action. (p. 19).

For Hume, no less than Arnauld and Nicole, it is impossible to maintain the suspension of judgement which was set up as an ideal by Pyrrho, the classical founder of scepticism. Hume thought the Pyrrhonian sceptic could be refuted by pointing out that he cannot maintain his sceptical state.[31]

Scepticism might also be taken as a *philosophical technique* or art. Pierre Bayle describes scepticism as 'the art of disputing about everything, without doing anything else but suspending one's judgement'.[32] A sceptic might then be taken as a philosopher who practises such a technique. In this sense one would consider any philosopher to be a sceptic in so far as he presents arguments which induce himself and others to question former beliefs. Hume considered Descartes to be a sceptic in this sense when, in the first of his *Meditations*, Descartes reflected upon the natural fallibility of our mental faculties. Hume seemed to think that there is no rational solution to the kind of doubt that Descartes proposed. In this case reason has undermined itself.[33] Similarly Hume thought that Berkeley had used reason to show that the belief in the external and independent existence of matter was self-contradictory. Hume called Berkeley's argument *merely sceptical* and held that, while Berkeley claimed to compose his book against sceptics as well as freethinkers and atheists,

most of the writings of that very ingenious author form the best lessons of scepticism, which are to be found either among the ancient or modern philosophers, Bayle not excepted. (E.155n.)

Hume did not consider Berkeley's argument (as Berkeley did) as a *reductio ad absurdum* of the position it attacked; rather, for Hume it shows that human reason and argument, when left to themselves, can lead to nothing but paradox and confusion. But he saw such arguments as useful in curbing the pretentions of reason itself. Hume's own sceptical arguments which I referred to in the first section of this chapter, those showing that reason cannot be the source of our belief in causation, have a similar function in showing the limits of reason. But it is worth noting that (at least when he wrote the *Treatise*)[34] Hume thought that the arguments of Berkeley and Descartes which attack reason itself went much further than his own.

But Hume is a sceptic in another sense, a sense in which he thought that Berkeley and Descartes were not. Hume must be thought to be putting forward a positive thesis about the indispensable origins of human belief. Hume holds that both scientific and moral beliefs rest in some way upon *human nature* as opposed to reason and argument. He does not want to deny absolutely the place of reason in scientific belief or ethics. That would be absurd. He does, however, want to stress that there would be no belief or notion of the world as the scientist thinks about it if there were no *natural judgements* or natural beliefs, however fallacious and in need of revision. He also wants to stress that there would be no such thing as morality if there were not certain *natural sentiments*, however personal and in need of universalisation.

It is as a sceptic in this final sense that Hume can provide a 'sceptical solution'[35] of the doubts raised by philosophers like

Descartes and Berkeley (and indeed Hume himself) who put forward sceptical *arguments*. For Hume did not think that excessive use of reason could provide any road to belief, or even truth. If justification is at issue one can say that Hume thought that nature was quite right in letting human nature do at least part of the job rather than leaving all to 'laboured deductions of the understanding' (E.55). Hume's defence against scepticism, the suspension of belief brought about by the excessive use of reason, involves an appeal to human nature which (he thought) provides a necessary foundation for science, and, even more importantly, for morality.

Unlike Arnauld, Hume does not *merely* refer the philosophical reasoner to his own good faith. He attempts to provide explanations of why certain beliefs cannot be withheld. This is the central function of Hume's accounts of the origin of beliefs. Through these accounts we should see how, in spite of the failures of reason, we come to form the natural beliefs which provide our connections with reality.

Philosophical scepticism as it appears in the writings of David Hume is not primarily a philosophy of knowledge (a philosophy of science) nor a philosophy of nature (a general metaphysic): it is a philosophy of man. Hume was mainly interested in the philosophy of knowing in so far as it tells us about the knowing being himself. According to Hume man is not a wholly rational being nor should philosophy treat man as if he were. Hume's philosophy of human nature begins with the recognition that we have extremely little insight into the nature of reality. But given this lack of insight, Hume wanted to ask how we come to have the beliefs that we do about that reality.

§4   *Conclusion*

Looked at from the point of view of the present-day conception of scepticism, Hume's concerns are primarily with the denial of belief. But in order to understand the full range of the sceptical problem as it appeared to Hume, we shall have to set aside our present conception of scepticism.

For, in the first place, when Hume and his predecessors doubted that they would ever have knowledge, they were employing a standard of evidence hardly conceivable to modern theoreticians of knowledge. For them, the idea of *a priori* knowledge of nature was a real but unrealisable ideal. In *The Problem of Knowledge*, A. J. Ayer states the view which is generally ascribed to Hume: 'the fact that all empirical statements are contingent, that even when true they can be denied without self-contradiction, is itself a matter of necessity' (p. 41). This is a view which Hume certainly did not hold. For he recognised a notion of necessity which was substantial, even if unrealisable, in the case of knowledge of cause. Like other eighteenth-century thinkers Hume connected his notion of genuine or necessary knowledge with a demand for intelligibility. In Hume's day the characterisation of 'empirical science' as a *scientific* method was still problematic.[36] This must be recognised if we are to appreciate the dynamics of the thought of a philosopher like Hume.

In the second place, in order to understand Humean scepticism we need to understand his development of a theory of ideas which was espoused by his predecessors. Like these earlier philosophers Hume considered ideas to be natural signs of an independent reality. But by tracing the contents of our ideas back to their natural origins in the data of sense, Hume claimed to be showing their *limits*. In Hume's hands the 'empirical' origin of our ideas contributes to a recognition of their imperfections. Rightly understood, (what is usually called) Hume's empiricism forms an intimate part of his sceptical denial of knowledge.

In the third place, the sceptical arguments put forward by Hume and other philosophers of his day do not *only* include those which call our attention to the limits of our information concerning the real natures of things. Those doubts that we considered in §1 can be reasonably construed that way. But in the course of his writings Hume uses other sceptical arguments such as those which show that we hold mutually contradictory beliefs, or that the principles we operate upon in determining one indispensable belief will oppose the principles we operate upon in determining another indispensable belief. In fact it is this inability to generalise the natural principles of the understanding which is the source of Hume's famous statement of scepticism in the conclusion to the first book of the *Treatise* (T.265–6). Hume's own statements of failure need to be seen in terms of his own philosophical project of deriving normative rules of the understanding from a discovery of underlying instinctive natural 'principles which are permanent, irresistable, and universal'.[37]

Finally, and most importantly, the present-day notion of scepticism leaves no room for an understanding of the sense in which Hume himself *is* a sceptic. Hume is a sceptic because he thinks that our fundamental beliefs about reality and our inferring procedures cannot be derived solely from scientific investigation; rather, he thinks that they derive from man as a natural organism. The problem of scepticism as we in the twentieth century generally conceive of it does not even allow for Hume's answer to sceptical argument – that of the philosophical sceptic. This is hardly surprising since the whole notion of a *natural* mental process, which is important in the writings of Hume and other philosophers of the seventeenth and eighteenth centuries, is so foreign to our conception of what is relevant to philosophy. Nevertheless it is absolutely essential for understanding Hume's concerns with scepticism, the problems which are posed for him and the answers which he gives.

In an important sense, Hume's questions precede those of contemporary philosophic enquiry. Instead of being primarily interested in justified or true belief he is interested in the source of belief as such. Instead of being primarily interested in right action he is interested in the source of action as such. Nevertheless, it is equally true that there is a sense in which our questions precede his. For, as we have seen, Hume does not really face the relativistic scepticism which confronts our own age. The philosophic enterprise as he conceives of it is informed by his concept of scepticism; ours is informed by our own. 'Concepts,' writes Wittgenstein, 'lead us to make investigations; are the expression of our interest, and direct our interest.'[38] It may be that different philosophical enterprises can throw a good deal of light upon each other. Nevertheless, much distortion arises from a failure to keep them separate.

Notes

1   See, for example, G. S. Pappas and M. Swain (eds.), *Essays on Knowledge and Justification*. A version of this analysis of knowledge is defended in the sixth chapter of R. M. Chisholm, *Theory of Knowledge*.

2 The account in this paragraph is based on A. J. Ayer, *The Problem of Knowledge*, pp. 28ff.

3 H. H. Price, 'The permanent significance of Hume's philosophy', *Philosophy*, 15 (1940); reprinted in A. Sesonske and N. Fleming (eds.), *Human Understanding: Studies in the Philosophy of David Hume*, p. 16.

4 D. G. C. Macnabb, *David Hume: His Theory of Knowledge and Morality*, p. 19.

5 E.152, lines 28–32; T.210, lines 10–15; T.213, lines 15–17; T.217, lines 30–5.

6 See, for example, T.132, line 5. Hume reserves the term 'philosophy' for a study of the causes of things, and divides philosophy into natural and moral (T.175). The term 'science' had both a narrower and a wider meaning for him. Sometimes 'science' is used to refer to those enquiries which can be carried on merely by comparison of ideas without appeal to experience (T.73; cf. Locke's use of the terms, cited in n. 36 below). But in Book II of the *Treatise* Hume speaks of 'philosophy' as that particular 'science' which is employed to 'explain the phaenomena' by means of hypotheses (T.319–20). Hume's use of the terms 'philosophy' and 'science' was not unusual in his day. See R. F. McRae, *The Problem of the Unity of the Sciences: Bacon to Kant*, p. ix, n. 6; and A. Thackray, 'The industrial revolution and the image of science', in A. Thackray and E. Mendelsohn, eds., *Science and Values: Patterns of Tradition and Change*, esp. p. 3.

7 T.104. On crucial experiments, see Rule 4, T.173. At E.74, Hume *appears* to deny that they are justified. But the view that one experiment can be sufficient for scientific induction is repeated at E.107n. (§1).

8 In an important sense I am in general agreement with writers such as D. C. Stove (see his *Probability and Hume's Inductive Scepticism*) who claim that Hume bases his 'inductive scepticism' on 'deductivism'. However, Hume's 'deductivism' is based on an eighteenth-century conception of what constitutes an *a priori* inference, a conception which is not considered by these writers.

9 In a letter written in 1754 to John Stewart, professor of natural philosophy at the University of Edinburgh, Hume says: 'I never asserted so absurd a Proposition as *that any thing might arise without a Cause*: I only maintain'd, that our Certainty of the Falshood of that Proposition proceeded neither from Intuition nor Demonstration; but from another Source' (H.L. I, 187). It seems to me indisputable that Hume had in mind the passage from T.132 and E.87 which I have been discussing.

   If the proposition *that any thing might arise without a Cause* (i.e., some events do not have a cause) is false, then the proposition *every event has a cause* must be true. Thus it seems plausible, as I suggest in the main text, that Hume thinks he has explained how philosophers reach the certainty that every event has a cause.

Hume's aim at T.132–3 is to explain how the reasonings connected with the causal maxim 'arise not *directly* from the habit, but in an *oblique* manner' (T.133). He attempts to show how the maxim ultimately arises in the fact that while an inconsistent experience causes us to remember opposing effects, habit produces a general tendency to believe that only one effect will occur.

10   There are two notable exceptions. One is in the book entitled *Hume*, written by the nineteenth-century biologist T. H. Huxley, esp. p. 79. Another is a more recent book by R. F. Anderson, *Hume's First Principles*. See Chapters 2 and 5 below.

11   E.73n. See also David Hume, *A Letter from a Gentleman to his Friend in Edinburgh*, pp. 28–9. I discuss this further in Chapter 4.

12   Hume derived his psychophysiology largely from N. Malebranche's *Recherche de la Vérité*, though he had English sources too. I discuss Hume's use of Malebranche's psychophysiology in §7(c), §18(b) and §19.

13   T.60. Hume's psychophysiology is also important at T.185, where he is explaining that scepticism can never undermine reason, and at T.202ff., where he is accounting for our natural belief in the continuing existence of our perceptions. In this latter account he makes a reference back to T.60.

14   *The Natural History of Religion*, G.G. IV, 316.

15   J. Passmore, *Hume's Intentions*, pp. 50–1. For a criticism of Passmore's view, see D. W. Livingston's important article, 'Hume on ultimate causation', *American Philosophical Quarterly*, 8 (1971). See also R. F. Anderson, *Hume's First Principles*, esp. pp. 102–10. Passmore thinks that Hume goes beyond Locke and Newton in rejecting all hypotheses in science. But the claim that Hume rejected hypotheses in science is as misleading for Hume as it is for Newton. See §18.

16   Kant's *Critique of Pure Reason* was first published in 1781, forty-two years after Hume's *Treatise*. See *Critique*, pp. 606–7.

17   Newton had written that 'inward substances are not to be known either by our senses, or by any reflex act of our minds' (*Sir Isaac Newton's Mathematical Principles of Natural Philosophy*, vol. 2, p. 546). Locke writes concerning causation by both mind and matter: 'Constant Experience makes us sensible of both of these, though our narrow Understandings can comprehend neither' (*Essay* 2, 23, 28). Newton and Locke were writing over forty years prior to Hume.

18   See *Critique*, pp. 121ff., particularly the following: 'The explanation of the manner in which concepts can thus relate *a priori* to objects I entitle their transcendental deduction; and from it I distinguish empirical deduction, which shows the manner in which a concept is acquired through experience and through reflection upon experience, and which therefore concerns, not its legitimacy, but only its *de facto* mode of origination' (p. 121).

19   Cf. J. Passmore, *Hume's Intentions*, pp. 90–1; A. Flew, *Hume's Philosophy of Belief*, p. 47; N. Kemp Smith, 'The naturalism of

Hume', *Mind*, 14 (1905), pp. 169–70. I discuss the nature of this foundation in Chapters 3 and 4.

20 Plato, *Theaetetus*, 151e–152e.

21 Ludwig Wittgenstein, *Philosophical Investigations*, §241.

22 Ludwig Wittgenstein, *On Certainty*, §262.

23 The quotations from Wittgenstein in this paragraph are taken from *Philosophical Investigations*, §§482, 485, 199.

24 'The Sceptic', G.G. III, 216. The important contemporary moral theorist R. M. Hare has written: 'It was Hume who taught us that our whole commerce with the world depends upon our *blik* about the world; and that differences between *bliks* about the world cannot be settled by observation of what happens in that world' ('Theology and falsification', a symposium with A. Flew, R. M. Hare, and B. Mitchell, in A. Flew and A. MacIntyre, eds., *New Essays in Philosophical Theology*, p. 101). In the context, these words misleadingly suggest that Hume conceived that there could be fundamentally different (e.g., moral) *bliks* or world-views, and that, *for him*, *bliks* could be arbitrarily chosen. Unlike Hare, Hume rejects freedom and stresses the origin of the fundamental structures of belief and action in *human nature*.

25 T.448; cf. T.415: The contradiction to truth and reason 'consists in the disagreement of ideas, consider'd as copies, with those objects, which they represent'. In his essay 'The Sceptic', Hume sees the operations of our reason as a means by which we seek to effect a correspondence between our conceptions and their objects: 'If I examine the *Ptolomaic* and *Copernican* systems, I endeavour only, by my enquiries, to know the real situation of the planets; that is, in other words, I endeavour to give them, in my conception, the same relations, that they bear towards each other in the heavens. To this operation of the mind, therefore, there seems to be always a real, though often an unknown standard, in the nature of things' (G.G. III, 217–18).

26 Thus for Hume the idea of a cause which functions only once is quite consistent. His point is that given the limits of our human faculties we should never form any belief that there was any causation if all causes were like this. Essential to Hume's notion of ontological causation is *production*, not *law*. Law and constant conjunction come in when one talks about conditions for human belief in causation. For we have no knowledge of the productive process itself.

27 This notion of *verisimilitude* or approximation to truth is implicit in Hume's attitude to his own scientific project: 'we might hope to establish a system or set of opinions, which if not true (for that, perhaps, is too much to be hop'd for) might at least be satisfactory to the human mind, and might stand the test of the most critical examination' (T.272).

28 Ernst Mach, *The Science of Mechanics*, p. 580. Compare the quotation from H. H. Price, in §1 above.

29 Compare T. K. Hearn, 'General rules in Hume's *Treatise*', *Journal of*

the History of Philosophy, 8 (1970).

30   Antoine Arnauld et Pierre Nicole, *La Logique ou l'Art de Penser*, p. 360 (often referred to as the *Port-Royal Logic*). Hume refers to a comparable passage of this work in his *Dialogues* (D.137 and note).

31   At the same time it must be recognised that Hume's ideas of natural and unavoidable belief do not seem *entirely* opposed to those of Sextus Empiricus, whose works survived as the most important statement of the scepticism of antiquity. While Sextus advocated suspension of judgement in theoretical questions, he also set as a goal 'moderate feeling in respect of things unavoidable'. See *Outlines of Pyrrhonism*, 1,12,25 (p. 19). The similarity of Hume's views to those of Sextus has been stressed by R. Popkin in his 'David Hume: his Pyrrhonism and his critique of Pyrrhonism', *Philosophical Quarterly* 1 (1951).

But in a recent article Terence Penelhum has noted that Hume, unlike Sextus, does not advocate suspension of judgement regarding theoretical questions. In fact, Hume characteristically denies the possibility of doing this. See T. Penelhum, 'Hume's skepticism and the *Dialogues*', in D. F. Norton, N. Capaldi, and W. L. Robison, eds., *McGill Hume Studies*. Also Penelhum's *Hume*, pp. 22–7.

32   Pierre Bayle, 'Pyrrho' (*Dictionary*, vol. 4, 653; Popkin, *Selections*, p. 194). The importance of Bayle as a formative influence on Hume has been well recognised; see, for example, N. Kemp Smith, *The Philosophy of David Hume*, esp. pp. 325ff. Hume refers to Bayle at T.243 . See also my opening remarks to Chapter 3 below.

33   E.149–50; T.180–7. Hume does not mention Descartes in the *Treatise* account, but clearly has him in mind. The doubt being considered here is based upon the principle that we should withhold belief in any faculty which has even once led us astray. On the importance of Descartes' *Meditations* in the writing of Hume's *Treatise*, see my opening remarks to Chapter 3.

34   The qualification must be made because it seems clear that by the time he wrote the *Enquiry* Hume was forced to recognise that others considered his arguments about the nature of probable reasoning to be Pyrrhonian (E.158ff.). This recognition is lacking in the *Treatise*, where Hume was centrally involved in his positive project of founding scientific reasoning in human nature. He does not seem self-conscious about the fact that the project had these Pyrrhonian implications. Nevertheless, it must be recognised that the claim that probability has a non-rational base is implicit in Hume's project from the beginning and is not, as some commentators think, an unforeseen consequence.

35   Cf. title to *Enquiry*, Section V.

36   Cf. Locke's claim that 'this *way* of getting, and *improving our Knowledge in Substances only by Experience* and History, which is all that the weakness of our Faculties in this State of *Mediocrity*, which we are in in this World, can attain to, makes me suspect, that natural

Philosophy is not capable of being made a Science' (*Essay*, 4, 12, 10).
37 T.225. One must, however, carefully distinguish between an
internal and external criticism of Hume's project. For Kant the
whole project was in *principle* a faulty one: his was an external
criticism. Kant claims that the rules which Hume seeks can only lead
to uncertain empirical knowledge: 'For whence could experience
derive its certainty, if all the rules according to which it proceeds,
were always themselves empirical, and therefore contingent? Such
rules could hardly be regarded as first principles' (*Critique*, p. 45).
38 *Philosophical Investigations*, §570.

TWO

Scepticism with regard to the senses

§5

There is another species of scepticism, *consequent* to science and enquiry.

– Hume, *Enquiry*, p. 150

§6

'Tis in vain to ask, *Whether there be body or not?* That is a point, which we must take for granted in all our reasonings.

– Hume, *Treatise*, p. 187

§7

We may well ask, *What causes induce us to believe in the existence of body?*

– Hume, *Treatise*, p. 187

§8

It seems that we ought to believe that there are [objects outside of us]. For we are naturally drawn to accept our natural judgment when we can not positively correct it by light and evidence.

– Malebranche, *Recherche*, III, 63

I begun this subject with premising, that we ought to have an implicit faith in our senses . . . . But to be ingenuous, I feel myself *at present* of a quite contrary sentiment.

– Hume, *Treatise*, p. 217

A central aim of the first book of Hume's *Treatise of Human Nature* is to show how certain fundamental beliefs about the world and the human mind are generated. A fundamental thesis of that book is that these ontological beliefs do not arise solely on the basis of rational or scientific considerations but that, on the contrary, they rest upon what Hume calls 'human nature'. These beliefs, which are themselves indispensable both for ordinary life and for science, cannot be based on the information which we derive from the world; rather, they have their source in natural propensities of the human animal. To appreciate Hume's philosophical scepticism it is important to separate the two sides of this thesis: the negative side wherein he attempts to show that the ontological beliefs which we naturally accept cannot be founded upon observation and rational considerations alone; and a positive side wherein he attempts to show that such beliefs have their origin in a natural instinct. It is also important to separate this question concerning the *origin* of an ontological belief from the questions of whether that belief is *justified* or whether it is *true*. Hume does think that the existence of a natural belief provides some *prima facie* justification for that belief; however, he does not think that such beliefs in themselves provide real insight into the nature of reality. Hume's considered view is that it is only when such beliefs are corrected by reason that they give us anything approaching truth.

The centrality which the question of the origin of ideas and beliefs plays in Hume's philosophy is easily misunderstood by those who approach his work from the point of view of contemporary philosophy. We have already noted in §1 the shift in the notion of knowledge which began with the work of Hume's successor Kant. Kant was also important in causing a shift in the fundamental question which philosophers raise concerning metaphysical concepts. He made a strict distinction between what he called questions of fact (*quid facti*) and questions of right (*quid juris*), and insisted that the important philosophical questions were of the latter sort.[1] According to Kant we need some sort of justification for the fact that in experience we employ concepts which cannot be derived from that experience. Kant claimed to discover the need for such a justification through his reading of the works of Hume. But, while it is certainly true that Hume denied that metaphysical concepts like those of causality and external existence arise from information which we receive in experience, his own claim is made in a context where he is primarily interested in a question of fact. Hume was primarily interested in the factual question of the way that our fundamental notions and beliefs actually arise.

A failure to bear in mind the primacy of this factual question can cause much confusion when one comes to consider a very difficult section of the *Treatise* entitled 'Of scepticism with regard to the senses' (T. 187–218). In that section Hume sets out to answer the question *'What causes induce us to believe in the existence of body?'* (T.187). Hume considers three possible origins of the belief in body – the senses, reason, and the imagination. He rejects the first two and opts for the third. In rejecting the senses and reason as sources of the belief in body, Hume is denying that belief arises from any information which we derive from the world. But in making this claim Hume draws on certain assumptions which can only be derived from an 'objective' point of view; that is, by already assuming the existence of body. Hume implicitly acknowledges that he is making this assumption when he announces right at the beginning of his section that the existence of body must be taken 'for granted in all our reasonings'. If he were denying our right to believe in body then there would be a kind of circularity in his procedure. But if, as is in fact the case, he is making a factual claim about the origins of belief, then there is no circularity. Hume sets out to show that such beliefs do not arise from experience. Similarly, if one thinks of Hume as simply answering a question of justification, then one distorts his own positive explanation of the source of our belief in body. For the natural propensity, which is the source of this belief, leads to a form of it which Hume unequivocally rejects as false. Hume's central aim is to discover that natural propensity, to show how the belief in body derives from the forces underlying human thought and behaviour.

In §5 I shall show how, from an objective scientific point of view, Hume attempts to show that the immediate objects of our senses are not themselves external objects. In §6 I shall show that Hume's whole argument to prove the subjective character of our perceptions presupposes the existence of independent external objects which are related to those perceptions. In other words, I shall show why, logically, Hume is forced to accept some form of representative theory of perception. In §7 I shall consider the nature of the forces which Hume thinks responsible for our natural belief in external existence. Finally, in §8 I shall explain the context in which the question of justification of belief in the external world actually does arise in Hume's discussion.

§5   *The senses*

In the discussion of these topics in his *Enquiry Concerning Human*

Understanding (E.149–54), Hume contrasts his own brand of scepticism with the pre-scientific scepticism of Descartes' first Meditation. Hume describes his own scepticism as of a kind which is '*consequent* to science and enquiry' (E.150). This is well illustrated in the *Treatise* in his discussion of the question of whether our belief in the distinct existence of the direct objects of sense can arise from the data of sense itself (T.188–93). Throughout this discussion Hume assumes that the direct objects of our sensory awareness are in fact internal and mind-dependent entities. In so doing he assumes the results of certain experiments which he presents only later in the chapter. Nevertheless it is on these objective scientific conclusions that Hume bases a central part of his argument that the senses present no appearance of external or independent existence.

Hume begins his discussion of the question of whether our senses present us with the idea that their immediate objects exist externally and independently, by noting that, if they did, it would be 'by a kind of *fallacy* and *illusion*'.[2] This, as he reminds us on the next page, is because all the strong and lively perceptions of our minds – sensations as well as pains, emotions, etc. – are really 'on the same footing'. From the context it is quite clear that he means that they are all internal and mind-dependent. Hume goes on to argue that it is impossible that we can have the illusion that sense-objects are external and independent, because we should then have to admit that 'even where we are most intimately conscious, we might be mistaken'. However, since these strong and lively perceptions (impressions) 'must necessarily appear in every particular what they are', and since 'every thing that enters the mind' is 'in *reality* a perception', it follows that it is impossible that 'any thing shou'd to *feeling* appear different' (T.190). In this remarkable argument Hume is presenting us with a conclusion about the way things *appear* to sense or feeling on the basis of a premise which makes a claim about *the actual nature of sense objects*: sense objects can't appear as external and independent because they actually are internal and dependent. Fallacy and illusion are not possible in this case.

The claim that Hume wants to draw a conclusion concerning the appearances of things from objective considerations concerning the nature of sense-objects is supported by his subsequent remarks; for he goes on to deny that objects actually appear (to our senses) as external to our own bodies. He denies, for example, that our own bodies are perceived in space, on the ground that when we perceive our bodies, we perceive only 'certain impressions, which enter by the senses' (T.191). Once again the common-sense view regarding the nature of sense-experience loses out against Hume's philosophical premise about the actual character of the immediate object of awareness.

Hume's doctrine that we do not directly perceive the parts of our own bodies seems to be taken over from Nicolas Malebranche's *Recherche de la Vérité*.[3] The significance of the close connection between Hume's ideas and those of Malebranche will emerge in the course of this chapter. While Malebranche is frequently considered a forerunner of Berkeley's idealism as well as Hume's scepticism, like Hume he held a firm belief in the independent existence of the material world. Both Hume and Malebranche make a clear distinction between our subjective sense-perceptions and the independent external objects. But both stress that we are only directly aware of the perceptions.

The passage of the *Treatise* which we considered on page 41 is commonly taken to show that Hume is committed to the view which philosophers call 'phenomenalism'. This has been described by John Laird as 'the doctrine that all our knowledge, all our belief, and all our conjectures begin and end with appearances; that we cannot go behind or beyond these; and that we should not try to do so'.[4] The interpretation of Hume as a phenomenalist is sometimes derived from his claim that all things of which we are intimately aware 'must necessarily appear in every particular what they are, and be what they appear'.[5] But, taken in the context of Hume's argument, this claim is used to show that things don't appear in the way that most of us unreflectively think that they do appear. Far from attempting to build up a picture of reality merely on the basis of the appearances of things, *Hume determines his conception of appearances on the basis of philosophic and scientific considerations.*

The primacy of the objective point of view over that of appearances in Hume's calculations is explicit when he turns to the question of whether the senses present us with any notion of *'independency'* (T.191). He answers that dependency or independency of sense objects is not anything that can itself be 'an object of the senses', but must, on the contrary, be determined by 'experience and observation'. He refers us to a later passage in 'Of scepticism with regard to the senses' where he purports to show, on the basis of experience, that the objects of sense are not in fact independent.

This argument to show that the immediate objects of our senses 'are not possest of any independent existence' occurs in a context where Hume claims to be showing the falsity of the direct realist view of common sense (T.210–11). According to this view the immediate objects of our sense awareness can continue to exist while unperceived. Hume thinks that he can undermine the common-sense view by showing that these immediate objects are mind-dependent entities. But Hume also clearly thinks that his arguments tell equally against any view (including the philosophical view of his predecessors like Descartes and Locke) which maintains that we are directly aware of independent existence in the act of sense perception.

Hume argues that direct realism is false on the basis of a few simple experiments which (he believes) show that our sensible objects are dependent for their existence upon our brains and nervous systems, or, as he puts it, 'on our organs, and the disposition of our nerves and animal spirits' (T.211). In his *Treatise* Hume relies heavily upon what might be called the 'double image' experiment. We might paraphrase his argument as follows. When I press my eyeball with my finger I become aware of two distinct and separate objects where I had only been aware of one before. I know that one of these objects came into being through a change in my organs of sight. This object did not exist prior to the pressure being applied to my eye, and will not exist after the pressure is removed. Thus it depends for its existence upon the state of my nervous system. But, says Hume, this sensible object is of the same nature as the other member of the set, the one which I do in fact (numerically) identify with the sensible object which existed prior to the application of pressure to my eye. He concludes from this that this latter object – in fact, any sensible object – is also dependent upon our physical state. Hume thinks that this conclusion is confirmed by other facts of human perception: the fact that the immediate objects of our senses increase and diminish in size as we move nearer to, or further from, the external object; that these objects change their colour and other sensible qualities when we are sick; and so on. He thinks that all these facts contribute to the conclusion that the sensible object is a physiologically dependent entity.

It is of some importance to note that Hume believes that these facts show not merely that certain perceptual *qualities* are partly or wholly dependent upon the perceiver, but that the very *objects* of which we are directly aware 'are not possest of any independent existence' (T.210). For Hume raises his problem in a context where he is enquiring into the type of existence which belongs to the entity of which we are aware when we take ourselves to be perceiving a particular object outside of us. Hume thinks that it is a factual question whether this entity, which *in this discussion* he calls indifferently an *'object* or *perception'*,[6] has a mind-independent existence. The ordinary unreflective man believes that it does: that 'this very table, which we see white, and which we feel hard' exists independently of us. On the other hand Hume thinks that the facts of perception to which he has alluded show that these 'existences . . . are nothing but perceptions in the mind' (E.151–2).

Hume's double image experiment is particularly suited to establish the conclusion that the perceptual object constitutes a mind-dependent entity. Unlike the other cases he cites, this phenomenon cannot be easily interpreted as showing that there is only a quality that is partly or wholly mind-dependent. For the displaced second image is quite distinct from the first and cannot be considered the distorted property of an independent object. It is an entity which clearly owes its very existence to some change in my bodily state. But since the displaced image is in other respects quite like the one which continues to occupy the normal position, it apparently follows that that one, too, is a mind-dependent existent which is distinct from the external object. Hume may also have thought that the cumulative effect of those other experiments to which he alludes may point in the same direction. Taken together they may show that *all* the qualities of our ordinary perceptual object are mind- or brain-dependent, and that there is nothing which is left over to constitute an unchanging independent perceptual object.

However, Hume's experiment does not appear to be conclusive. Its primary defect seems to lie in its implication that we have no reason to consider the two perceptions (those resulting from the pressure to the eyeball) as different in nature. For one of the two does seem to be the normal perceptual object and the other to be a less real image. The one that seems to be normal occupies the position within our perceptual field to which we had previously assigned what we took to be the perceptual object. This would seem to provide a reason for considering the two perceptions to be different in nature.

Nevertheless, I think that it must be recognised that Hume's experiment has some weight. We might consider what sort of experiment, drawn up along the lines of this one, would be conclusive. Let us suggest an experiment which, while it is rather fanciful in terms of current scientific knowledge, is not completely implausible. Suppose that our knowledge of psychophysiology had progressed to such a state that by stimulating certain parts of the brain we could produce complete visual hallucinations as elaborate as anything we now sense. Such perceptions would be of the same nature as our ordinary perceptions in the presence of a physical object. I think that, given the positive results of such an experiment, we would be very much inclined to conclude that we are always only perceiving existences which are not independent of our own nervous systems. It is, I think, this sort of conclusion that Hume was trying to establish from his own less spectacular experiment.

When we say that Hume thought of the perception as mind-dependent, it is important to recognise that for him, at least in this context, there is no clear distinction between the mind and the body. (At the beginning of Book II of the *Treatise*, Hume speaks of impressions such as pains and pleasure as arising originally 'in the soul, or in the body, *whichever you please to call it*' (T. 276; italics mine).) He seems to think of perceptions as literally *in* our bodies, or perhaps as modifications of our bodies. In his *Enquiry* Hume speaks of these philosophic reflections as showing that what is present to the mind is nothing but an image which is conveyed through the inlets of the senses. Elsewhere in the *Treatise* he speaks of 'the image and idea' as 'extended in the *retina*, and in the brain or organ of perception'.[7] Sensible images and even their ideas are considered to be very literally extended and located in our bodies.

From the conclusion that our sensible perceptions are physiologically dependent, Hume thinks that it naturally follows that they cannot continue to exist while unperceived. For if they are dependent for their existence upon our physiological state they will go out of existence when we cease to be in that state. This leads Hume to say that they are 'interrupted, and perishing, and different at every different return' (T.211). A simple example will illustrate his meaning. I place a book before me on the table; I shut my eyes for a few seconds; finally I re-open my eyes and see a book which exactly resembles the first book. Unreflectively I think of myself as looking back at the same book, the *same* perceptual object as existed prior to my closing my eyes. But according to Hume, I should realise that this is not possible, when I recognise that my perceptual objects are dependent on my physiological state. The sensible object cannot continue to exist after I cease to be aware of it. What I previously took to be a book goes out of existence when I shut my eyes. For when its existence is *interrupted* it completely *perishes*. And it follows that I cannot be seeing numerically the same sensible perception when I re-open my eyes. This is what Hume means when he says that my sensible perceptions are *different at every return*. A break in the observation of my book-perception corresponds with its destruction and it cannot be the same as any subsequent existent.

By means of such considerations Hume thinks that he has shown the falsity of the direct realist theory of common sense. As we shall see in the third section of this chapter, Hume thinks that the crux of that theory lies in its numerical identification of distinct perceptual objects. It is that false identification of what is in fact numerically distinct which originally leads us into the belief that there is something which continues to exist while we are not sensibly aware of it. Hume's explanation of how we identify distinct perceptions supplies his solution to the problem of the origin of our belief in external existence. But through his experiments Hume thinks that he has shown that it is false that we can encounter numerically identical perceptual objects upon distinct occasions. Thus the natural and original direct realist conception of external existence is shown to be false. As we have seen, Hume assumes the falsity of this theory right from the beginning of 'Of scepticism with regard to the senses'.

Hume's unequivocal rejection of direct realism has commonly been disregarded by major commentators on his theory of knowledge. Those who interpret Hume as a 'phenomenalist' claim that he argues that 'material objects consist entirely of "perceptions".'[8] But if by 'perception' is meant that of which we have direct awareness in sense perception, and by 'material object' that which is continuous and independent, then there is no doubt that Hume denies that perceptions are or constitute material objects distinct from the perceiver. Sometimes those who interpret Hume as a 'naturalist' also maintain that he sets out 'to defend and to uphold' the natural direct ·realist view of common sense.[9] But while Hume recognises that the view is 'the most natural of any' he tells us in no uncertain terms that it is 'false' (T.213). While Hume argues that that natural view is the origin of our belief in an independent and continuous existence, he makes no effort to uphold the truth of that view.

By showing the 'interrupted' nature of the direct objects of our sensory awareness, Hume thinks that he has undermined the direct realist view of common sense; but it is important to realise that, if his experiments show what he thinks that they show, he has also undermined a more sophisticated version of that view which, it may be claimed,[10] was held by his predecessors such as Descartes and Locke. According to these writers, sense perception gives us an awareness of the confrontation between a passive state of our own minds on the one hand, and an active world of material objects on the other.[11] The activity and independence of the objects that we perceive is revealed in sense perception. But, as we have seen, Hume clearly thinks that experiments such as those which he has described show that we have no such awareness of the 'independency' of those objects. For he thinks that his objective scientific experiments have shown that the objects of which we are aware in perception are in fact mind-dependent existences; and from this it follows that it is false that we have any impression of the efficacy of independent objects upon our minds.

Descartes had stressed the fact that sensation takes place without, and frequently contrary to, one's own will. This fact contributed to his proof of material bodies only because he claimed to have a clear and distinct idea of himself as a self-active being, quite apart from all sensation. For Descartes, when I have a sensation, I am already intermingled with my body. But for Hume, I have no veridical sense of my own activity with which I can contrast the passivity of sensation: 'no impression, either of sensation or reflection, implies any force or efficacy' (T.160). Hume's conclusion that we have no genuine awareness of ourselves as self-active beings, like his conclusion concerning our inability to have any direct awareness of the activity of the world upon us, is drawn from objective scientific investigation. According to Hume, scientific inquiry teaches us that there is no less necessity involved in human behaviour than in the behaviour of material objects; in both cases our notion of a necessity is drawn from the observation and discovery of a regularity (T.399 ff.). It is on these grounds that Hume rejects the view that the immediate impression we have of our own liberty is veridical (T.408, lines 32ff.). Here again objective scientific investigation takes precedence over the immediate appearances. The result for Hume's theory of perception is his assumption that I have no veridical awareness of the activity of my own will with which I can contrast my passive relation to the activity of external objects.[12]

§6   *Reason*

Descartes was so confident that he had a clear and distinct awareness of his own activity as a thinking being on the one hand, and of his passive relation to external and independent objects on the other, that he thought the fact of sensation could furnish him with an absolute certainty concerning the existence of these objects.[13] The 'proof' depends upon reason in that it depends upon the development of clear and distinct ideas of what is presented in our immediate awareness. Locke, too, held that our assurance that things exist independently of us *'deserves the name of knowledge'* (*Essay* 4, 11, 3). Hume's scepticism is commonly thought to arise from his development of the inevitable consequences of the 'theory of ideas' held by such authors; but I have already given some grounds for thinking that Hume's account of sense perception was substantially different from that of Descartes and Locke. In fact Hume's discussion of the senses is probably far more influenced by his reading of the rejection of Descartes' proof of material existence that is to be found in the sixth 'Eclaircissement' of Malebranche's *Recherche*. Like Malebranche,[14] Hume rejects the claim that we have any idea of the activity of external objects upon us, and insists that our perceptions constitute a realm of existence distinct from that of external material objects.

In Chapter 3 we shall see how Hume's whole scepticism concerning knowledge is bound up with his acceptance of an indirect realist theory of sensory perception which draws a numerical distinction between perceptions and distinct independent objects. It is important to recognise that, far from undermining such a theory, as is so commonly thought, Hume's scepticism is intimately bound up with his acceptance of its truth. My aim in the present section is to show that while Hume denies that reason *alone* can be the source of this theory, it is nevertheless (justifiably) presented by him as the most reasonable one. Moreover, we shall have to explain Hume's polemical remarks against the theory – remarks which have been taken by others to indicate his rejection of it.

(a) Can reason be the source of our belief in body?
So far we have seen that Hume bases his claim that the *senses* cannot be the source of our conception of a continued and independent existence upon the ground that, in sense perception, we are only aware of that which is fleeting and dependent. But he argues on the same ground that *reason* cannot be the primary source of the belief in body (T. 212). We are certain, says Hume, only of the existence of the perceptions of which we are immediately aware. In order to infer the existence of external objects we would have to rely upon an argument from cause and effect; we would have to be able to argue that our perceptions are causally dependent upon independent objects which resemble them in at least certain respects (i.e., are extended, solid, figured, mobile, etc.). But in order to make such an inference we would have to have already established some connection between the objects and perceptions. But this, according to Hume, is not possible, because in sense perception we are only aware of perceptions, of that which is fleeting and dependent. We never have the direct awareness of the continuous and independent objects which would be required in order to establish their connection with perceptions. Thus it is impossible to infer the existence of independent objects from the existence of our perceptions.

In order to appreciate the exact force of this argument it is important to note that there is an ambiguity in Hume's use of the word 'perception' when he claims that we are aware only of the perceptions of which we are immediately aware. If he had meant that it is certain that we are only aware of mind-dependent existences, then, as we shall see below, it is equally certain that there are independent distinct external objects. But in point of fact, *neither* of these claims is, strictly speaking, certain. What is certain is that we are aware of something which may itself be either an external object or a mind-dependent entity, something which has the sensible qualities that we associate with perceptions. All Hume's argument really shows is that the 'philosophical' system (which assumes a double existence of mind-dependent perceptions and distinct independent external objects) has no *primary* recommendation to reason – that is, that it does not derive from reason *alone*. The argument does not show that the philosophical system does not derive at all from reason and science; indeed, Hume has just shown that it does!

Hume bases his scepticism with regard to the senses upon his rejection of the senses and reason as sources of belief in the existence of external objects. He has argued, in effect, that our conception of and belief in independent material objects does not arise from the information which we derive from experience.[15] It is this reflection on the 'imperfections' of the human senses and reason which provides the central basis for the scepticism which Hume presents in the sections of his works which we are considering.

(b) The premises of Hume's argument for scepticism

It is important to bear in mind that while this scepticism depends upon the claim that we have direct awareness of fleeting and mind-dependent perceptions, that claim in turn is dependent upon reason and observation. It is commonly thought that Hume's scepticism either entirely undermines the truth of the claim that there exist continuous and independent objects,[16] or at least undermines the indirect realist view of perception which Hume attributes to philosophers.[17] But Hume, as we have seen, tells us right at the beginning of his section 'Of scepticism with regard to the senses' that the existence of body must be taken for granted in all our reasonings.[18] A careful examination of the logic of his argument for the dependent and discontinuous existence of perceptions reveals that he does indeed premise the existence of body in that argument. Thus it would be wrong to think that he subsequently shows that opinion to be false or absurd. (For, unlike the argument against the modern conception of matter which Hume presents in a subsequent section of the *Treatise* entitled 'Of the modern philosophy', his argument in the present section can*not* reasonably be construed as a *reductio ad absurdum*.) Similarly, Hume regards his argument for the dependent and discontinuous status of perceptions to have equal force in establishing a numerical distinction 'betwixt perceptions and objects' (T.211). The claim that there exist both perceptions and objects is the fundamental thesis of the indirect realist theory which Hume himself espouses at a number of points in his *Treatise*. [19] It is of some importance to recognise that, whatever the limitations of that theory which Hume presents in his present discussion, he himself puts it forward as the most reasonable one possible.

In fact, Hume has as much reason to believe in the existence of distinct independent objects as he does to believe that that of which we are immediately aware in sense perception is itself neither independent nor continuous. Or, to put the same point in another way, Hume's scepticism with regard to the senses has no more basis than his indirect realism. In order to see this, it is helpful to consider the form of argument for the dependent and discontinuous status of perceptions which Hume presents in the *Enquiry*. In that work he grounds his argument upon a consideration of the phenomena of changing perceptual size to which he briefly alluded in the *Treatise*. The argument runs as follows:

The table, which we see, seems to diminish, as we remove farther from it: but the real table, which exists independent of us, suffers no alteration: it was, therefore, nothing but its image, which was present to the mind. (E.152)

Hume draws the conclusion that we are aware only of mind-dependent images. [20] But he *also* goes on to draw the conclusion that these images are 'nothing but . . . representations of other existences, which remain uniform and independent'. Our present question is whether the premises of the argument actually warrant this conclusion that there are *both* fleeting perceptions *and* independent unchanging external objects. It seems clear that they do. In order to see this we might state the form of Hume's argument more generally as follows: there is a change in the perceptual object due to a change in the subject; but (as anyone would admit) there is no change in the real and independent object in these circumstances; hence, we can conclude that the perceptual object is not the real and independent object, and that what underwent the change was a mere perceptual object which is dependent upon the subject. The argument is one which shows the non-identity of two objects, by showing that the one has a property which the other does not have. This establishes the 'double existence' of the indirect realist theory, as well as establishing that we are only directly aware of perceptions.

While we may admit that the premises of Hume's argument are sufficient to establish the double existence of perceptions and external objects, we may wonder if they are both necessary to draw the conclusion that we are only aware of mind-dependent perceptions. For if we can dispense with the premise which states that there is an independent object which is unchanging, then we should be able to infer the mind-dependent character of perceptions, without also inferring that there are independently existing unchanging objects. But a little reflection will convince us that this is not possible. Let us suppose that we do dispense with the troublesome premise. Then we should still have to recognise that our perceptions change in size owing to changes in the perceived spatial relation of subject and object. But the fact that there is this dependence of the size of the perceived object upon its relations with the subject does not establish that the perceived object does not have an independent existence. The wax which expands as it warms up in my hand is not *ipso facto* a thing which has no independence. The fact that the properties of a thing are dependent upon the subject, or upon the relation of the thing with the subject, does not establish that the thing itself has no independent existence. Without the assumption that the independent object itself does not undergo the relevant change in the circumstances, it is impossible to conclude that the immediate objects of perception do not have the kind of existence which permits their continuing existence while unperceived.

To make this point clearer let us reconsider the example which Hume employed in his *Treatise* argument – the double image experiment. Here again, if we fail to make the assumption that the independent object does not undergo the relevant change, then we do not have a sufficient basis to deny the independent existence of what we directly perceive. Certainly, if we fail to make this assumption, then we shall still have to admit that the object which is directly perceived undergoes remarkable changes due to changes in the perceiving subject. We shall be forced to admit that the object splits like an amoeba when we manipulate our eyeballs in a certain manner. But without the assumption that the independent external object does not split, the phenomena of double perception have little more significance than the fact that I can take a hammer, break a stone, and then glue it back together again. Certainly we should have to admit that the manipulation of my body has a remarkable influence on external objects; we should have to construe external events in a different way from the way that we do now. But we should not be forced to conclude that these perceptual objects do not continue to exist after my bodily state ceases to have these remarkable influences upon them. In order to conclude that the perceptual object is not an independent entity, we must assume, as Hume does, that the independent object does not undergo the relevant changes in these circumstances.

We have seen that Hume's argument establishing the mind-dependent character of perceptions rests upon the assumption that there are independent objects which do not undergo certain changes under certain circumstances. We have also seen that once this assumption is granted, the argument has equal force to establish the indirect realist theory which postulates the existence of both mind-dependent perceptions and independent objects. I shall show the exact nature of this assumption in a moment; we shall see that it involves a belief in independent existence which is neither that of the common man nor that of the philosopher. First let us consider the significance of our discovery that Hume's reasonings commit him to the system of philosophers.

Any understanding of Hume's scepticism with regard to the senses must take into account the fact that the belief in the mind-dependent character of perceptions is no more certain than the belief in the existence of independent objects. Thus it is wrong to think of Hume as having shown that we are not epistemically justified in believing in external objects. Hume's scepticism is based upon the assumption that there are independent external objects, the assumption which he takes for granted. It is true that Hume speaks of certain 'extravagant sceptics' who, having recognised that we have no direct evidence for the belief in external existence, opt to believe only in the existence of their fleeting perceptions (T.214). The refusal of these sceptics to believe in external existence is in itself perfectly consistent. However, it is important to note that *if* these sceptics claim to found their refusal to believe in external existence upon Hume's reasonings, *then* they are involved in a self-contradiction. For, as we have seen, those reasonings presuppose the existence of an independent external object which has certain properties. Hume himself stresses the objections of these extravagant sceptics against reason in order to support his own claim that the belief in independent existence has its *origin* in certain natural irrational processes of the imagination.

Has Hume undermined the belief in indirect realism simply by showing that, if that theory is true, the belief in external existence can never be proved? Many have thought so, simply because they have attributed to Hume a verification theory of meaning: unless a belief can be founded upon immediate evidence, or is derived simply from the evidence of the senses by reasoned argument, it is meaningless. But on these grounds all of the major beliefs which Hume seeks to found in the *Treatise* would be nonsense. Hume denies that we derive our idea of necessary connection from the external senses or reason, and yet he insists that the relation of necessary connection is the most important part of our conception of causation (T.77). Similarly, he denies that our notion of independent existence can ever be an object of the senses, or be derived simply from reasoning on the basis of what does appear. It is a major theme of the *Treatise* that such fundamental beliefs do not rest upon any sort of direct evidence. But there is no reason to think that Hume rejected these beliefs on these grounds.

It may be thought that Hume presents the most telling objection against the indirect realist theory of perception when he points out that this system (which he calls the philosophical one) can only be reached 'by passing thro' ' the direct realist view of the common man (T.211). Hume stresses this dependence of the indirect realist system on the view of the common man. He goes so far as to say that the indirect realist theory 'at once denies and establishes the vulgar supposition' (T.218). And he notes more generally that the indirect realist system is dependent in a number of respects upon principles of imagination which cannot be refounded upon reason and experience. Many have concluded from these remarks that Hume entirely rejects the indirect realist theory which he attributes to philosophers, or seeks some compromise between that view and the direct realist theory of the common man.

(c) How indirect realism is dependent on the natural belief
In weighing this objection it is important to determine the exact nature of the dependence of the indirect system upon the natural belief of the common man. For it should now be clear that the scientific system arises in a perfectly logical way from the rational criticism of the common man's belief that our perceptions themselves are independent existences. But we have seen that the whole argument leading to the indirect realist belief in dependent perceptions and distinct objects depends for its conclusion upon the premise that there are independent objects which do not change along with our perceptions. Now the logic of the argument demands that this be a *neutral* realist claim which presupposes neither the view of the independent perceptions of the *direct* realist, nor the view of distinct independent objects of the *indirect* realist. Otherwise, the conclusion would contradict a premise, or the argument would be patently circular. The second premise of the argument (as I have given it on p. 52) merely asserts that the real and independent object does not change; in itself, it leaves neutral the question whether that independent object is a perception or a distinct independent object. Now this means that *logically* speaking the belief in indirect realism does not depend upon the belief in direct realism. The major propositions of these theories are in fact contradictory. But Hume purports to show that the belief that there is an independent object which does not change along with our perceptions is *psychologically* derived from the false belief of the ordinary man, the belief that it is *perceptions* which have this independent existence. Thus the *source* of the *general* belief that there are independent unchanging objects is the direct realist belief of the common man.

But that specific belief cannot be assumed by the indirect realist (or the sceptic when he chooses to reason) without contradiction. *It is the general belief in body which is taken for granted in the reasonings which leads to the establishment of the indirect realist system.* From a logical point of view, it is a neutral belief, presupposing neither direct nor indirect realism, which we in fact 'take for granted in all our reasonings' (T.187).

It is now clear that when Hume insists on the priority of the direct realist belief in independent existence, he can only be referring to a psychological priority. He claims to search for, and not to be able to find, any other basis for the general view that there are objects which exist independently of us (T.212–13). This is a necessary part of his claim for the priority of the vulgar system. But it is only the neutral general view which is presupposed by the argument of the indirect realist. Here we see the importance of separating Hume's own question concerning the *origins* of a belief (the question which always takes precedence in his inquiries) from the question of the truth or falsity of a belief. What is distinctive in the direct realist view is false, but that view, in general, is the source of any belief that we have in external existence. Thus we see clearly that the indirect realist in no way assumes the truth of what is peculiar in the system of the direct realist. The reflective man rejects the particular form of belief in external existence of the common man, and yet his view is dependent for its origin upon that belief.

Of course there are other ways in which the indirect realist system is dependent upon the same natural processes as the direct realist one. In any particular judgement where he ascribes continuing existence to an object, the philosopher will have to rely upon the same criteria as the unreflective ordinary man. Both will re-identify objects after a break in observation using those criteria which Hume calls constancy and coherence.[21] In this respect the indirect realist system, no less than the direct realist system, will illustrate a basic theme of the first book of the *Treatise*: that the criteria for ascribing so-called inconstant relations (causality, identity, and relations in space and time) must ultimately be drawn from certain natural processes of the imagination. While the philosopher may reason in a more rigorous way in his re-identification of objects, he will not be able to refound his fundamental criteria of re-identification upon real insight into the processes of nature. In this respect his system will be no more rational than the purely instinctual one of the common man.

Hume thinks that the close connection between the system of the philosopher and that of the common man is also demonstrated by the fact that the philosopher believes that his perceptions resemble distinct independent objects – at least in certain respects (T.216–17). This belief, Hume maintains, cannot be founded upon reason. Since no beings can be present to the mind but perceptions, it is impossible to have the direct awareness of the external objects which would be required to establish that the former resemble the latter. According to Hume, this belief is based upon a fundamental principle of the human imagination, the principle that all our thought-contents or ideas are derived from prior sensible perceptions or impressions which they resemble. When the philosopher forms his *idea* of the distinct objects which correspond to his sensible perceptions, he forms the idea of something which totally resembles those perceptions. Thus Hume says, rather paradoxically, that the philosopher thinks of his distinct object as a perception (T.218). Hume is stressing that, while the external *object* of the indirect realist system of the philosopher is numerically distinct from the immediate objects of the senses, it is generally thought of as being just the same *kind* of entity. 'Generally speaking', the philosopher considers his distinct objects to be coloured solid entities with just the same sorts of sensible characteristics as his perceptions (cf. T.68). It is only later, and through a form of reasoning which Hume seems to regard as somewhat problematic, that the philosopher comes to claim only a partial resemblance between perception and object. In 'Of scepticism with regard to the senses' and in an earlier section entitled 'Of the idea of existence and external existence', Hume explicitly limits himself to a consideration of the more natural indirect realist or representative view which requires the total resemblance of perception and object.

It appears that, in a variety of ways, the indirect realist system illustrates the general reliance of the scientific thinker upon the natural processes of the human imagination, and the impossibility of surpassing them. At the same time, the indirect realist system must be recognised as the rational correction of the false features of the system of the common man. For the philosopher shows the falsity of the common man's view that perceptions are independent objects. In these respects the indirect realist system, the one which regards our objects as resembling our perceptions, perfectly fits the standard for our 'philosophical decisions' which Hume proposes at the end of his *Enquiry*, namely, that they 'are nothing but the reflections of common life, methodised and corrected' (E.162). The theory appears to be the proper one for the *'mitigated* scepticism or *academical* philosophy' which Hume himself adopts at the end of that work (E.161).

At the same time, it is important to understand why Hume was not content with merely describing the indirect realist system as the rational correction of that of the common man. In his *Treatise* Hume sought to found philosophy in the principles of the imagination 'which are permanent, irresistable, and universal' (T.225). He does not consider the reasoning of science (or philosophy) to be *sui generis*; it is itself founded upon the principles of the imagination. When this reasoning undermines the primary and natural belief in the external world, Hume regards the conflict as one between two indispensable principles of the imagination, neither of which can be entirely universalised. Both the belief in the external world and our reasonings from cause and effect are absolutely necessary for human life; yet the principles upon which each is founded come into conflict in the scientific criticism of the natural belief in external existence. It is from this point of view that the indirect realist system appears as the 'monstrous offspring of two principles, which are contrary to each other, which are both at once embrac'd by the mind, and which are unable mutually to destroy each other' (T.215). But properly understood, this objection raises more difficulties for Hume's project of founding the understanding on mutually compatible principles of the imagination than it does for the indirect realist system itself. In any case it is important to recognise that the supposed objections which Hume presents to the indirect realist system are drawn from such a perspective.

It is commonly thought that Hume rejects both the direct realist system of ordinary men and the 'double existence' theory of philosophers. It is certainly true that, from a certain point of view, Hume lays his greatest strictures on the latter theory. But those who see Hume as rejecting that theory usually disregard that point of view and, in any case, fail to get beyond Hume's polemic to a clear understanding of the logical structure of his arguments. There is an essential asymmetry between Hume's attack on the system of ordinary unthinking people and his attack on the theory of philosophers. While he purports to show that the system of the ordinary man is *false*, he only claims that the theory of the philosophers lacks verification and is psychologically derivative. Anyone who has studied the least logic should know the importance of the distinction between falsification and lack of verification! Hume himself was certainly not confused about this distinction. He quite justifiably continued to assume the truth of the philosophical theory, even after he produced arguments to show that it was impossible to verify it directly, and that it arose only from the discovery of the falsity of the ordinary man's belief in the independent existence of the direct objects of perception. In the conclusion to this chapter we shall consider further the point of view from which Hume attacks the epistemic justifiability of the philosophical theory.

§7   Imagination

(a) The problem

Hume's criticism of indirect realism is not that it is false, but that it has *'no primary recommendation to reason or the imagination'* (T.213). Hume thinks that the view which is *primary* is the direct realist view of common sense, which arises directly from the imagination. According to this view 'those very sensations, which enter by the eye or ear, are . . . the true objects' (T.202). While Hume premises his positive account of the origin of belief in external existence on the assumption that 'all impressions are internal and perishing existences' (T.194), he seeks to explain how, in our non-scientific state of mind, we think that those impressions actually are independent objects. Hume is asking how certain entities which *in fact* depend for their existence upon events in our brains, come to be *thought* to exist independently of ourselves. He is attempting to explain the origin of a false belief. However, as we saw in the last section, Hume holds that this false belief is the psychological source for any belief that we have in the existence of things independent of ourselves.

As we have already seen in §5, Hume thinks not only that all our impressions are internal and perishing entities, but also that they 'appear as such'. He seeks to explain how, in spite of the fact that they all are and appear as internal and perishing, we come to form a 'notion' of the external and continuing existence of certain of these impressions (T.194). According to Hume, that notion derives from the processes of the mind or imagination itself. In giving an account of these processes Hume attempts to show *'what causes induce us to believe in the existence of body'* (T.187).

Hume purports to discover these causes by way of inference from the features of the stimulus objects which bring them into play. It is this aspect of his account which he regarded as most characteristic of his use of experimental method.[22] At the same time we must recognise that Hume does draw conclusions about the mental causes operating in the formation of the belief in externality which are more than inductive generalisations of the phenomena. Indeed, as I shall argue later on in this section, Hume's explanatory account draws on a psychophysiological theory which he inherited from his predecessors. Without this theory, his account of the forces involved in the formation of the belief in external existence makes little sense.

Hume begins his attempt to discover these forces with a preliminary inquiry into the features which are common to *all* and *only* those impressions to which we ascribe an external existence. Hume assumes at the outset that it must be some formal difference between the impressions of sight, hearing, and touch, on the one hand – and desires, emotions, pleasures and pains, on the other – which stimulates the imagination to ascribe an external existence to the former and not to the latter. He thinks that while all impressions 'appear' to the mind in the same way, as internal, there must still be some feature of the first type which provides the stimulus on the basis of which the imagination forms the notion of, and belief in, their externality.

Hume rejects what he considers to be the usual view that the mind ascribes external existence 'upon account of the involuntariness' of impressions, or on the basis of 'their superior force and violence'. He argues that this view is untenable because pains and other impressions which 'operate with greater violence', and which are as involuntary as our impressions of sight, hearing, and touch, are nevertheless not supposed to have any existence independent of us (T.194).

Hume's objection to the usual view is based upon a systematic confusion which is worth making clear in order to understand how this theory of belief in external existence relates to that of his predecessors. For Descartes and Locke, Hume's presumed counter-example would have provided no exception to the claim that the mind ascribes external existence on the basis of the involuntary nature of impressions. For both these authors, pain is no less external than our impressions of sight and touch.[23] They conceived of 'involuntariness' and 'force and violence' as ways of distinguishing the ideas of sensation from those of the active imagination (i.e. those which 'I can at Pleasure re-call to my Mind').[24] Our idea of pain and other such lively ideas fall under the category of ideas of sensation. Unlike Hume, Descartes and Locke held that even in an unscientific state of mind, we ascribe external reality to an idea by thinking of it as *being caused* by a distinct object. Thus a pain, or the colour of a visible surface, are both ideas of what is external to the mind. They are external to the mind in the sense that their 'involuntariness' is a sign of an active power independent of it which they represent.

Hume's objection really applies to the views of Malebranche and Berkeley who, like Hume later, made a sharp distinction between the philosophical conception of external existence and that of ordinary men. Malebranche held that in our unscientific state of mind, we believe that the 'same stars which we immediately see are outside the soul and in the heavens' (R. I, 156). Berkeley, too, described the view of ordinary men as the view that 'ideas or objects of perception' have 'an existence independent of, and without the mind' (*Principles*, I, 56). Both authors claim that, prior to scientific reflection, people ascribe external independent existence to the immediate objects of perception themselves. These perceptions are not considered as the sign of any objective existence. They themselves are thought to exist independently of our perception of them. But Malebranche and Berkeley also maintain that this unreflective belief in the externality of our perceptions is based upon a recognition of the 'involuntariness' of the perceptions.[25] It is this second assumption with which Hume takes issue. For if ordinary people really ascribed external existence on the basis of involuntariness, then they would think that pains and other such involuntary sensations themselves exist independently of us. They would think of pains as continuing to exist after we cease to perceive them. But of course they do not think of pains that way. Thus, while accepting Malebranche and Berkeley's characterisation of the common man's conception of external existence, Hume rightly takes issue with these philosophers' claims as to the criterion on the basis of which such existence is ascribed.

Thus we see that, at the outset of his discussion, Hume rejects the criterion of belief in externality which was universally accepted by his predecessors, namely, 'involuntariness'. In so doing he denies that the distinction between internal and external can be based upon a consideration of what was, according to orthodox Cartesianism, the proper activity of the mind itself – namely, the conscious operation of the will.[26] In fact we shall find that, while Hume speaks of the 'actions of the mind' in his account of the causes of our belief in external existence, he does not mean the actions of the conscious mind itself. What Hume does mean by such activity of mind will become clear in the course of our discussion later in this section (see note 39 below, and the corresponding text).

When Hume turns to his own account of the distinctive features of those impressions to which we ascribe an external existence, he in fact describes certain properties of the objects of those impressions. He labels these properties *constancy* and *coherence* (T.194–5). When Hume speaks of constancy, he has in mind the fact that the gross features of many objects in our world are relatively stable, and that they do not undergo changes due to our observation of them:

These mountains, and houses, and trees, which lie at present under my eye, have always appear'd to me in the same order; and when I lose sight of them by shutting my eyes or turning my head, I soon after find them return upon me without the least alteration. (T.194)

The constancy of external *objects* results in the fact that their *impressions* form complex patterns which are frequently repeated in our experience. Moreover these patterns are not affected by 'any interruption in my seeing or perceiving them' (T.195). I can continuously perceive unchanging objects over a period of time, or experience them in an interrupted way at different points in time. Similarly, when Hume speaks of coherence he describes the fact that other objects in our world change in regular and predictable ways, and that their impressions occur in regular sequences whether I observe them continuously or not.

Has Hume really isolated features which distinguish our 'inner' impressions from 'outer' ones? It does not appear to me to be clear that he has. Certain emotions may as regularly attend our observation of familiar objects as do their accompanying visual patterns. These emotions are as much a part of the recurring patterns which we observe as are the aspects to which we ascribe a continuous existence. I feel joy and a flock of related emotions whenever I see certain landmarks associated with happy childhood memories. Yet we in modern western society are not, for that reason, inclined to think that the joy goes on existing in our absence. Similarly, while Hume agrees that emotions have regular sequences and follow one upon the other in regular patterns, he denies that such sequences go on in the same way independently of our observation of them. However this assumption appears gratuitous. It is quite possible that our unconscious emotional life goes on in the same way whether we attend to it or not, something that might be suggested by the common aphorism that 'time heals all wounds'. Yet it is clear that we ordinarily do not assume the continuous and unperceived existence of our emotional lives.

It is probable that when Hume spoke of *constancy* he had in mind a feature of the impressions themselves which is not explicit in his initial account. It is not only the case that those mountains, houses, and trees outside Hume's study in La Flèche appear to him in similar patterns after a break in his observation of them; it is also the case that he can attend to them over a period of time without any great lapse in his attention. Hume seems to believe that this feature of our perception of 'outer' impressions is repeatable in imagination. He speaks of our ability to 'imagine . . . a change in the time without any *variation* or *interruption* in the object' (T.201). Hume seems committed to the view that, among our 'inner' perceptions, emotions do not have this sort of constancy. In Book II of the *Treatise* Hume characterises human nature as *inconstant* and maintains that 'changeableness is essential to it'. He stresses that our passions are continually changing: 'no sooner one arises than the rest immediately follow' (T.283). Hume seems to hold that passions, unlike outer impressions, cannot be felt continuously, in an unchanging way, even for a short period of time.

'Constancy', for Hume, means continuous and unchanging existence. Hume conceives of a constancy both of external objects *and* of the impressions of these objects. Both kinds of constancy are important for his discussion of our judgement of external existence. Since *objects* are constant we have impression-patterns which resemble one another at different points in our experience. But, as we have just seen, the constancy of objects also results in a constancy of the 'outer' impressions themselves; they can be experienced as unchanging over a period of time. Both the resemblance of impressions at different times, and their own constancy over a continuous time, are important for Hume's account of the origin of our belief in external existence.

It is at least plausible to assume that these two features, constancy and resemblance, distinguish 'outer' from 'inner' impressions. Although our impressions of physical pain can be all too constant, they do not usually reappear in similar patterns after an absence. Emotions and desires, while they reappear in similar patterns after an absence, do not themselves have any constancy. Many 'outer' impressions of sight, on the other hand, appear to exhibit similar patterns at different times, and can themselves be continuous and unchanging over a period of time. Thus these features seem to supply sufficient conditions on the basis of which we ascribe 'outer' existence to our impressions.

Hume seems to think of constancy *and* coherence as supplying individually sufficient and disjunctively necessary conditions of the impressions to which we ascribe an outer existence. But since the principle of the imagination which Hume postulates as operating in conjunction with the coherence of impressions seems particularly *ad hoc,*[27] and in any case he himself ultimately regards this principle as operating with little force (T.198–9), I shall concentrate on his account of the effects of *constancy*.

(b) The natural propensity to believe in a continuous unperceived existence

The crux of Hume's positive account of the origin of our belief in external existence lies in his description of the 'natural propensity of the imagination'[28] which leads us to identify numerically our resembling but temporally distinct impressions. Because of the constancy of external objects, a number of resembling sensible objects (or impressions) are frequently repeated in our immediate experience.[29] When we observe these resembling sensible objects in similar environments, especially after frequent exposures, we have a natural tendency to think of them as temporal parts of one and the same continuously existing thing. To understand why Hume speaks of a 'natural propensity' in this context it is of value to consider how, quite spontaneously, without any reflection, one slowly comes to recognise certain buildings in a new city. It is often only after seeing a building on a number of occasions that one comes to re-identify it. Hume would say that this is an entirely non-rational process which depends upon a certain natural propensity of which we ordinarily have no consciousness.

Hume claims that our natural propensity actually causes us to imagine that our temporally distinct resembling impressions constitute one continuous impression-object. At first sight this seems entirely implausible. It is difficult to believe that there is any sense in which we think that our impressions are continuous when they appear discontinuously. Yet Hume holds that we must have some idea of the continuous existence of these impressions, or else we would not judge them to be identical. For he thinks of judging as a particular way 'of conceiving our objects' – that is, as a particular way of having ideas.[30] There must be some idea-content or contents corresponding to the continuity we judge to exist. Hume thinks we have a continuous content which constitutes our judgement of the numerical identity of an object. Moreover he holds that we normally believe in the continued existence of the very entities which we immediately perceive – what are really impressions. Thus we must form an idea of the continuous existence of our resembling impressions. These very impressions must be *thought of* as continuous, even though they do not *appear* that way.

Hume thinks that the natural propensity, which makes us numerically identify our resembling impressions after a gap in our observation, leads us to form the notion of their unperceived and independent existence. This notion consists of two distinct perceptions, that of *imagination* and that of *sense*. He claims that the source of our belief in the unperceived and independent existence of our resembling impressions lies in our tendency to *imagine* (form an idea of) a single temporally continuous perception when what we actually *sense* (have an impression of) are two or more temporally discontinuous resembling perceptions. The natural propensity of the imagination leads us to think of our resembling impressions as one continuous appearance. The idea of the imagination must be derived from our previous constant impressions of this or similar objects.[31] This is why we ascribe continuous existence only to impressions which themselves appear as unchanging over a period of time. (As we have seen, Hume denies that passions ever appear this way.) Nevertheless, in the present case, these impressions are actually discontinuous in their appearance to the senses. The perceptions of imagination and sensation result in a 'contradiction' (T.205) and the notion of an unperceived independent existence results from its resolution. Through a kind of 'confused reasoning'[32] we combine the contradictory perceptions of imagination and sense, and so judge the unperceived existence of our resembling impressions. We are forced to think of them as existing in the gap between their appearances. Thus we think of these impressions as existing independently of their appearance – as being independent external objects.

In order to understand how Hume thinks that a new notion can come to be formed out of two very different perceptions, it is helpful to take a look at a fairly clear example taken from what Hume called 'the metaphysical part of optics',[33] an example which he may well have studied when he read Malebranche's *Recherche*. According to Malebranche it is by way of a 'natural judgement' or 'compound sensation' that, in spite of the decreasing size of my retinal image when a man walks away from me, 'I always see him as the same size'. Malebranche speaks of a compound sensation because the judgement depends upon different visual cues. The decreasing size of the image of the man walking away from me is combined with the 'impression of the distance' which is received simultaneously (R. I, 97). This latter impression derives largely from the 'change which occurs in the situation of our eyes' as the angle, which is formed by drawing lines from each eye to the point of focus on the object, decreases in size. This impression of distance is comparable to that which is derived from the disposition of the arms of the blind man as he 'senses' the distance of objects in front of him using two sticks.[34] A recent commentator has suggested that Malebranche regards this impression of distance as unconscious.[35] This may be so in general, though he seems to regard it as sometimes becoming conscious as a kind of 'effort of the muscles' when one looks very closely at a tiny object.[36] In any case it is certainly true that Malebranche regards the natural judgement as taking place 'in our eyes and in our brain' through a physiological process of which we ordinarily have no consciousness (R. I, 120). We make the judgement of size constancy without being conscious of the process by which the separate stimuli are combined.

In the case of Hume's example, one of the two perceptions which are combined is derived from the imagination instead of sense. But in other respects the examples are quite parallel. The actual resembling sensible impressions of a constant external object are discontinuous, just as the actual images of a receding object grow smaller. But a secondary perception enters, in Malebranche's case from the slight change in the focus of the eyes as the object recedes, and in Hume's case from my previous continuous observation of this object or other ones like it.[37] The secondary perception causes us to form a natural judgement, in the former case that what we see does not change size, in the latter case that there is a real continuity of the temporally separate resembling impressions. Finally, in Hume's case as well as that of Malebranche, both the secondary perception and the underlying causal processes lie in a pre-conscious or unconscious realm.

It is the pre-conscious nature of the judgement about the continuous existence of our resembling impressions which accounts for the fact that we tend to disregard its obvious falsity. We saw earlier, at the beginning of §5, that Hume holds that impressions 'must necessarily appear in every particular what they are, and be what they appear' (T.190). But this needs to be qualified in the case of ideas. Hume does indeed say that ideas are 'determinate' (T.35; cf. T.19), but this must be understood compatibly with his observation that 'many of our ideas are so obscure, that 'tis almost impossible even for the mind, which forms them, to tell exactly their nature and composition' (T.33). The judgement that our resembling impressions have a continuous existence springs from obscure ideas of this sort. We are therefore not really able to focus upon the source of this judgement. That would depend upon 'a strict attention, of which, generally speaking' the mind is 'wholly incapable' (T.203).

(c) The causes which induce us to believe in the existence of body
Hume thinks of these obscure ideas as arising from psychophysiological processes of which we normally have no consciousness, except perhaps as an obscure feeling. This part of his account may not be entirely explicit, yet it is essential for a clear understanding of the kind of causal explanation which Hume thinks he is providing when he turns to the faculty which he calls the imagination. At the beginning of his explanation of our 'mistake' in substituting an idea of continuous existence for that of our resembling impressions, Hume refers his reader back to an earlier account of such mistakes where he found it necessary to give a neurophysiological account of their causes.[38] In this account Hume had explained how related ideas, since they are located in contiguous brain-traces, tend to be confused one with the other: the motion of the nervous fluids 'naturally turns a little to the one side or the other' and, instead of running 'precisely into the proper traces' and stimulating 'that cell, which belongs to the idea' which was required, they run into contiguous traces and excite a related idea (T.61). Hume claims that this process is particularly common among the ideas of things which are strongly related by resemblance. We tend to use the idea of the resembling thing as if it were the one we originally intended. To take a simple example, if I try to think of a house where I met someone at some earlier time, I might actually go on and think of a resembling house and connect the person with things and events which are in fact unrelated to him. Hume would say that such an error is based upon certain natural brain processes. Actually Hume is primarily thinking of more general sorts of error where the idea of one kind of perception is systematically substituted for the idea of another kind of perception which has a close relation to it. He is particularly interested in those cases where the substitution occurs not only because of a resemblance of the perceptions themselves, but also because the *'act of the mind'*[39] in conceiving the two kinds of perceptions is very similar.

This brain-account is implicit in Hume's explanation of the formation of the false idea of the temporal continuity of our discontinuous resembling impressions. According to Hume, the *action of the mind* when we conceive of two or more resembling objects is so like the action of the mind when we conceive of a continuous one that we tend to substitute the idea of the latter when we perceive the former. The act of mind by which I conceive of my house (say) as enduring through a period of time, is so like the act of mind by which I conceive of different resembling perceptions of my house as I return to it every evening, that I tend to form the idea of the continuous uninterrupted house whenever I have the new house-impression. Hume explains this similarity of conception in the following way. When I form the idea of a single thing enduring through time, I form a single 'image or idea of the object' and think of it as participating in a succession of co-existent events which mark out the different periods of its existence. In characterising this *act of mind* Hume speaks of the 'repose' of the faculties as they fix upon the image of the enduring object. 'The passage from one moment to another is scarce felt' because there is no 'different direction of the spirits' (i.e. the 'animal spirits' or nervous fluids) such as would be required by a change in idea (T. 203). Similarly, when we conceive of different resembling impressions of the same object, the passage of the mind is so 'smooth and easy, that it produces little alteration on the mind, and seems like the continuation of the same action'. Since this act of mind is properly connected with the conception of the single object enduring through time, we tend to 'attribute sameness to every succession of related objects' (T. 204). The implication is that because of the 'smooth and easy' transition of the mind, the animal spirits fall into the traces connected with the idea of the continuous appearance of the object, rather than those connected with the idea of its successive appearance. The brain-traces connected with these different forms of appearance are contiguous, and the ideas connected with them are apt to be confounded with each other.

Whatever the obscurities of this account, it is at least quite clear that it refers to a psychophysiology which would have been familiar to Hume's contemporaries. His talk of the 'smooth and easy' transition of the mind echoes Locke's talk of a 'smooth path' being wrought between brain traces by the frequent motion of animal spirits due to 'Custom': this smooth path allows subsequent motions of these nervous fluids to become 'easy'.[40]

Malebranche, too, accounted for association by means of the formation of a path through which the animal spirits can pass more easily (*plus facilement*) (R. I, 223). It seems clear that, in his attempted explanation of the cause of our ascription of numerical identity to resembling impressions, Hume was attempting to apply a model of brain processes which he shared with his predecessors.

When we look at the probable origin of Hume's own explicit neurophysiological account of the source of the 'mistakes' caused by resemblance, we can more clearly understand how he thought that the notion of independent existence arises through the combination of the perceptions of imagination and sense. In the second book of the *Recherche*, that entitled 'Of the Imagination', Malebranche had given an account of 'the most common cause of the confusion and falsity of our ideas' which is strikingly similar to that which is to be found in Hume.[41] Malebranche, like Hume, explains how the animal spirits flow into the traces of resembling ideas. For both authors, ideas become confused due to their resemblance. The main difference between the two explanations is that Malebranche thinks that the animal spirits move into traces which have been cut deeply into the brain by frequent experience. He presents an interesting example of how such a process can lead to perceptual illusion:

the reason why one commonly sees a face in the moon, and not just the irregular blotches which are there, is that the traces of faces in our brains are very deep; for we look at faces frequently and with great attention. Thus when the animal spirits find resistance in other places in the brain, they turn easily from the direction [of those traces] that the light of the moon impresses upon them when it is observed, to enter into the traces which are naturally connected with the idea of a face. (R. I, 276)

Malebranche stresses that the operative principle in causing this physiological error is the *resemblance* between the shape and the size of the image of the moon and the image of a head at a moderate distance. The physiological connections between the traces of these resembling ideas actually cause us to see a face in the moon. The idea created by the imagination enters into our perception of the external object. The case is parallel to Hume's account of the formation of our notion of the independent existence of impressions. For we actually think that we see sensible objects to be numerically the same when we 'return' after a break in observation. The idea of the continuous existence of our resembling impressions which has its origin in the imagination actually enters into our perception of the world, in the same way as the outlines of a face when we look at the moon. We actually *see* impressions *as* continuously existing objects, just as we *see* the moon *as* a head at a moderate distance. In both cases the illusion arises from a trick of the imagination which causes the animal spirits to move in a pre-determined way through pathways formed in the brain.

(d) How we believe in the appearance and non-appearance of a single object

Having provided an explanation of how we think of impressions as continuing to exist while unperceived, Hume is left with the subsidiary problem of explaining how we think of an impression as sometimes appearing and sometimes not appearing, without thinking that it undergoes some intrinsic change. From an objective scientific point of view the appearance of an object involves the 'new creation' of an impression in the mind or brain; its absence involves the 'annihilation' of such an entity. We conceive of the object as remaining essentially unchanged, while there is some change in the perceiver which accounts for the appearance and non-appearance of the object. But Hume stresses that, from a non-scientific point of view, our 'perceptions' are our 'only objects'. Our impressions are conceived as 'the real body or material existence' (T. 206). We have no conception of something separate to account for the difference between the house as experienced and the house as unexperienced. How then do we think of our impressions as being sometimes present to the mind and sometimes absent from it without thinking of 'any real or essential change' in the impression-object itself (T. 207)?

In order to explain how we come to think of a perception as present to the mind, Hume relies upon his theory of the formation of the idea of a unified self-identical mind. According to Hume, our idea or notion of our own mind arises when we reflect 'on the train of past perceptions' (T. 635–6). When we think about these past perceptions in an act of memory, because of certain close associational links between them, the 'transition of the mind' is so 'smooth', that we tend to think of them as constituting one single self-identical continuous perception. This 'fiction' is the source of the idea of our own selves.[42] Conceived as a member of this set, our 'outer' impressions are conceived as present to the mind, as experienced. In fact they and the mind are not distinguished. Along with our 'inner' impressions they constitute the mind. Thus 'becoming present to the mind' is not conceived as involving any intrinsic change in the impression-object itself; rather it is conceived as the acquiring of a set of relations to certain other perceptions.[43] The conception that an impression is (or was) present to the mind arises when we reflect on the train of past perceptions in *memory*.

But we have another way of conceiving of our past perceptions and this, according to Hume, allows us to think of them as absent from the mind. We can think of *any* given impression in isolation from the other impressions along with which it appeared. At various points in the *Treatise* Hume stresses this ability of the mind to conceive or *imagine* any impression separately – in association with other impressions than those originally conjoined with it in space and time (e.g., T.8–10). In the present context Hume draws on this ability in order to explain how it is that we conceive of our sensible perceptions as absent, or separate from the set of perceptions and relations which constitute our own notion of the mind. When we conceive the impression apart from those relations, we conceive it as absent from the mind, without thinking that that impression itself undergoes any intrinsic change. The explanation depends upon Hume's distinction of *imagination* from *memory*.

Thus Hume claims to have shown how we find 'no contradiction' in conceiving one and the same impression-object as both perceived and unperceived. It is important to recognise that Hume claims to be doing no more than that in the present discussion. Here he is not (as many seem to think) giving a positive explanation of how perceptions can form a distinct mind-independent system of outer objects. Indeed, in a certain sense he has already done that in explaining how the imagination fills in the gap when we 'remove the seeming interruption' in our impressions by 'feigning a continu'd being'. At this stage of his explanation Hume claims to show only how 'we may easily indulge our inclination to that supposition' (T.208).

Since Hume's account of the mind as a 'bundle or collection of different perceptions, which succeed each other with an inconceivable rapidity' (T.252) is commonly supposed to be incompatible with a conception of mind as consisting of brain processes, it is perhaps not inappropriate here to make a few tentative remarks on this subject. It is certainly true that Hume holds that, from a purely subjective point of view, we have not 'the most distant notion of the place' where our perceptions appear, nor 'the materials, of which it is compos'd' (T.253). At the same time we have seen that, when Hume speaks of the 'actions' of the mind which cause us to form our judgement of the identity of our resembling impressions of external objects, he conceives of certain neural processes in the brain which result in the formation of the judgement. While there is no explicit reference back to the neurophysiological account when Hume explains how we develop our idea of the continuous identical self, his language concerning the smooth transition of the mind suggests that that account may be relevant here too. Further, we have seen the importance of memory in Hume's account of the origin of the idea of self. While his remarks on memory in the *Treatise* are generally concerned with his attempt to discover the criterion by which we distinguish memory from imagination, he has elsewhere left some notes which suggest that he subscribed to a physiological account of memory which he associated with Cartesianism.[44] According to the Cartesian account, memory consists in the formation of physical traces in the brain. Since the origin of our idea of self, according to Hume, depends upon the smooth transition of the mind from one perception to another *in memory*, there is certainly good reason to believe that he would have thought of this transition as being possible on account of the formation of such traces. There certainly is no incompatibility between Hume's account of the origin of our ordinary conception of our own minds and an account which considers mental events to be closely tied up with such processes. I believe that when we understand the close tie which philosophers such as Malebranche and Hume believed to exist between the continuous motions of fluids in the brain and the dynamics of our mental lives, we can form a genuine insight into the origin and nature of Hume's idea that the self is no more than a continuous series of perceptions related in certain ways.

In the end, Hume's discussion of the formation of the judgement of external existence forces us back to his conception of the psychophysiological processes which he conceived to occur in the brain. The obscurities in Hume's account of our belief in external existence result from the inevitable difficulties which are involved in a theoretical account of this kind. Hume had the idea that our neural pathways cause us to form different sorts of natural judgements because they cause us to relate ideas in certain kinds of ways. Natural relations, which are themselves really neural in character, cause us to believe things which are, strictly speaking, false: such are the belief in the external existence of our 'outer' perceptions and the belief in the absolute unity of the perceptions which constitute ourselves. It is less important to understand the details of Hume's accounts of the formation of our ideas of external existence and the self than to understand the basic vision of mental processes which clearly guides those accounts. In Chapter 5 we shall see more fully how Hume's account of human nature, as based upon relations of association of ideas, closely fits the dream of a science of man as expounded by Malebranche. We shall also see the important differences which show the uniqueness of Hume's own vision of human nature.

§8   *Conclusion*

In the article on 'Pyrrho' in his *Dictionary Historical and Critical* Pierre Bayle claimed that there is not 'one good proof of the existence of bodies'. He derived this conclusion from the premise that 'the objects of my senses cannot be the cause of my sensations'. It follows that I might 'feel cold and heat, see colours, figure, extension, and motion, tho' there was not one body in the world'. In support of his view Bayle referred his reader to the sixth 'Eclaircissement' of Malebranche's *Recherche* – the one in which he attacked Descartes' claim to prove the existence of an external world.[45] But Bayle does not go on to consider the fact that, in the place of Descartes' proof, Malebranche did present an argument which (he thought) led to the conclusion that the existence of external objects is 'very probable'.[46]

Malebranche argued that we have 'an extremely strong propensity'[47] to believe that we are surrounded by material objects and that this propensity, by its very existence, gives some justification for the belief that these objects exist (R. III, 62). For

Malebranche holds that we ought to believe that which we have a strong inclination to believe, unless that belief can be shown to be false by reason.[48] On the other hand, Malebranche also holds that 'we have no sensation of external objects which does not contain some false judgement . . .' (R. I, 156). In particular, like Hume, Malebranche stresses the falsity of the 'judgement of sense or compound sensation' which leads us to believe that sensations themselves exist outside of us (*ibid.*). Unlike Hume, Malebranche does not go into any details about the nature of this judgement, or how it is 'compounded' out of different sensations. But he does insist that we can hardly prevent ourselves from forming the judgement that the sensations which we have on the occasion of certain movements in the brain are themselves outside of us and in the external cause of those movements (R. I, 157).

When Hume tells us at the end of 'Of scepticism with regard to the senses' that he is unable to conclude, as he intended, that 'we ought to have an implicit faith in our senses', his remarks should be placed in the same framework as those of Malebranche. The word 'ought' here operates as a concept of epistemic justification. There are two considerations which lead Hume to hesitate in concluding that we are justified in believing in our senses: he has only been able to discover 'trivial qualities of the fancy' which lead to the belief in the external world, and he claims that we are led to the belief 'by such false suppositions' (T.217). In the first place, this indicates that, like Malebranche, Hume held that the existence of a strong natural propensity provides *prima facie* justification for the belief to which that propensity leads. But Hume claims that he finds himself '*at present* of a quite contrary sentiment'. Because he can withhold the belief in external existence, at least for a brief time, this weakens the sort of justification which he thought he could supply. Secondly, Hume seems to have gone even further than Malebranche in stressing the false suppositions which accompany our natural belief in external existence. For it is a gross error, according to Hume, to believe that our temporally distinct impressions are one continuous entity; but it is this very error which leads us to our original belief in external existence, to the belief in the external existence of the very impressions themselves.

In the *Treatise*, when Hume turns to consider the question of the justification of the philosophical system, he considers it basically from the point of view of a natural propensity. The philosopher only believes in the identity of objects corresponding to his impressions because he originally has the false natural belief in the identity of the temporally distinct resembling impressions themselves. He believes that his ideas represent external objects only because he originally has the false natural belief that these objects entirely resemble his impressions. Without the natural propensities, according to Hume, the philosopher has no basis for any belief at all in external existence. And yet the philosopher himself recognises that these natural propensities lead to false beliefs. In the *Treatise* Hume underlines the fact that, since the view which the philosopher constructs on the basis of reason has no direct appeal to any natural propensity, it has not even that justification which supports the view of common sense.

When Hume criticises the philosophical system in this fashion he chooses to ignore the fact that, according to his own account, that system is built up on the basis of the correction of the false aspects of the natural belief of the ordinary man. Hume doesn't ignore these facts elsewhere in the *Treatise,* where he presupposes the philosophical system. And in his *Enquiry* he states his point regarding the philosophical system far more judiciously when he notes that while it represents the 'more rational opinion', it nevertheless departs from the 'natural propensities' and is not entirely able to 'satisfy . . . reason' (E. 154). What the *Enquiry* account lacks is Hume's own attempt to show the exact character of these natural propensities. Certainly in his *Enquiry* Hume stresses that our ordinary belief in external existence is based upon a 'blind and powerful instinct of nature' (E. 151); but he makes no attempt to show how such an instinct operates. In that book one loses sight of just what Hume intended when he sought to found our fundamental beliefs on *human nature.*

Notes

1   *Critique of Pure Reason,* p. 120.
2   T. 189; italics mine. The direct realist view of common sense is also referred to as false at T. 192, T. 209, T. 217, and again as a 'fallacy' at

T.210. The falsehood of the theory, however, is not Hume's sole reason for rejecting the senses as a source of belief in externality; he goes on to consider whether the belief may not arise by way of fallacy and illusion. This is a good example of the priority which psychological (as opposed to ontological) questions always have for him.

3 Hume writes: 'properly speaking, 'tis not our body we *perceive,* when we *regard* our limbs and members' (T.191; italics mine). This passage is clearly derived from the sixth 'Eclaircissement' of Malebranche's *Recherche.* Malebranche writes: 'On dira peut-être, que nous voyons ces corps hors de nous, et même fort éloignez de celui que nous animons . . . Le corps materiel que nous animons, prenons y garde, n'est pas celui que nous *voyons,* lorsque nous le *regardons'* (R. III, 60–1; my italics). The words *'voir'* and *'regarder'*, which are echoed by Hume, had a technical meaning in Malebranche's philosophy. This will be discussed in John Yolton's forthcoming book *Perceptual Acquaintance from Descartes to Reid.*

The section of the *Treatise* which we are now discussing clearly shows the influence of Berkeley, as well as that of Malebranche. Hume's entry under *'Thirdly'* (T.191) indicates that he had been reading Berkeley's *Principles of Human Knowledge* I, 43 (see Roland Hall, 'Hume's actual use of Berkeley's Principles', *Philosophy* 43 (1968)) or *Three Dialogues between Hylas and Philonous* (see *The Works of George Berkeley,* vol. 2, p. 201). But the phrase 'distance or outness' which is used by both Hume and Berkeley has its origins in Malebranche's sixth 'Eclaircissement' where he writes that 'there are outnesses (*des dehors*) and distances . . . in the intelligible world which is the immediate object of our mind' (R. III, 61; see also A. A. Luce, *Berkeley and Malebranche,* p. 46). In spite of the fact that Hume follows the *words* of Berkeley there is no indication that he commits himself to anything but doctrines which Malebranche and Berkeley hold in common. The intelligible world of distance which Malebranche says he *immediately* perceives is in fact known through a natural judgement or reasoning (see below p. 66, and p. 245, n. 74). As various commentators have pointed out, Hume was not influenced by Berkeley's doctrines on our apprehension of external existence. In the passage we are discussing Hume disregards the central point on which Berkeley takes issue with Malebranche – that distance is not 'judged of by lines and angles' (*Principles* I, 43; cf. T.58 and T.636). He never even considers Berkeley's own view that it is through *touch* that we acquire any awareness of externality, and the awareness of distance through sight arises from association (*Principles* I, 44 and *An Essay Towards a New Theory of Vision,* §147). In general, I agree with John Passmore that the whole spirit of Berkeley's enterprise was 'alien to Hume' (*Hume's Intentions,* p. 87; cf. Passmore's discussion of T.58 and T.636) – though I entirely disagree with the value judgement which he wants to draw from this difference in their philosophical enterprises.

4   *Hume's Philosophy of Human Nature*, p. 25. Laird often refers to Hume as an imperfect phenomenalist. On my view the imperfection arises because Hume never aimed to be a phenomenalist at all! Hume has also been considered a phenomenalist in a weaker sense by John Passmore. According to Passmore, Hume is a phenomenalist because he held that we cannot be certain of anything but perceptions and cannot even infer the existence of anything else (*Hume's Intentions*, pp. 89ff.). Literally Hume *is* a phenomenalist in Passmore's sense. However once one understands the exact force of Hume's claim that we are only certain of perceptions, one is forced to recognise that there is no important sense in which the term 'phenomenalist' applies to Hume. See pp. 49ff., below.

5   T.190. See for example, D. M. Armstrong's interpretation of what he calls 'Hume's Principle' in *Perception and the Physical World*, pp. 37ff. Armstrong's 'Hume's Principle' was not held by Hume.

6   T.202. Hume claims to withhold the distinction between object and perception *only* from T.202, line 21 to T.211, lines 16–17. While Hume sometimes uses the word 'object' to mean direct object of the senses (i.e., impression), the distinction between perceptions (i.e., impressions and ideas) on the one hand, and external objects on the other, is operative throughout the rest of the *Treatise*. Hume is very explicit about this in the passage cited here.

Hume speaks explicitly of making 'ideas themselves our objects' at T.245. Here he means 'intentional object', not 'external object'. Hume often uses the word *object* in the former sense in his *Treatise*. It seems to have led to untold confusion for many readers of Hume, but it was a perfectly familiar use of the word throughout seventeenth- and eighteenth-century philosophy.

7   T.372. See the important discussion by R. F. Anderson, 'The location, extension, shape, and size of Hume's perceptions', in D. W. Livingston and J. T. King (eds.), *Hume, A Re-evaluation*, esp. pp. 165–7.

David Berman has pointed out that Hume's double image experiment had already been employed by Arthur Collier in his *Clavis Universalis* (1713) ('An early essay concerning Berkeley's immaterialism', *Hermathena*, 109 (1969), n. 3). It is important to note the differences as well as the similarities between the two accounts. In section ii of Chapter 1 Collier argues that neither of the double images are external; however, unlike Hume, he draws no conclusion about *physiological* dependence of perceptions. Nor does he think that the argument leads one to draw a distinction between perceptions and external objects. While Collier draws the conclusion that the visible world cannot be external, he does not analyse externality, like Hume, in terms of 'distinct or independent existence'.

8   H. H. Price, *Hume's Theory of the External World*, p. 223. Price recognises elsewhere (p. 101) that Hume 'officially' rejects the direct realist view, and that his (Price's) analysis is only a reconstruction of

Hume's text.

9 N. Kemp Smith, *The Philosophy of David Hume*, p. 453.

10 See, for example, J. W. Yolton, 'Ideas and knowledge in seventeenth-century philosophy', *Journal of the History of Philosophy*, 13 (1975). The view which Yolton is inclined to attribute to Descartes and Locke is most clearly found in Antoine Arnauld's criticisms of Malebranche. In *Des Vraies et Des Fausses Idées* (1683), Arnauld notes that 'toutes nos perceptions sont des modalités essentiellement *représentatives*' (*Oeuvres de M. Antoine Arnauld*, vol. 38, p. 199). But Hume, like Malebranche, clearly considers the relation to an object to be something which is *in fact* extrinsic to the perceptions (i.e., the Malebranchean 'modifications of the mind') themselves. Hume says that 'the reference of the idea to an object' is 'an extraneous denomination, of which in itself it bears no mark or character' (T.20).

Hume's theory of ideas is very close to that of Malebranche. Malebranche stressed that 'all sensations of which we are capable can subsist without there being any object outside of us' (R. I, 42). Ideas, for Malebranche, have 'a very real existence' and differing from other ideas by their properties come to represent different things (R. I, 415; cf. R. I, 423). Similarly, Hume writes that 'since all our perceptions are different from each other, and from every thing else in the universe, they ... may be consider'd as separately existent, and may exist separately' (T.233). At T.239, Hume clearly regards our conceptions of the qualities of the objects to be derived from the 'qualities of a perception'. Yolton regards the section from which these latter passages are taken ('Of the immateriality of the soul') as a 'satire' on the representative theory of Malebranche (see Yolton's 'Perceptual acquaintance in eighteenth century Britain', *Journal of the History of Ideas*, 40 (1979), esp. pp. 226ff.). But, in fact, Hume *assumes* the representative theory throughout the section, where his *purpose* is to show that the difficulties which apply to the Spinozist conception that external *objects* 'inhere' in a unitary substance (i.e., God) also apply to the common view that *perceptions* 'inhere' in a unitary substance (i.e., the soul). Hume's argument relies upon the assumption that any conclusion (except those we derive 'by an irregular kind of reasoning' (T.242)) we derive about objects 'will most certainly be applicable to impressions' (T.241). This assumption, together with Hume's corresponding assumption that objects may have an essential nature different from perceptions (see Chapter 4 below), presupposes an indirect realist theory of perception. Hume holds that our conclusions about the essential nature of objects are derived from our rational analysis of the perceptions. Thus anyone who argues for the incoherence of the Spinozist view that *objects* inhere in a single substance must accept the incoherence of the view that perceptions inhere in a single substance. That is Hume's point.

11 Descartes, sixth Meditation, H.R. I, 190–1. Locke, *Essay*, 4, 11, 5.

Compare Descartes' remark in his Letter to Hyperaspistes, August 1641: 'I proved the existence of material things not from the fact that we have ideas of them but from the fact that these ideas present themselves in such a way as to make us aware that they are not produced by ourselves but come from elsewhere' (A. Kenny (trans. & ed.), *Descartes: Philosophical Letters*, p. 115). In ascribing to these authors the view that matter is 'active' I do not mean that it has genuine 'active powers' in their sense. Bodies have what Locke called 'passive power' (§16 below). They are active in the sense that their role is to transmit power to another object, but this power is passive inasmuch as they derive their own motion from another object.

12   See also §7(*a*).

13   *Principles of Philosophy* IV, 206: 'There are some, even among natural things, which we judge to be absolutely, and more than morally, certain. . . . Of this nature [is] the knowledge that material things exist' (H.R. I, 301–2).

14   'Au reste j'ai fait cette remarque, principalement afin que l'on fasse une serieuse reflexion sur ces veritez: Que les corps ne peuvent agir sur les esprits, ni se faire voir à eux' etc. (R. III, 65).

15   It is important to remember that 'experience' and 'sense perception' themselves involve a process of *transdiction* which takes us beyond the data of the senses. Yet through such full-bodied experience Hume claims to show the exact nature of the *data* upon which experience itself is based.

16   This claim stems from Hume's contemporary critic, Thomas Reid. Reid writes: 'supposing certain impressions and ideas to exist in my mind, I cannot, from their existence, infer the existence of anything else: my impressions and ideas are the only existences of which I can have any knowledge or conception; and they are such fleeting and transitory beings, that they can have no existence at all, any longer than I am conscious of them. So that, upon this hypothesis, the whole universe about me, bodies and spirits, sun, moon, . . . all things without exception, which I imagined to have a permanent existence, whether I thought of them or not, vanish at once' (*An Inquiry into the Human Mind,* in *The Works of Thomas Reid, D.D.,* vol. 1, p. 96).

17   Cf. H. H. Price, *Hume's Theory of the External World,* p. 104.

18   I should not be taken to be claiming that Hume's 'must' connotes logical force in the context of this statement, only, that he goes on to do what he said he would do. I believe Hume's 'must' indicates a psychological necessity and an epistemic attitude. See the conclusion to this chapter.

19   See quotations on p. 87. Note that Hume's distinction is between perceptions (ideas *and* impressions) on the one hand, and external objects on the other. Commentators who explicitly recognise that Hume accepted some form of representative or indirect theory of perception include John Passmore and Antony Flew. See the

references given in Chapter 1, n. 19.

Hume's statements of indirect realism are embedded in contexts wherein he goes on to raise problems about the exact relation between perceptions and external objects; but these problems about 'specific' or qualitative difference must not obscure Hume's firm commitment to a numerical difference. Throughout 'Of scepticism with regard to the senses' Hume's conception of external objects is one which takes them to resemble perceptions totally; they are 'specifically' the same as those perceptions. See T. 188, lines 26–8. It is only at the end of the section (T. 218) that Hume lumps this view, that external objects have the same nature as perceptions, among those views which are false. I think it is important, for understanding Hume's sceptical philosophy of knowledge, to recognise that he allowed a specific difference between perceptions and objects (see further §11 below). But in the section we are discussing, Hume is interested only in establishing the psychological priority of the view that perception and objects are specifically the same.

20 Thomas Reid criticised this argument, mistakenly claiming that it was the sole argument put forward by Hume in support of his conclusion that we only perceive ideas in our minds. See his *Essays on the Intellectual Powers of the Human Mind* in *The Works of Thomas Reid, D.D.*, vol. 1, p. 302. The argument which Reid purported to find here is the following: 'the table we see seems to diminish as we move farther from it: that is, its apparent magnitude is diminished; but the real table suffers no alteration, – to wit, in its real magnitude; therefore, it is not the real table that we see'. Reid made short work of this argument. It has an ambiguous middle term: 'apparent magnitude is the middle term in the first premise; real magnitude in the second.' Thus the conclusion does not follow, and Hume has made a simple logical error (*ibid.*, p. 304).

But Reid has mischaracterised Hume's argument. In Hume's version the second premise states that the real independent object undergoes no change. This would exclude the change in apparent size that Reid would ascribe to the independent object. In fact, what Reid is doing is to deny the second premise of Hume's argument. Let us suppose that we follow him here and insist that the real and independent object does undergo a change here, namely, a change in apparent magnitude. But this would be a change in an *extrinsic* or relative property of that object. But the object which we see undergoes a change in an *intrinsic* property. Thus we must again conclude that the object we see cannot be the real and independent object.

21 See below, pp. 62ff.

22 Compare, for example, his discussion of the causes of pride and humility at T. 280ff. I discuss this further in §18 (*b*).

23 See Descartes' *Principles of Philosophy* II, 2 (H.R. I, 255).

24 Locke, *Essay*, 4, 11, 5; Descartes, sixth Meditation, esp. H.R. I, 186.

25 Malebranche's view is not really consistent and it is tempting to
think that it was in reading the *Recherche* that Hume came to
recognise the difficulties of the view he criticises. At R. I, 157,
Malebranche claims that the reason why we believe that our
immediate sense objects are outside the soul 'is that it is not in the
power of the soul to see them when it pleases'. But two chapters
earlier Malebranche recognised that we judge that '*lively* sensations
such as pain and pleasure' are 'within us' (R. I, 140; italics mine). In
fact he holds that it is on account of the*feebleness* of the sensations of
light, colours, and mediocre sounds that the soul 'disrobes itself . . .
in order to clothe [the external objects] with them' (R. I, 138). In this
earlier passage Malebranche recognises that the most forceful and
least voluntary sensations are not considered external to us. In an
important sense Malebranche has already recognised the point later
made by Hume, but he has not connected it with his own remarks on
involuntariness in the next chapter but one!

26 I have discussed the importance of this principle in Cartesianism in
my 'Hysteria and Mechanical Man', *Journal of the History of Ideas*, 41
(1980), p. 238.

27 The principle is 'that the imagination, when set into any train of
thinking, is apt to continue, even when its object fails it, and like a
galley put in motion by the oars, carries on its course without any
new impulse' (T.198). The same principle is used to account for our
belief in infinite divisibility of space (T.47–8; see pp. 96–7, below).

28 T.210. On the same page Hume speaks of 'a strong propensity or
inclination'; at T.205 and T.209 he speaks of 'a propension' and at
T.205 of 'natural propensities'.

29 Hume himself does not make this explicit until the latter part of his
account where he explains the 'liveliness' which constitutes our
belief in the continued existence of body (T.208–9). Still, it is not
really clear from his discussion whether he thought repetition is
only requisite for the 'liveliness' of the idea, or for the very existence
of the propensity. What exactly is the role of memory in Hume's
account? This is not made clear.

30 T.96–7n. All 'acts of the understanding' are 'nothing but particular
ways of conceiving our objects. . . . The act of the mind exceeds not a
simple conception.' Cf. Chapter 5, n. 74, below.
   The same point may be made in a slightly different way about
Hume's analysis of the concept of belief. 'The idea of an object is an
essential part of the belief of it . . .' (T.94). Thus, if I believe in some
proposition *p*, then it is required that I have some contents which
account for my belief in *p*. Yet it is important to note that, for those
beliefs based on what Hume calls fictions, there is no single
self-consistent idea-content which corresponds with our belief or
judgement.

31 Hume is not explicit about this, but it seems to be required by his
fundamental principle that any idea must be derived from a
corresponding impression which it resembles. Without such

unchanging and continuous impressions we could not form any idea of a continuous appearance. See also n. 29, above.

32 This apt expression is from Malebranche (R. I, 127) where it is used in a different but parallel context. Hume himself refers to this as 'an irregular kind of reasoning' (T.242).

33 T.374. The example which Hume goes on to mention, *'that objects appear greater or less by a comparison with others'* (T.375), probably relates specifically to Malebranche's discussion at R. I, 120. Malebranche himself suggested that our judgement of external existence is a natural judgement at R. I, 191n. But he never explained how such a judgement was formed.

34 R. I, 109. This example is from Descartes' *Dioptrique* (A.T. VI, 137). See pp. 223–4 below, for a discussion of the passages of this work which are relevant for the development of the concept of natural judgement.

Hume adopted the Cartesian conception of size perception in the text of the *Treatise* (T.58), although he rejected it in the Appendix (T.636). Berkeley claimed to show the falsity of the theory in his *Essay towards a New Theory of Vision*.

35 F. Alquié, *Le Cartésianisme de Malebranche*, p. 168: 'Mais, en fait, une seule sensation nous est offerte, et c'est la sensation correcte. Le redressement se situe en deça des limites de notre conscience.' Norman Kemp Smith opted for a similar view: since it is God and not the individual who draws the inference, 'it is a matter of indifference whether or not the signs [of distance] are apprehended at all' ('Malebranche's theory of the perception of distance and magnitude', *British Journal of Psychology*, 1 (1905)).

36 See 'Eclaircissement' XVII, 32 (R. III, 333).

37 See notes 29 and 31 above.

38 T.202, final paragraph. The footnote refers the reader back to T.53–65, and the contextually relevant passage is T.60–2.

39 T.205n., italics mine. Compare the use of the expression 'the actions of the mind' at T.61. The close connection between this expression and Hume's psychophysiology is also apparent in its use at T.185 where the *'action of the mind'* becomes forc'd and unnatural' owing to the fact that 'the spirits being diverted from their natural course, are not govern'd in their movements by the same laws . . . as when they flow in their usual channel'; and at T.98, where *'the action'* of the mind has 'more or less vigour and vivacity' as 'the spirits are more or less elevated, and the attention more or less fix'd'. All the italics in passages cited in this footnote are my own.

40 *Essay* 2, 33, 6; see p. 218 below.

41 R. I, 275. The account given by Malebranche seems to have become fairly generally accepted as an account of recollection in eighteenth-century England. See, for example, Bernard de Mandeville, *Treatise on the Hypochondriack and Hysterick Passions* (London, 1711), p. 130 and Isaac Watts, *Philosophical Essays on Various Subjects* (London, 1733), pp. 92–3. However, I have found no

other writer but Hume who follows Malebranche's use of this psychophysiology to explain the 'confusion and falsity of our ideas'.

The general psychophysiological mechanism of association employed by Hume at T.60–1 is particularly close to that presented by Joseph Addison (see Chapter 5, n. 42). Like Addison, Hume claims that associated ideas are located in contiguous brain-traces. The expression 'proper traces' in Hume's account appears to be derived from Addison.

42   T.254. Compare T.260, line 17 where Hume speaks of the 'easy transition of ideas'.

43   Hume thinks that we conceive of becoming 'present to the mind', or 'perceiving' in terms of the causal relations of an impression to subsequent perceptions: our impressions cause 'present reflexions and passions' and store 'the memory with ideas' (T.207). It is these close causal links which, when reflected upon in a memory sequence, result in the formation of the notion of the unified self, and give us the idea of the impression-object as present to the mind.

44   The following note is to be found in the ninth volume of Hume manuscripts in the Royal Society of Edinburgh: 'There is a remarkable Story to confirm the Cartesian Philosophy of the Brain. A Man hurt by the fall of a Horse forgot about twenty Years of his Life, & remember'd what went before in a much more lively Manner than usual.' This note is reprinted in E. C. Mossner, ed., 'Hume's early memoranda 1729–1740: the complete text', *Journal of the History of Ideas*, 9 (1948), p. 502. Mossner thinks that these notes date from a period well before the publication of the *Treatise*. For a contrary view, based on the manuscript watermarks, see Kemp Smith's note to *Dialogues* p. 35.

The Cartesian theory of memory is expounded by Malebranche in the *Recherche* at R. I, 224–5. See the passages from Descartes' *Treatise of Man* discussed in Chapter 5 §19 (c), below; also *Descartes: Philosophical Letters*, p. 112.

45   *Dictionary*, vol. 4, 654a, n. 12; see also Popkin, *Selections*, pp. 197–8.
46   'tout-à-fait vrai-semblable', R. III, 64.
47   'un penchant extrême', R. III, 62; cf. R. III, 63 where Malebranche speaks of 'une inclination forte'.
48   'Nous n'avons rien qui nous prouve qu'il n'y . . . a point [de corps au dehors], & nous avons au contraire une inclination forte à croire qu'il y en a. Nous avons donc plus de raison de croire qu'il y en a, que de croire qu'il n'y en a point. *Ainsi il semble que nous devions croire qu'il y en a*. Car nous sommes naturellement portez à suivre nôtre jugement naturel, lorsque nous ne pouvons pas positivement le corriger par la lumière & par l'évidence' (R. III, 63; italics mine). Compare Malebranche's expression 'il semble que nous devions croire' with Hume's expression cited at the beginning of the next paragraph.

THREE

Knowledge and objective scepticism

§9

'Tis an establish'd maxim in metaphysics, *That whatever the mind clearly conceives includes the idea of possible existence*. . . . We can form no idea of a mountain without a valley, and therefore regard it as impossible.

– Hume, *Treatise*, p. 32

§10

I say then, that since we may suppose, but never can conceive a specific difference betwixt an object and impression; any conclusion we form concerning the connexion and repugnance of impressions, will not be known certainly to be applicable to objects.

– Hume, *Treatise*, p. 241

§11

Vice and virtue, therefore, may be compar'd to sounds, colours, heat and cold, which, according to modern philosophy, are not qualities in objects, but perceptions in the mind: And this discovery in morals, like that other in physics, is to be regarded as a considerable advancement of the speculative sciences; tho', like that too, it has little or no influence on practice.

– Hume, *Treatise*, p. 469

§12

Truth or falshood consists in an agreement or disagreement either to the *real* relations of ideas, or to *real* existence and matter of fact.

– Hume, *Treatise*, p. 458

On 26 August 1737, shortly after leaving La Flèche in Anjou, where he wrote most of his *Treatise of Human Nature*,[1] Hume composed a letter to a friend in Britain suggesting four works which would be of help in understanding the 'metaphysical Parts' of his reasoning.[2] These works included Malebranche's

Recherche de la Vérité, Berkeley's *Principles of Human Knowledge*, the
more metaphysical articles of Bayle's *Dictionary* such as those on
Zeno and Spinoza, and finally Descartes' *Meditations*. In his letter
Hume noted that the other parts of his reasonings 'have so little
Dependence on all former systems of Philosophy' that his friend
can judge them by his good sense. While this latter claim need not
detain us at present, we might well be puzzled by Hume's
suggestion that the metaphysical reasonings of his predecessors
can throw any light on his own. Our problem is not with Bayle,
whose own scepticism may seem a natural preparation for the
sceptical system of Hume. But what of Malebranche, Descartes
and, above all, Berkeley? In what sense can the metaphysical
reasonings of these 'dogmatic' philosophers help us to
understand the central ideas of Hume's *Treatise*? For each of these
thinkers claimed to have access to a mode of reasoning which led
to genuine *knowledge* of the structure of reality. In answering our
question in this and the next chapter, we shall find that we can
throw a great deal of light upon Hume's whole conception of
human knowledge and its relation to his own fundamental
beliefs about the nature of reality. We shall see that it is the
divergence between the metaphysical reasonings of his
precedessors and his own original reasonings, both of which he
considered to have *prima facie* objective validity, that forms the
fundamental basis for Hume's scepticism concerning human
knowledge.

In the last chapter I discussed those sections of the *Treatise* and
Enquiry in which Hume is commonly taken to be undermining the
view that there exist external objects which are distinct from
perceptions. I showed that, on the contrary (just as he announces
at the beginning of 'Of scepticism with regard to the senses'),
Hume takes for granted the *existence* of body in all his reasonings.
I showed that Hume's whole argument leading to the conclusion
that we are only aware of perceptions – that is, brain-dependent
entities – presupposes that there exist independent objects which
sometimes do not undergo the subjective changes of our
perceptions (pp. 51ff. above). In fact, we did not need to take this
rather circuitous route to establish the fact that Hume
distinguishes between perceptions on the one hand, and external
objects on the other. When he operates outside of his discussions
of scepticism with regard to the senses, Hume is fully explicit in

making a distinction between perceptions and external objects. For example, toward the end of Book I of the *Treatise*, after the whole discussion of scepticism with regard to the senses, Hume states clearly that

The most vulgar philosophy informs us, that no external object can make itself known to the mind immediately, and without the interposition of an image or perception. (T.239)

Similarly, near the beginning of the *Treatise*, Hume notes that

'tis universally allow'd by philosophers, and is besides pretty obvious of itself, that nothing is ever really present with the mind but its perceptions or impressions and ideas, and that external objects become known to us only by those perceptions they occasion. (T.67)

In fact, it is apparent from this latter passage that it is in the context of the double existence of perceptions and objects that Hume poses his central problem of human knowledge. He says that we have knowledge of the objects only through the perceptions they occasion. Do we then have genuine knowledge of the objects?

Unfortunately there is no simple answer to this question in Hume's philosophy. Many have thought that Hume either reduces knowledge of objects to knowledge of perceptions, or else argues that the external object is entirely unknowable, and so becomes irrelevant. But Hume accepts neither of these resolutions to the problem of knowledge. The difficulty of establishing the reality of human knowledge does play an intrinsic role in Hume's overall philosophy. However, this does not mean that he reduces objects to perceptions, or else dogmatically asserts that the external object is unknowable.

Hume's views concerning knowledge are often identified with those of Berkeley. Berkeley argued against a double-existence view of sense objects on the ground that such a theory leads to the impossibility of knowledge concerning the external world:

We have been led into very dangerous errors, by supposing a twofold existence of the objects of sense, the one *intelligible*, or in the mind, the other *real* and without the mind: whereby unthinking things are thought to have a natural subsistence of their own, distinct from being perceived by spirits. This which, if I mistake not, hath been shewn to be a most groundless and absurd notion, is the very root of *scepticism*; for so long as men thought that real things subsisted without the mind, and that their knowledge was only so far forth *real* as it was conformable to *real things*, it follows, they could not be certain that they had any real knowledge at all. (*Principles* I, 86)

Berkeley solved this problem by denying the 'twofold existence of the objects of sense': there is no real numerical distinction, according to him, between perceptions (i.e., *ideas* in Berkeley's terminology) and objects. Thus the problem that objects might be unlike perceptions does not arise. Berkeley appears to solve his problem of scepticism by adopting a form of phenomenalism. By reducing objects to perceptions, he denies that there is anything in the natural world which is unknowable.

As we have seen, Hume made no attempt to do away with the distinction between objects and perceptions. In order to understand why, it is important to recognise that, unlike Berkeley, Hume did not seek any solution to the problem of human knowledge as such. He sought a solution to scepticism, but unlike Berkeley, he did not conceive of scepticism merely as a challenge to human knowledge. He conceived of scepticism, more generally, as a challenge to *belief* based upon the paradoxes of reason and science (cf. above, pp. 27ff.). Far from trying to minimise the problem of knowledge through a reinterpretation of reason and science, as did Berkeley, Hume stressed the problem in order to show that belief in the fundamental properties of our world is based not upon reason but upon a quite different source – namely, on natural instinct. Hume was satisfied with pointing out the problematic features of the representative theory of knowledge because they helped him show that our conception of objects is not derived from rational insight into the nature of reality. Our fundamental beliefs are not based upon genuine knowledge.

In order to see that Hume did not attempt a solution to scepticism along the lines of Berkeley it is important to recognise that he clearly subscribed to a representative theory of knowledge. At the beginning of Part II of Book I of the *Treatise* Hume sets forth his account of the conditions of human knowledge:

Wherever ideas are adequate representations of objects, the relations, contradictions and agreements of the ideas are all applicable to the objects; and this we may in general observe to be the foundation of all human knowledge. (T.29)

Hume ties his conception of human knowledge to that of *adequate representation*. When ideas adequately represent objects, those properties of the ideas which are discoverable by reason (relations, contradictions, and agreements) also apply to the objects. Conversely, when these 'reasoned' properties are not common to both objects and ideas, then those ideas will be inadequate, and we will lack genuine knowledge. Hume clearly makes knowledge dependent upon a contingent relation between idea and object which is bound up with the notion of adequate representation.

In this chapter and the next I shall argue that, by retaining the representative theory of knowledge and a notion of adequacy derived from his predecessors, Hume could make sense of the claim that we lack knowledge of the real nature of things. In the *Treatise*, Hume's rejection of knowledge-claims is closely connected with his belief that, in certain respects, we lack adequate ideas of objects. In these respects the reasoned properties of the ideas (or perceptions) are not those of the objects. Thus, by retaining a distinction between perceptions and objects, Hume left himself open to accept a set of beliefs about objects which differs from those implied by the rational analysis of the perceptions themselves. As we shall see, Hume usually accepted the metaphysical reasoning of one or other of his predecessors, but maintained that such reasoning applies only to the perceptions. I shall show that Hume was opposed to, or agnostic about, certain ontological beliefs to which a complete identification of perceptions and objects would otherwise commit him.

A consideration of Hume's attitude to human knowledge gives us a different perspective on his reasons for holding the 'double-existence' theory from the one discussed in the previous chapter. From the point of view of knowledge, the theory appears as an explanatory hypothesis (albeit one which has the support of the experiments we considered in the last chapter) which allows Hume to withhold judgement on, or hold a belief contrary to, that implied by the perceptions. The numerical distinction between perceptions and external objects becomes the basis for a belief in what Hume calls a 'specific difference' between these entities. The objects are allowed to be different in species or *essence* from the perceptions. It is this essential difference between perceptions and objects which forms what I shall call Hume's objective scepticism. In contrast to the material (or existential) scepticism which we considered in the previous chapter, Hume really did accept objective scepticism. His views seem to be in accord with those of Sextus Empiricus, who in his *Outlines of Pyrrhonism* wrote: 'we question whether the underlying object is such as it appears, [but] we grant the fact that it appears.'[3] Like Sextus, Hume took for granted the existence of the external object, and questioned whether it was like its appearances.

However, when Hume began writing his *Treatise*, he clearly thought that we do possess genuine knowledge – no matter how limited. He thought that in some cases, the rational analysis of perceptions does reveal the essential nature of objects. I shall begin the discussion of Hume's conception of knowledge and objective scepticism by considering his account of our ideas of geometry. The examination of this account gives us occasion to consider the basic notion of adequacy operative in Hume's philosophy and to show how it relates to the metaphysical reasoning of his predecessors. In §10 I shall note the fact that Hume clearly thinks that the correct rational analysis of our ideas will lead to a *Cartesian* as opposed to a *Newtonian* conception of space and time; and yet we shall see that Hume rejects conceivability as an infallible basis for the determination of what really exists. Here we shall see the close connection between Hume's objective scepticism and his own attempts to show how metaphysical beliefs arise in human nature. In §11 I shall argue that Hume's attitude to what he considers to be the basic principle of modern philosophy is at best ambiguous. There are no conclusive reasons for thinking that he follows Berkeley in rejecting the view that material objects have only primary qualities. Hume's objective scepticism gives him the option of accepting the modern notion of matter, though he denies that it is 'conceivable'. Finally, in the conclusion I shall reconsider the essential difference between Hume's philosophy and that of Kant in the light of the latter's claim that Hume failed to challenge the conception of metaphysical knowledge which he derived from his predecessors. I shall argue that it was Hume's retention of that conception which gave him the option to accept a genuine scepticism concerning the real nature of things.

§9 Quantity

It is important to note that Hume was prepared to claim that, in certain respects, our perceptions are adequate representations of external objects, and hence that we possess genuine knowledge. At the beginning of Part III of Book I of the *Treatise* Hume lists four 'philosophical relations' which are 'the objects of knowledge and certainty' (T.70). These relations are said to 'depend entirely on the ideas, which we compare together' (T.69). Hume seems to have thought that these relations are the objects of knowledge, only because the ideas we compare together in order to determine them are *adequate*, and therefore the relations of the objects are directly represented by the ideas.

This point of view is clearly expressed in Hume's discussion of our ideas of quantity in Part II of Book I of the *Treatise*. Here Hume attempts to argue for the objective validity of the ideas we have of geometrical objects. He *opposes* the view held by many philosophers and mathematicians of his day that the lines, surfaces, and points whose proportions are compared in geometry are 'mere ideas in the mind' which 'not only never did, but never can exist in nature' (T.42). Hume argues that our ideas of these items are adequate, and hence that objects corresponding to them can have a real existence in nature. In this discussion Hume does not claim to establish that our geometrical ideas correspond with some independent standard, a task whose impossibility he fully recognises.[4] Rather, he attempts to show that our ideas of such objects are not mere mental abstractions, and hence are of a kind which can represent real entities.

Hume's use of the word 'adequacy' in his definition of knowledge is closely related to its use by Descartes. In his reply to the fourth set of Objections to his *Meditations* (which would probably have formed part of the volume of that work to which Hume refers in his letter), Descartes claimed that while we do not have *entirely* adequate ideas of things, since only God possesses that, our knowledge has 'sufficient adequacy to let us see that we have not rendered it inadequate by an intellectual abstraction' (H.R. II, 98). Moreover, Descartes held that when we determine that we have not arrived at an idea by abstraction, we are able to establish that it can represent a real substantial thing. These thoughts are closely related to his claim, in his third Meditation, that ideas possess more or less *objective* or (which amounts to the same thing) *representative* reality (H.R. I, 162). Ideas possess more or less objective reality, in this sense, according to Descartes, in so far as they are less or more abstract, and so can be used to represent a greater or lesser reality of things. A clear and distinct idea is one which can represent a thing or substance, because it is not itself an abstraction. On the other hand, ideas which cannot be thought in distinction from others are abstract, and so can represent only modes or accidents, items which are not in themselves complete or real beings. When the mind conceives of these items 'it conceives the thing inadequately' (H.R. II, 22).

In order to justify his view that we have ideas of quantity which are adequate representations of external objects, Hume appeals to (what he calls) the 'establish'd maxim in metaphysics' (T.32). The principle which he employs is a version of the fundamental Cartesian principle of metaphysical reasoning espoused in Descartes' *Meditations*;[5] namely, the principle that 'whatever can be conceiv'd by a clear and distinct idea necessarily implies the possibility of existence' (T.43). Hume also employs the converse, that whatever is inconceivable is impossible: we can, he says, 'form no idea of a mountain without a valley, and therefore regard it as impossible' (T.32; cf. H.R. I, 181). The upward slope without the downward slope is a mere mental abstraction and so cannot have any real independent existence. As we shall see both in this and the next chapter, the principles to which Hume here alludes were used by Descartes and his followers to make fundamental claims about the nature of reality.

In his discussion of our ideas of geometry Hume employs the established maxim of metaphysics in a Cartesian way, to argue that, since we have clear and distinct ideas of the minimal parts of extension, it follows that objects can exist corresponding to them. His discussion is most immediately directed against Bayle, who, in the article on Zeno of Elea in his *Dictionary*, argued that three-dimensional bodies, as well as geometrical lines and surfaces, 'cannot exist any other way than ideally' – that is, as abstractions in the mind.[6] Bayle based his argument on the claim of the authors of the *Port-Royal Logic* that bodies must be considered to be infinitely divisible. He used this claim to support his own scepticism, insisting that infinite divisibility leads to paradoxes, such as the conclusion that no two objects, no matter how close together, can ever be contiguous. Bayle argued that, if matter is infinitely divisible, there will always be an infinite number of parts between any two objects. He met such paradoxes by claiming that our ideas of extension can exist only in the mind. We shall see that, in other cases, this is the route chosen by Hume. But, on this question, Hume opposes Bayle's sceptical conclusion by insisting against the Port-Royal authors that we do in fact have a clear and distinct idea of finitely divisible parts of matter. For he insists that 'our ideas are *adequate representations* of the most minute parts of extension' (T.29; italics mine). Moreover, by applying the Cartesian principle of idea-analysis, he concludes that infinite divisibility of matter 'must be *really* impossible and contradictory' (T.29). Thus Hume is prepared to draw an ontological conclusion, a conclusion about what can and cannot exist, on the basis of claims about the nature of our ideas.

Of course we must recognise that the Cartesians drew a very different conclusion about divisibility of matter from Hume. Nicole and Arnauld, the authors of the *Port-Royal Logic*, insisted that infinite divisibility is clearly conceivable, though we can never 'comprehend' the infinitely divisible parts. But their arguments for infinite divisibility were based on 'demonstrations'.[7] Hume opposes these demonstrations by appeal to what he takes to be the clear and distinct ideas of the parts of matter. He regards himself as the defender of the definitions of Euclid against these presumed demonstrations of infinite divisibility to be found in the *Port-Royal Logic*. According to Hume the definition of a point as that which has 'neither length, breadth nor depth' would be invalid if matter were indeed infinitely divisible (T.42). Hume thought it was paradoxical that geometry should, through its demonstrations, destroy its own fundamental ideas. Thus, in this context, Hume regards himself as the real upholder of the fundamental Cartesian principle of metaphysical reasoning.[8]

Hume opposes the claims of infinite divisibility with his insistence that 'the ideas of quantity' are all 'particular, and such as are suggested by the senses and imagination' (E.158n.). He claims that we have a clear and distinct idea of finite minimal parts of extension derived from what he calls 'impressions of atoms or corpuscles' (T.38). Hume argues that we have a non-abstract complete idea of the atomic parts of extension, on the ground that when we view (or have impressions of) objects disappearing off in the distance, they reach an absolute minimum and then entirely disappear (T.27). Our impressions do *not* go on decreasing *ad infinitum*. This fact about our impressions is the source of our idea of points (Hume calls them coloured or tangible atoms) which themselves have no extension, but which combined together can form extended lines, surfaces, or solid bodies (T.38–9).

In defending the real objective existence of finitely divisible geometrical objects by appeal to the properties of sense impressions, Hume followed a path which had already been laid down by Berkeley. In *A New Theory of Vision*, first published in 1709, Berkeley had argued that 'whatever may be said of extension in abstract, it is certain sensible extension is not infinitely divisible' (§54). In this section Berkeley also spoke of 'a Minimum Visibile, beyond which sense cannot perceive'. In his *Principles of Human Knowledge*, first published in the following year, Berkeley rejected the infinite divisibility of *conceived*, as well as *sensed*, geometrical figures (*Principles*, I, 124); like Hume later, Berkeley connected this rejection with his attack on abstract general ideas (*Principles*, I, 126, 127). Berkeley's own objection to Newton's ideas of infinitesimals in his *Analyst* of 1734 was of importance in the historical development of the calculus.[9] This objection was closely connected with Berkeley's belief that the world consists of minimal finite objects. Hume, who (unlike Berkeley) was not an accomplished mathematician, seems to have accepted Berkeley's results as showing that genuine knowledge of the finitude of matter is, at least in principle, possible.

Hume accepted Berkeley's sensory criterion of conceivability, and hence Hume's application of the established maxim of metaphysics led – at least on the question of the divisibility of matter – to a substantially different result from its application in the hands of the Cartesians. For both Hume and Berkeley, what we can conceive or imagine is no different from what we can sense. All ideas, as Hume frequently reminds us, are derived from corresponding sense impressions which they resemble. This principle is closely related to the central principle which Hume derived from Berkeley – the principle that there are no abstract general ideas – that is, ideas which do not resemble the particular and determinate ideas of the senses (cf. T.17 ff).

It is, I believe, wrong to exaggerate the importance of the differences between the criteria of conceivability employed by Berkeley and Hume on the one hand, and the Cartesians on the other. While Descartes insisted that we can form a clear and distinct idea of our own minds and of God without employing the senses or imagination, he nevertheless believed that these faculties were necessary in order to form the conception of an extended object. In his *Regulae* Descartes insisted that, in order to form an idea of a corporeal thing, we must 'form the idea of that thing as distinctly as possible in the imagination' (H.R. I, 40; cf. 57–8). This, he says, is best effected by exhibiting the object to the senses. It must be admitted that Descartes also stressed the 'errors' which result from our belief that external objects resemble the ideas of the senses. Nevertheless he always insisted that we should properly 'call extended only what is imaginable and has parts outside other parts of a determinate size and shape'.[10] As we shall see in the next section, 'imagination' plays a not unimportant role in Descartes' theory of conceivability of external existence.

We have seen that Hume employed the Cartesian maxim of metaphysical reasoning, combined with a criterion of conceivability derived from Berkeley, in order to determine that extension is composed of finite discrete minimal parts. Hume argues along similar lines in order to establish that time, too, is composed of *minima*. Here he employs an observation of Locke and Newton: since there is a threshold beyond which we cannot observe the successive parts of some change, it follows that our idea of time is composed of minimal parts which succeed each other. From these authors[11] Hume learned that when 'you wheel about a burning coal with rapidity, it will present to the senses an image of a circle of fire' (T.35). The example shows that we perceive simultaneity when events take place successively beyond the threshold of our perception. From this fact Hume concludes that we have an idea of the minimal parts of succession, and that our idea of duration is derived from nothing but our awareness of the succession of these parts. Hume seems to regard these temporal *minima* as the basic units which form our ideas of number (T.30–1). He seems committed to the view that arithmetic presupposes the existence of minimal units which have objective validity.

But while Hume argues on the basis of criteria of conceivability that reality is composed of minimal parts of space and time, he clearly holds that such criteria do not go very far in helping to establish the basic principles which underlie the sciences. If one seeks what Hume considers to be genuinely distinctive in his reasoning concerning the foundations of geometry, one must examine his *rejection* of conceivability as the basis for the determination of the axioms and postulates of that subject.

Hume claimed that in most respects, we *lack* knowledge of the fundamental structure of space. As we have seen, Hume does maintain that 'our ideas are adequate representations of the most minute parts of extension' (T.29). But, by showing that our impressions reach a minimum, Hume only claims to have shown how objects can be conceived to be composed of parts which cannot be divided. Our ideas are adequate representations of objects in this one respect. But Hume also claims that we discover 'by reason, that there are other objects vastly more minute' than the smallest objects which appear to the senses. Thus our senses 'represent as minute and uncompounded' objects which are 'really great and compos'd of a vast number of parts' (T.28). Representation is merely proportional. Hume holds that because we lack ideas which represent the actual size of the minute parts of extension, we are not able to have real insight into the composition of points which compose geometrical objects. He maintains that the order of points which constitutes the difference between a straight and a curved line is 'perfectly unknown' (T.49). Hume appears to believe that the principle that a straight line is the shortest distance between two points is not known to be necessarily true. He attributes our lack of knowledge of this and other fundamental principles of geometry to the fact that our ideas 'can never afford us any security, when we examine the prodigious minuteness of which nature is susceptible' (T.71).

Hume claims that the fundamental propositions of geometry are derived from what he called the 'general appearance' of things (T.71). Hume's use of this phrase is somewhat puzzling; but very clearly he intends to contrast *appearances* with the properties which we discover when we examine our clear and distinct ideas. According to Hume, we arrive at the conclusion that a straight line is the shortest distance between two points 'by

accident' when we consider its 'particular appearance' (T.50).
This conclusion does not follow from an examination of the ideas
themselves. Hume also denies that our ideas of minimal parts of
extension play any practical role in our geometrical reasonings.
Because we draw our judgements of the equality of two lines
from a comparison of their 'general appearance', we find that we
sometimes have to correct these judgements, and determine that
what we thought was equal was not really so (T.47–8). Through a
natural propensity we come to believe that such corrections can
always be made: we believe that we can always discover that one
of the lines is composed of more parts than the other. This seems
to be the source of the false idea that any part of matter can always
be further divided. But Hume claims that this idea is no less
natural than any of the other fundamental principles of
geometry, all of which are derived from the 'general appearance'
of things. Thus we should, according to Hume, deny that
geometry is 'a science exact enough to admit of conclusions so
subtle as those which regard infinite divisibility'.[12]

These reasonings are difficult to follow, but they are clearly
meant to contrast the sorts of conclusions we derive from the
rational analysis of ideas with those based upon a natural
propensity of human nature. In this discussion Hume regards
knowledge of the real nature of things to be derivable only by the
former means; the fact that we rely upon 'general appearance'
and a natural propensity is only the sign of the lack of 'exactness
and certainty' of geometry (T.71). At the same time the general
foundation of geometrical axioms, such as they exist, is clearly
not based upon the 'establish'd maxim in metaphysics', even
when that maxim is interpreted along with the criteria of
conceivability provided by Berkeley. Generally speaking, Hume
rejected conceivability as the actual foundation for the
fundamental principles of geometry. He was only willing to
accept that foundation in relation to his claims regarding the
objective existence of geometrical objects themselves.

In the next chapter we shall find that there are even reasons to
think that Hume was forced to abandon the view that space and
time consist of distinct discrete parts. Hume's rejection of the
rational analysis of human ideas as a genuine guide to the real
nature of things will then seem complete. Nevertheless, we shall
find that this ideal of human knowledge is never abandoned by

Hume and always forms the basis for the claim that we lack knowledge of the structure of reality. Paradoxically, it is Hume's *acceptance* of the conception of knowledge connected with the Cartesian maxim of metaphysical reasoning, which forms the real basis of his scepticism.

It is somewhat ironic that the views of mathematics which are most associated with Hume's name are ones which he himself would not have considered distinctive at all.[13] In his *Enquiry Concerning Human Understanding* Hume abandoned his earlier conception of knowledge, which tied up the notion of certainty with that of 'adequate representation'. He claimed that the certainty of geometrical propositions does not depend upon the existence of geometrical objects:

Propositions of this kind are discoverable by the mere operation of thought, without dependence on what is anywhere existent in the universe. Though there never were a circle or triangle in nature, the truths demonstrated by Euclid would for ever retain their certainty and evidence. (E.25)

The view which Hume expressed in his *Enquiry* echoed that expressed by Descartes in his fifth Meditation:

when I imagine a triangle, although there may nowhere in the world be such a figure outside my thought, or ever have been, there is nevertheless in this figure a certain determinate nature, form, or essence, which is immutable and eternal. (H.R. I, 180)

In fact, both philosophers stepped beyond these positivist-like claims concerning the actual existence of geometrical objects. While, in his fifth Meditation, Descartes maintained that the certainty of geometry does not depend on the actual existence of corporeal substance, in his sixth Meditation he showed that, as a matter of fact, it does exist.[14] Thus geometry gives us knowledge of an actually existing object. Descartes went on to maintain, quite notoriously, that he did not require 'any other principle in Physics than in Geometry or abstract Mathematics' (*Principles of Philosophy* II, 64; H.R. I, 269). Hume, of course, was quite explicit in rejecting the Cartesian claim that the first principles of physics were reducible to geometry. Nevertheless, even in the *Enquiry*, he was as confident as any Cartesian in his belief in the objective validity of geometrical principles. He maintained that through geometrical reasonings one can arrive at 'the just dimensions of all the parts and figures which can enter into any species of machine' (E.31). As Antony Flew has suggested, it is an anachronism to maintain that Hume actually put forward the positivist view that purely mathematical propositions are analytic, and do not present any substantial truths about objects.[15] In fact Hume's remarks on geometry in the *Enquiry* are so brief that it is difficult to tell *what* he believed! In that book there is no discussion of the foundation of the fundamental postulates and definitions of the mathematical sciences.

When he wrote his *Treatise* Hume clearly held it to be a requirement of geometrical knowledge that geometrical propositions be necessary and that they apply to reality. We have seen that he denied that we have such knowledge on the ground that the actual fundamental propositions of geometry are merely contingent. Hume *explained* this lack of knowledge by the fact that our ideas of the minimal parts of extension do not adequately represent the size of the parts of extension itself. In his *Enquiry* Hume clearly abandoned the view put forward in the *Treatise* that the *certainty* of geometrical propositions depends upon the real existence of their objects; but he did not *deny* that these propositions actually do apply to the real world of objects. He merely reverted to the view, held by many philosophers of his day, that geometrical propositions are necessary, and that their necessity does not *depend upon* the existence of geometrical objects. Nevertheless, he *assumed* that Euclidean geometric relations apply to all actually extended objects. It is of some historical importance to recognise that it was this theory of mathematics found in the *Enquiry* which was ascribed to him by his contemporary, Kant.[16]

Kant credited Hume with having made the discovery that there are judgements which are fundamental to scientific inquiry which are not known through analysis of ideas.[17] But the German philosopher thought that Hume merely concentrated on the causal principle and never considered that knowledge of pure mathematics also could not be founded in this way. Kant's misreading of Hume's views on mathematics is accounted for by the fact that only the *Enquiry*, not the *Treatise*, was available to him in its entirety: Kant naturally concluded from the former work that Hume had always held the common view that the fundamental principles of geometry were derived from idea-analysis, and he believed that Hume would be troubled by the discovery that geometry did not have the objective validity warranted by such analysis. Kant thought that if Hume had recognised that, according to the old account of knowledge, mathematics was in no better condition than the causal maxim, he would have been saved from scepticism by 'his good sense'. Kant thought that Hume should have recognised the need for an entirely new conception of mathematical and metaphysical knowledge.

We have seen that, in the *Treatise*, Hume did not abandon the Cartesian principle of idea-analysis as a foundation for knowledge: yet he was willing to go against Kant's 'good sense' in order to claim that we lack genuine knowledge of the structure of space. No less than Kant, Hume recognised the 'synthetic' character of the fundamental propositions of geometry: but he held to the view that this character was a mark of the fact that we lack real knowledge of objects. Kant held that geometrical propositions give us knowledge of the form in which objects *must* be intuited in space by finite creatures such as ourselves.[18] But Hume retained a clear distinction between objects and perceptions, and claimed that geometrical axioms are derived from certain facts of human perception and imagination which might well be other than they are. The development of non-Euclidean geometries in the nineteenth century and their subsequent application in physics would seem to show that Hume's 'good sense' – which led him to question the objective validity of the fundamental principles of geometry – was at least equal to that of Kant.

§10   *Space and matter*

According to the *Port-Royal Logic* the 'certainty and evidence of human knowledge' depends upon the principle that *'everything that is contained in the clear and distinct idea of a thing can truly be affirmed of that thing'*.[19] According to this principle it is the rational analysis of our ideas which gives us knowledge of reality. Descartes wrote along similar lines that 'we cannot have any knowledge of things except by the ideas we conceive of them'. Conversely, he claims that 'whatever conflicts with these ideas is absolutely impossible and involves a contradiction'.[20] As with

Hume, who may have followed him here, Descartes conceives of contradiction as closely tied up with the notion of abstraction: 'by abstraction we . . . obtain the idea of a mountain, or of an upward slope, without considering that the same slope can be travelled downhill'.[21] An abstract idea represents what is in itself impossible because it cannot be conceived clearly and distinctly.

In various scientific and philosophical writings Descartes determined one of the most central claims underlying his physics – the claim that there is no such thing as empty space or a vacuum – by appeal to a claim about the nature of our idea of space or extension. According to Descartes, it is impossible to conceive of extension without matter; extension is only conceived apart from the extended thing through a distinction of reason.[22] Descartes claimed that when we think of an extended place apart from body we are only thinking of 'extension in general', not something particular which can exist in its own right (*Principles of Philosophy* II, 12 (H.R. I, 260)). In his *Regulae*, Descartes stressed the need for *imagination* in order to form a clear and distinct idea of body (H.R. I, 40). He claimed that persons who think that space can exist if all the matter in the universe were annihilated base their belief on a *'false judgment of the intellect working by itself'* (H.R. I, 57; italics mine). They mistake an abstraction of the intellect for something that can exist as a real thing or substance.

While the Cartesian analysis of the idea of extension may seem rather artificial to us today, it seems to have played an important role in later seventeenth- and eighteenth-century philosophical and scientific debates about the existence of absolute space. Newton and Locke defined body in terms of resistance or solidity, ideas derived from the sense of touch when an effort is made to force two bodies into the same place. Locke claimed that, whether or not the vacuum exists, it is certain that we have 'an Idea of Space distinct from Solidity' (*Essay* 2, 13, 26). Newton was commonly held to have proved that a vacuum is 'absolutely necessary' in order to explain the motion of the planets.[23] However, Bayle, who was widely read in England as well as on the continent, insisted that Newton demonstrated *'the existence of what is contrary to the most evident notions of our intellect'*.[24] For according to Bayle, we 'have a clear and distinct idea' of extension as that which is divisible, mobile and impenetrable. These properties are bound up with our conception of the essence of extension. However the Newtonian space, of which we have no clear and distinct idea, is indivisible, immovable, and penetrable. Bayle claims that the Newtonian notion of absolute space is 'repugnant to our clearest ideas' (*ibid.*).

It is rather surprising to discover that Hume, writing nearly forty years after Bayle, also supports the Cartesian view that absolute space is inconceivable. 'We can', claims Hume, 'form no idea of a vacuum, or space, where there is nothing visible or tangible' (T.53). Hume thinks that our ideas of space and time are 'no separate or distinct ideas, but merely those of the manner or order, in which objects exist' (T.39–40). Like Descartes, Hume holds that space and time considered apart from the spatial and temporal ordering of actual objects are mere mental abstractions. Space and time are conceived as mere modes or 'manners' in which things exist: they are not conceived as things in their own right. It is, says Hume, 'impossible to conceive . . . a vacuum and extension without matter' (T.40). Likewise time cannot be conceived without our conceiving a succession of changing objects (T.36). For Hume, no less than a Cartesian, the Newtonian notions of absolute space and time are inconceivable.

Hume's discussions of our conceptions of space and time are remarkably similar to those of Descartes. Hume even attempts to show how these conceptions are derived by abstraction through a comparison of visible surfaces of different colours, and a comparison of tangible surfaces with visible ones. We 'found an abstract idea merely on that disposition of points, or manner of appearance, in which they agree' (T.34). His account of how we arrive at our abstract notions of space and time is closely related to his own earlier account of how we form a *'distinction of reason'*. There he gave as examples of these distinctions the Cartesian 'modal' distinctions between 'figure and the body figur'd; motion and the body mov'd'. Hume argued that such distinctions only arise in the act of reasoning by which we compare one idea with another. In this way we form a distinction of what 'really is, perfectly inseparable'. Hume insists, no less than Descartes, that such abstract notions cannot be conceived apart from the complete thing (T.24–5).

The question now arises whether Hume followed the Cartesians in applying to the objective world the result of this analysis of our ideas of space and time. Did Hume maintain – as

he did in the case of his discussion of the finite parts of matter –
that our *ideas* provide an accurate touchstone of what objectively
exists? In this case, as we have seen, the 'establish'd maxim in
metaphysics' should lead anyone who accepts the Cartesian
idea-analysis to deny the existence of absolute space and time.
For according to this analysis, which Hume did accept, space and
time cannot be conceived distinctly apart from material things
which are extended and changing. Hence, the only question is
whether Hume believed that the analysis of our ideas is an
accurate guide to the way things exist objectively, apart from our
human conceptions.

Hume's answer to this question is unambiguous. He clearly has
no intention to settle the question of the existence of absolute
space and time in an *a priori* manner by means of ideas. In the
Appendix to the *Treatise* he states that there are 'no very decisive
arguments on either side' of the ontological dispute between the
Newtonians and the Cartesians.[25] He thinks that the subject is
one which exceeds 'all human `capacity', and notes that, in
relation to such subjects, it is best to opt for a 'modest scepticism'
(T.639). But Hume fully recognises the implications of his stand.
He states that his *'intention never was to penetrate into the nature of
bodies'* (T.64; italics mine). While Hume fully accepts the Cartesian
account of the analysis of our ideas of space and time, he rejects
that account as the basis for decisions concerning the actual
nature of objects. In this discussion Hume clearly *rejects* the
'establish'd maxim in metaphysics' and allows for the possible
existence of that which is conceived to be absolutely impossible –
namely, absolute space.

Hume firmly denied that we have any ideas of absolute space
and time, and was committed to the view that such notions are
contradictory. Yet he firmly held that we all have a *natural belief* in
the existence of what corresponds to these contradictory notions.
He believes that it is the Newtonian rather than Cartesian views
which accord with 'vulgar and popular notions' (T.639). While
Hume denies the conceivability of absolute space and time, he
proceeds to explain how we come to believe in their existence.
Our belief is based upon what he elsewhere (T.48; T.209) calls a
mere *fiction* of the imagination, rather than upon a clear and
distinct idea.

Hume's account of the origin of our belief in absolute space is exactly parallel to his account of the origin of our belief in the continuous unobserved existence of body, which is the basis of our belief in external existence. Indeed, it is in Hume's account of the formation of our belief in empty space where he declares his psychophysiological model indispensable for an understanding of what he is doing.[26] Here he explains how we superimpose the image of a full space when we observe nothing between two objects (T.58–9). Once again our belief arises from a confused reasoning resulting from an opposition between the perceptions imposed upon us by imagination and sense. The confusion results from the similarity of 'the actions of the mind' when we conceive closely related ideas: the motion of the animal spirits gets diverted when we attempt to conceive of the distance between two stars in the sky, and 'falling into the contiguous traces' they present the idea of a similar distance which is filled with sensible objects (T.61). The details of Hume's account of the similar 'actions of the mind' need not concern us here: it suffices to say that they closely parallel the account of belief in continuity which we considered in §7 (c).

As in the case of our belief in the independent existence of body, Hume holds that the natural origin of the belief in empty space provides some justification for that belief. In the Appendix to the *Treatise* he states that he favours the Newtonian view simply because it is the one that accords with the vulgar and popular notions. This common-sense view must be justified by the fact that it has its source in a natural instinct. But, as we have already seen, Hume goes on to qualify his support and opts for a 'modest scepticism'. *Reason* opposes the common-sense view of empty space no less than it opposes the common-sense view of external existence. The opposition of reason to the existence of empty space is drawn from the rational analysis of our ideas – not from experimental reasoning, as in the case of our belief in external existence. But Hume does not entirely abandon reason in the present case, any more than he did in his discussion of external existence. The balance between reason and natural instinct leaves him totally suspended between the Cartesian and Newtonian views of space. In this case there is not even room for a reconciliation.

If Hume did not entirely abandon idea-analysis as a guide to objective existence, he clearly held that it was a very problematic guide. Unlike Locke, he did not insist that he had a better rational analysis of space than the Cartesians; rather, he claimed that the rational analysis of ideas might apply only to the perceptions, not to the world of objects. Hume denied that the 'objective reality' of our ideas need be a guide to the nature of what actually exists.

It is clear then that Hume holds that what is inconceivable – absolute space and time – *may* exist. In the case of space and time he clearly allows that our human conceptions may not be an accurate guide to 'possible existence'. At the same time it is not necessary to conclude that Hume abandons his *Treatise* conception of knowledge. Indeed, it is within terms of that conception that we can understand his objective scepticism concerning our ideas of space and time. For Hume holds that such ideas might be *inadequate* and that therefore the contradictions of ideas are not necessarily those of reality. His official reason for claiming that there is such inadequacy in the case of our ideas of space and time is the existence of the opposing natural instinct. However, it is tempting to think that the real reason has more to do with the fact that Newtonianism was the scientific philosophy becoming dominant in Hume's own day. In either case Hume had reasons for claiming that our ideas were inadequate and that we lack knowledge of the real nature of space and time.

However, the conclusions of Hume's analysis of absolute space and time can also be stated in terms of his reinterpretation of the concept of knowledge in the *Enquiry*. We have seen that in that work Hume sharply distinguished knowledge of essence from that of existence. In line with his conception of knowledge in the *Enquiry*, we may say that Hume never denied that we have knowledge of the essential connection between space and matter, and time and changing things. He only denied that we have knowledge that any object exists which corresponds to these *natures* or *essences*. *A priori* we have no guarantee that time exists only as the measure of change, any more than that triangles exist whose angles are equal to 180 degrees. In both cases we have knowledge of a certain essence, but it is merely an essence which belongs to our perceptions. Space and time, as they are in themselves, might not only exist as the order of the parts of matter; they may have the absolute existence attributed to them by Newton and his followers.

Hume's views concerning absolute space stand in marked contrast to those of Berkeley, and help to show the essential difference between the ontological commitments of the two philosophers. Like Hume, Berkeley followed the Cartesians in claiming that the idea of pure space without body is a merely abstract idea (*Principles*, I, 116). But Berkeley drew an ontological conclusion from his criticism of the Newtonian theory. As Popper has noted, Berkeley believed that 'Newton's doctrine of absolute space . . . must . . . be rejected as a physical theory'.[27] But, as we have seen, this is just the conclusion that Hume did not draw. Hume, whose central interest was in the source in human nature of our confused notion of empty space, allowed for the possibility that it, rather than our clear and distinct idea, might be the true guide to physical reality. Unlike Berkeley, Hume abandoned the Cartesian principle of idea-analysis as an infallible guide to what really exists.

It is clear then that Hume thought that the objective or representative reality of our ideas of space and time might not be any guide to their real existence. Hume agrees with Berkeley and the Cartesians that our separate and distinct notions of space and time are mere abstractions or distinctions of reason; yet he allows (with Newton) that they may represent a real or independent existence. Hume is clearly committed to the view that we can *suppose* the existence of that which is *inconceivable*. Consider his own words toward the end of Book I of the *Treatise*:

I say then, that since we may *suppose*, but never can *conceive* a specific difference betwixt an object and impression; any conclusion we form concerning the connexion and repugnance of impressions, will not be known certainly to be applicable to objects. (T.241; italics mine)

Here we find Hume's clearest statement of *objective scepticism*. Its importance in Hume's philosophical reasoning cannot be underestimated. In the final analysis Hume regarded the 'establish'd maxim in metaphysics' to have a purely problematic application to reality. What is necessarily connected in our perceptions (i.e., impressions and ideas) need not be necessarily connected in reality. What is repugnant to our clearest ideas – for example, the notion of space without matter – may be supposed to exist in reality.

Inconceivable suppositions play an important role in Hume's own philosophical reasonings. Throughout the *Treatise* Hume argues that our fundamental beliefs are of this kind. According to Hume such beliefs are based upon an 'irregular kind of reasoning' which makes us ascribe 'a connexion or repugnance betwixt objects, which extends not to impressions' (T.242). In other words, Hume thinks that we are led to attribute properties and relations to objects which are contrary to those which belong to the essential nature of our impressions. The reasoning which makes us do this is 'irregular' or confused, but it is essential for the formation of our actual beliefs about objects. We naturally form suppositions concerning the distinct existence of space or bodies themselves, which, as the Cartesians and Berkeley show us, 'extend not to impressions'. As we shall see in the next chapter, Hume also thought that it was through such 'irregular' reasoning that we form the judgement of a causal *connection* between objects, even though their impressions are in themselves entirely distinct. We shall see that our supposition of causal connection, no less than our supposition of empty space or the independent existence of body, involves a belief in what is inconceivable.

§11 *Matter and sensible qualities*

Hume does not always discuss the ontological implications of his ideas, as he does in the case of the vacuum. But our examination of this discussion helps us to clarify a general theme that runs throughout the *Treatise*. For we may say that, in general, objective scepticism concerning the ontological implications of analysis of ideas arises when such analysis conflicts with a natural judgement. Hume's faith in natural judgement seems to vary a good deal: in the case of the vacuum he does not put absolute faith in it, and is satisfied to balance the natural judgement against the Cartesian idea-analysis. On the other hand, as we shall see in the next chapter, Hume puts complete faith in the natural judgement of causal connection and comes to reject the idea-analysis which opposes it. But sometimes the conflict between idea-analysis and natural judgement is not made entirely clear by Hume, and he even appears to favour the ontological judgement formed on the basis of idea-analysis. This is the case in Hume's discussion of the modern conception of matter. He is sometimes thought to reject this notion on the basis of analysis of ideas. In this section I shall argue that there are reasons to think that, even here, Hume was willing to reject the ontological implications of idea-analysis.

What Hume called 'the fundamental principle' of modern philosophy – namely, the principle that matter has only 'primary qualities' such as 'extension and solidity, with their different mixtures and modifications; figure, motion, gravity, and cohesion' (T.226–7) – had been attacked by Berkeley. According to Berkeley, the whole theory is based upon the incorrect assumption that these primary qualities 'may be abstracted from all other sensible qualities' and be considered to exist alone in reality. While he agreed with the Cartesian view that one cannot distinctly conceive extension without material body, he went further and argued that matter itself could not be conceived without secondary or sensible qualities such as colour or sensations of touch. Berkeley argued that the modern conception of matter, as consisting of only primary qualities, was a false abstraction. He concluded that 'where the extension is, there is the colour too', namely, in one's mind. Both qualities are 'alike *real*' and their reality consists in their being perceived (*Principles* I, 99).

Since (as we have seen in §9) Hume accepted Berkeley's sensory criterion of conceivability, he too concluded that the modern notion of matter was conceived by abstraction. In his section 'Of the modern philosophy' Hume reminds us that his own earlier analysis of extension in Part II of the *Treatise* showed that "tis impossible to conceive extension, but as compos'd of parts, endow'd with colour or solidity' (T.228). The indivisible parts of extension 'must be non-entities, unless conceiv'd as colour'd or solid'. Hume goes on to note that solidity cannot be conceived without sensible ideas of sight or touch (T.228). His argument, as he himself acknowledges in the *Enquiry*, closely follows that of Berkeley (E.155n.). But it leads to a conclusion which *Hume* regards as entirely paradoxical.

Hume thinks that the analysis of our idea of matter leads to the conclusion that primary qualities, like secondary ones, are 'in the mind, not in the object' (E.154). Hume conceives of the argument as operating in two distinct stages. The second of these depends upon idea-analysis. But the first depends upon the principle of 'cause and effect', a principle whose natural origins are stressed by Hume. It is the combination of these two principles which he thought leads to the paradoxical conclusion that there is 'nothing in the universe' which exists independently of our perception of it (T.231).

Consider the first part of Hume's argument, the part which leads to what Hume calls the fundamental principle of modern philosophy. By basing his argument for this principle on causal reasoning, Hume was led to a version of it which differs in an important way from the principle as espoused by Descartes and Locke. Nevertheless, Hume's argument was particularly appropriate for the sceptical conclusion he drew from it. He argued that sensible qualities 'such as hard, soft, hot, cold, white, black' are non-representative: they are 'without any external archetype or model, which they represent' (E.154). Following Bayle[28] and Malebranche,[29] Hume based his argument on the claim that we can perceive contrary sensible qualities (e.g., hot and cold, depending upon the differing disposition of our two hands) in one and the same object: he concluded that these sensible qualities cannot represent any single feature in an object which causes them (T.226–7). Hume concluded that sensible qualities are mere perceptions in the mind. This conclusion differs markedly from that of Locke and Descartes who concluded only that there is nothing in objects which resembles ideas of secondary qualities;[30] these authors nevertheless held that these ideas are representative and are accurate guides to qualities existing in the object.[31] Through his causal argument Hume concluded without equivocation that sensible qualities are entirely subjective.

Having drawn this conclusion Hume finds it easy to argue along with Berkeley that the primary qualities, which (according to the version of idea-analysis that both accepted) are not conceivable apart from secondary ones, must also be in the mind. Thus Hume reaches the paradoxical conclusion that we cannot conceive of anything existing independently of us.

Did Hume then accept Berkeley's ontological claim that the being of objects consists in their being perceived? We have good reason to think he did not do so. As we saw earlier Hume regards Berkeley's writings as forming 'the best lessons of scepticism, which are to be found either among the ancient or modern philosophers'. Hume describes as 'merely sceptical' Berkeley's argument showing that we cannot form a conception of anything independent of the mind. He notes that such arguments 'admit of no answer and produce no conviction' (E.155n.).

In his *Treatise* Hume regards Berkeley's conclusion as resulting from two natural operations of the mind which are 'directly contrary' (T.266). On the one hand, we have a natural belief in the independent existence of the objects of our senses, which is based upon the principles of the imagination which we considered in §7. On the other hand, arguments based on another natural principle – that of causal reasoning – have led modern philosophers to conclude that our sensible perceptions are 'nothing but internal existences' (T.227). Moreover, as Berkeley had pointed out, extension and other primary qualities cannot be conceived apart from these sensible qualities. Thus *reason* in the guise of the latter two principles opposes *the senses* as represented by the former. In the conclusion to Book I of the *Treatise* Hume regards both the senses and reason as 'natural and necessary', and yet as balanced in an irresolvable opposition (T.266). Here he clearly does not consider, as a possible resolution, Berkeley's claim that both secondary and primary qualities 'are alike real' and that their reality consists only in their being perceived. Rather he thinks he has discovered the irreconcilability of the principles of imagination on which are based our fundamental beliefs about external objects.

There are, I believe, good reasons to think that Hume was in sympathy with the fundamental principle of modern philosophy, which he regarded as intimately tied up with the claim that all changes in nature 'are nothing but changes of figure and motion' (T.227). We find over and over again that he favours causal explanations expressed in terms of these categories; he shows no tendency to resurrect the theory of substantial forms which this theory was designed to replace. Thus far it might be said that Hume's views differ little from those of Berkeley who, in his *Siris* (1744), also maintained that 'all the phenomena in nature are produced by motion'.[32] But in Book III of the *Treatise*, in presenting his own theory that our judgements of vice and virtue have their source in human nature, Hume draws an analogy with the view of modern philosophy that 'sounds, colours, heat and cold . . . are not qualities in objects, but perceptions in the mind'. He says that both views represent *'a considerable advancement of the speculative sciences*' (T.469; italics mine). These words suggest that Hume was as fully committed to the second theory as to the first. Referring to this passage in a letter to Francis Hutcheson, written just prior to publication of Book III of the *Treatise*, Hume says the following: 'I wish from my Heart, I coud avoid concluding, that since Morality . . . is determin'd merely by Sentiment, it regards only human Nature & human Life' (H.L. I, 40). Hume goes on to indicate his belief that the claim concerning the subjectivity of moral qualities has serious ontological implications regarding the moral indifference of God or Nature. Hume's analogy with the theory of modern philosophy suggests that he believed that the real nature of things excludes sounds, colours, heat and cold, etc., just as it excludes moral qualities. This leaves us with the conclusion that real material existence consists of those primary qualities which Berkeley showed to be inconceivable without secondary ones.

In Book I of the *Treatise* Hume clearly recognises that the 'speculative' foundations of modern physics require that we should 'suppose in general' what it is 'impossible for us distinctly to conceive' – namely, that objects are different 'in their nature' from perceptions (T.218). He recognises that in considering external objects as composed of primary qualities without sounds, colours, etc., we have to suppose them *'specifically different'* from our perceptions (T.68). However, when we remind ourselves that all the fundamental beliefs which Hume seeks to found in the *Treatise* are based upon such inconceivable suppositions, then his objections to the modern theory of matter seem negligible. One merely needs to assume an objective scepticism regarding Berkeley's analysis of our idea of matter in order to answer these objections. Like space without matter, extension and solidity without secondary qualities might exist – even though they cannot be distinctly conceived. Once again analysis of ideas may prove to be no guide to actual existence. Such a resolution is especially plausible in the present case because Hume considers the fundamental principle of modern philosophy to be founded upon the 'natural principle' of causal reasoning. This natural principle clearly has a strong legitimacy in Hume's philosophical system.

Hume's objective scepticism is obscured in this discussion by the fact that his central aim is often to stress that the fundamental principles of the speculative sciences have 'little or no influence on practice' (T. 469). Hume claims that 'generally speaking we do not suppose' objects 'specifically different' from our perceptions (T. 68). As we saw earlier (pp. 57–8) Hume attempts to show how natural principles operate in making us think of external objects either as perceptions or as objects resembling perceptions. This stress on 'practice' is in accord with the central positive project of Part IV, Book I of the *Treatise*. Hume aimed to show that our fundamental beliefs can, in practice, be little affected by the conclusions of the speculative sciences. Just as (in Book III) Hume stressed that moral practice cannot be brought to a halt by the reflection that moral properties exist only in human nature, so (in the last part of Book I) he stressed that our belief in external existence cannot be impeded by the proofs of the inconceivability of matter. But Hume's stress on practice must not simply be taken to indicate his ontological commitments. He clearly accepted the theoretical conclusion that moral qualities do not exist independently of the structure of the human mind. There is good reason to think that Hume held that the secondary qualities have a similar subjective character. He clearly recognised that one gains a good deal theoretically by characterising reality in terms only of primary qualities. In order to do this one need merely *suppose* what one 'never can *conceive*', namely 'a specific difference betwixt an object and impression'.

§12   *Conclusion*

We are now in a position to form a clear answer to the question I formulated at the beginning of this chapter – the question concerning Hume's debt to his predecessors for the metaphysical parts of his reasoning. Following these thinkers, especially Berkeley, Hume showed that rational analysis of our ideas leads to paradoxical conclusions about reality which oppose the conclusions formed on the basis of the natural processes of the imagination. Hume clearly thought that, in a certain sense, these natural processes are a necessary guide to what really exists. Without such processes, fallible and faulty as they are, we would be led into 'the most extravagant scepticism' (T. 228) Yet it would be wrong to think that Hume abandoned the idea-analysis of his predecessors as a criterion of knowledge, as Kant later purported to do. Hume retained the *ideal* of knowledge based upon the 'establish'd maxim in metaphysics'. All knowledge depends upon clarity and distinctness of ideas. However, Hume claimed that, in important respects, our ideas may not be *adequate representations* of objects, and hence that what we determine on the basis of the established maxim may be only the rational structure of our perceptions, and not that of the independent external objects. We lack knowledge of the real nature of things.

The significance of Hume's claim that we lack adequate representations of objects is clear when his philosophy is contrasted with that of Kant. As we have seen, Hume claimed that we can conceive of space and time only as 'the manner, in which impressions appear to the mind' (T.36). But while he claims that we can only *conceive* space and time in this way, Hume does not deny that they have an objective existence apart from the ordering of appearances, or even apart from the ordering of any objects in space and time. Kant, on the other hand, claimed that space and time are *only* the forms in which things appear to us. In his *Critique of Pure Reason* he wrote: 'It is . . . indubitably certain, that space and time . . . are *merely* subjective conditions of all our intuition' (p. 86; italics mine). Kant removed his 'thing-in-itself' from the spatio-temporal world and regarded it as a pure object of thought. Thus the rules of ordering of things in space and time (i.e. the principles of Euclidean geometry), which refer *only* to the way things must appear to us, are absolutely certain. For Kant, there is nothing about space and time which is unknown. When Hume denies the adequacy of our idea of space, partly on the ground that the fundamental principles of geometry are merely contingent, he allows that space and time in their objective constitution can have a structure which is unknown to us. Objects, as they exist apart from perceptions, can have spatial and temporal structures which are not knowable.

In Hume's philosophical system the unknowable independent object is finite, with properties more or less like our perceptions. The object is spatially and temporally qualified: however, it is impossible for us to discover the nature of its spatial and temporal properties. The problems concerning the unknown properties of this object are engendered by the opposition between natural judgement and rational analysis of ideas. Natural judgement makes us suppose that the object is infinitely divisible; whereas rational analysis of ideas convinces us that it is composed of discrete minimal parts. Natural judgement makes us form a notion of space and time existing independently of bodies; whereas rational analysis of ideas convinces us that space and time are mere modes of ordering of such bodies. In each of these cases we have at least some notion of the alternative properties which may belong to the unknown external object. These alternatives relate to genuine questions concerning the real nature of objects which were disputed by natural philosophers in Hume's day. In the latter case Hume clearly regards the dispute as genuine though undecidable. A more serious problem concerning the nature of the unknown object derives from the reasonings of Berkeley: natural judgement makes us think of objects as independent entities which resemble our impressions; yet rational analysis of ideas, along with the causal maxim, convinces us that all the properties which we can conceive in objects, both primary and secondary, are totally mind-dependent. But as we have seen, Hume regards Berkeley's reasonings as completely paradoxical; and he certainly does not follow Berkeley in concluding that primary qualities really have no mind-independent existence.

For Kant, the thing-in-itself or noumenal object – which lies beyond the realm of all appearances – is absolutely unlimited. It is not conditioned by space and time. The doctrine that the thing-in-itself lies outside of all space and time is essential to Kant's philosophy.[33] The unknowable object, as thus understood, becomes irrelevant for our strict scientific understanding of nature, though it can serve as a regulative concept.[34] At the same time this object becomes an essential presupposition for our understanding of our actions as moral agents, who stand in a realm of freedom outside the limitations imposed on finite efficient causes.[35] Kant's thing-in-itself plays an entirely different philosophical role from that of Hume's unknown independent object. As we shall see in the next chapter, this latter object, as conceived by Hume, is absolutely determined through finite necessary principles.

For Kant, the world of finite objects (phenomena) is entirely knowable. This is related to the fact that he puts forward what amounts to a coherence theory of truth: 'in respect of its . . . form . . . logic, in so far as it expounds the universal and necessary rules of the understanding, must ... furnish criteria of truth' (*Critique*, p. 98). These formal rules serve to distinguish (true) objective perceptual orderings from subjective ones. The phenomenal object is no more than a perceptual ordering which is formally structured under the rules of the understanding. Thus, like Berkeley, Kant effectively reduces objects to perceptions.[36]

I began this chapter by stressing Hume's representative theory of knowledge; it is perhaps fitting that I should close it with a consideration of his correspondence theory of truth. Here again Hume's representative realism plays a large role in his conceptions. At one point in Book II Hume goes so far as to consider 'truth' in terms of a very literal 'copy' theory of representation. He says that a contradiction to truth and reason 'consists in the disagreement of ideas, consider'd as copies, with those objects, which they represent' (T.415). But perhaps the most illuminating definition of truth which Hume presents is at the beginning of Book III of the *Treatise*: 'Truth or falshood consists in an agreement or disagreement either to the *real* relations of ideas, or to *real* existence and matter of fact' (T.458). Here, Hume not only presents his important distinction between relations of ideas and matters of fact, but does so in a context where it is clear that they are both equally ways of considering reality itself. Just as there is *real* existence and matter of fact to which our ideas can correspond, so there is a possible correspondence or agreement to *real* relations of ideas. According to the analysis of Hume's thought which I have presented in this chapter, it seems clear that there can be real relations of ideas of which we have no knowledge. This will be due to the inadequacy of *our* ideas. The relations of our human ideas will often be false in so far as our concern is with the real intelligible nature of the world (i.e., *'real* relations of ideas'), but at the same time these ideas may be sufficient for us to determine real existence and matter of fact. These ideas are then considered as either false or true, depending upon the 'two kinds' of truth which Hume distinguishes (T.448). In the next chapter we shall discover that our ideas of cause and effect are clearly inadequate ideas of this kind.

Notes

1   'My own life', H.L. I, 2.

2   This letter first appeared in T. Kozanecki, 'Dawida Hume'a nieznane listy w zbiorach Muzeum Czartoryskich (Polska)', *Archiwum Historii Filozofii I Mysli Spolecznej*, 9 (1963), p. 133. It is reprinted in R. H. Popkin, 'So, Hume did read Berkeley', *Journal of Philosophy*, 61 (1964). The original transcription contains frequent misprints and in the brief quotation below I have assumed that Hume wrote 'systems' rather than 'system'.

3   Sextus Empiricus, vol. 1, p. 15.

4   See above, p. 49; and E.153.

5   For example, in his sixth Meditation Descartes writes 'I know that all things which I apprehend clearly and distinctly can be created by God as I apprehend them' (H.R. I, 190).

6   Bayle, *Dictionary*, vol. 5, 611b (Popkin, *Selections,* p. 363). Hume's geometrical realism is in accord with the views of a well-known British mathematician to whom reference is made in the *Treatise*; namely, Isaac Barrow, Newton's predecessor in the chair of mathematics at Cambridge. In *The Usefulness of Mathematical Learning Explained and Demonstrated*, the work to which Hume refers at T.46, Barrow says that 'all imaginable Geometrical Figures are really inherent in every Particle of Matter, I say really inherent in Fact and to the utmost Perfection' (p. 76). In his article on Zeno the Epicurean (*Dictionary*, vol. 5, 622a; Popkin, *Selections*, p. 363), Bayle claims that Barrow's view is unusual among mathematicians, and proceeds to take issue with it.

7   See *La Logique ou L'Art de Penser*, p. 365. Three proofs of infinite divisibility are presented. The first of these depends on the incommensurability of the sides of a square with its diagonal: 'par consequent il est impossible que ces deux lignes soient composées d'un certain nombre de parties indivisibles.' The second is based on a similar argument. The third proof is based upon the claim that indivisible parts, having zero extension, could not be combined to form any extended whole.

As I understand him, Hume denies the premise of this final argument and claims that the indivisible parts of extension, while they are not themselves extended, form the *units* of any extended line or surface. If he had had the terminology, Hume might have said that it is a category mistake to say that the indivisible parts have zero extension; for it is only through the combination of such points that one can correctly speak of extension at all.

8   Descartes' own considered view of the divisibility of matter is in fact more cautious than that of the Port-Royal authors. In his *Principles of Philosophy* I, 27 (H.R. I, 230), he maintained only that the limits of divisibility 'if they exist, cannot be discovered by us'. For any given bit of matter, be it ever so small, a further division can be imagined.

9   See C. B. Boyer, *The History of the Calculus and its Conceptual Development*, pp. 226ff.

10 Letter to Henry More, 5 Feb. 1649, *Descartes: Philosophical Letters*, p. 239.

11 Hume's reference is to Locke, and the relevant passage seems to be *Essay* 2, 14, 8–9. The specific example of the burning coal which Hume uses is to be found in Newton's *Opticks*, p. 347 – though Hume may have had another source. In the General Scholium to his *Principia* Newton spoke of an 'indivisible moment of duration'. See *Sir Isaac Newton's Mathematical Principles of Natural Philosophy and his System of the World*, vol. 2, p. 545. On the other hand, at least in the *Opticks*, he considered absolute space to be 'divisible *in infinitum*' (p. 403).

It is probably important to point out that, while Locke (unlike Hume and Berkeley) claimed that we cannot frame an idea which is not composed of parts, he does speak of the least parts of space and time 'whereof we have clear and distinct Ideas'. The small part of duration he calls a 'Moment', and of extension, a 'sensible Point'. This latter is the 'least Particle of Matter or Space we can discern' (*Essay* 2, 15, 9). Locke appears to be claiming that there exist *minima sensibilia*, though he also claims that smaller parts can be *conceived* – at least obscurely. Berkeley and Hume accepted Locke's claims about sensible *minima* and rejected his distinction between the sensible and conceivable.

12 A.658. For a recent discussion of the reasons for attributing this anonymous work to Hume, see P. H. Nidditch, *An Apparatus of Variant Readings for Hume's Treatise of Human Nature*, pp. 47–9.

13 A major change in view in the *Enquiry* involves Hume's adoption of the distinction between abstract and 'mixed mathematics' at E.31. However, this distinction is clearly expressed in the article 'Mathematics' in Ephraim Chambers' *Cyclopaedia, or Universal Dictionary of Arts and Sciences* of 1728. Chambers claims that 'mix'd *Mathematics*' considers 'Quantity as subsisting in material Beings, and as continually interwove'. In his article 'Geometrical' Chambers stresses the uncertainty of mixed mathematics: but he claims that 'the Errors . . . we fall into in Astronomy, Music, Mechanicks and the other Sciences to which Geometry is applied, do not properly arise from Geometry which is an infallible Science'. Chambers cites the authority of Malebranche's *Recherche* in support of the view he is putting forward. If there is any difference between Chambers' view and that of Hume's *Enquiry*, it seems to me that it lies in Hume's continuing tendency to treat geometry as if it gives the *a priori* structure of matter. See the quotation toward the end of this paragraph in the main text.

It is interesting to note that the Malebranchian view of mathematics disappeared in the second edition of the *Cyclopaedia* which was published in 1738. The whole article 'Geometrical' is eliminated in the later edition, and the claim about 'mix'd mathematics' disappears from the article 'Mathematics'.

14 'All things which, speaking generally, are comprehended in the object of pure mathematics, are truly to be recognized as external objects' (H.R. I, 191). Similarly, in the *Port-Royal Logic*, the authors write that if judgements like the judgement that the angles of a triangle are equal to two right angles 'ne regardoient pas les choses en elles-mêmes, mais seulement nos pensées . . . nous sçaurions seulement que nous les pensons être de telle sorte; ce qui détruiroit manifestement toutes les sciences' (*La Logique ou l'Art de Penser*, p. 389).

15 *Hume's Philosophy of Belief*, pp. 64ff. Flew follows Reichenbach, taking the essence of the positivist view of mathematics to be found in the principle that 'all knowledge is either analytic or derived from experience: mathematics and logic are analytic, all synthetic knowledge is derived from experience' (p. 64; quoted from H. Reichenbach, *The Rise of Scientific Philosophy*, p. 86). Earlier (p. 63), Flew cites Einstein: 'As far as the laws of mathematics refer to reality, they are not certain, and as far as they are certain they do not refer to reality.' It seems to me that Chambers (see n. 13) comes much closer to Einstein's position than Hume who, in the *Enquiry*, does not appear to doubt that geometry gives us *a priori* laws of actual spatial relations. The point that Hume asserted the synthetic nature of mathematical judgements was recognised by John Laird in *Hume's Philosophy of Human Nature*, pp. 53ff.

16 Compare L. W. Beck, 'A Prussian Hume and a Scottish Kant', in D. F. Norton *et al.* (eds.), *McGill Hume Studies*, pp. 68–9, n. 20: Kant 'continued to ascribe to Hume only the mathematical teaching of the *Enquiry*'. It seems likely that Kant's acquaintance with the *Treatise* was almost totally through a German translation of James Beattie's *Essay on the Nature and Immutability of Truth* which reproduced substantial portions of that work. Beck refers to a number of commentators who have argued for this likelihood. See also N. Kemp Smith, *A Commentary to Kant's Critique of Pure Reason*, pp. xxvff.

17 *Critique of Pure Reason*, p. 55.

18 'The constant form of . . . receptivity . . . is a necessary condition of all the relations in which objects can be intuited as outside us. . . . Our exposition . . . establishes the *reality*, that is, the objective validity, of space in respect of whatever can be presented to us outwardly as object' (*Critique of Pure Reason*, p. 72). Kant set out to show how it is possible that we have knowledge of principles like that which states that a straight line is the shortest distance between two points. See his *Prolegomena to any Future Metaphysics*, pp. 16–17. Kant's assumption that we have knowledge of the objective validity of such a judgement in spite of its synthetic character should be contrasted with Hume's account of the same principle at T.49–50 and his scepticism concerning the objective validity of such principles at T.71. Hume stresses that the principle is contingent

(T.50); but he also stresses that the 'order' of points which constitutes the difference between a straight and a curved line 'is perfectly unknown' (T.49). I take Hume to be implying that, in reality, it might be false that a straight line is the shortest distance between two points. For our belief that the proposition is not false is only drawn from the general appearance of objects. Lewis White Beck writes that 'there is so striking a resemblance between Kant's explanation of why "a straight line is the shortest distance between two points" is not analytic (*Critique of Pure Reason*, B.16) and Hume's explanation of why it is not a definition . . . that one can hardly believe that Kant did not know of Hume's argument' (*McGill Hume Studies*, p. 69n.). This may be so, but it is important to recognise that the central point of Hume's analysis is antithetical to Kant's assumption that we have knowledge of such geometrical principles.

19 *La Logique ou l'Art de Penser*, p. 388. This passage is seriously mistranslated in a current English translation, *The Art of Thinking*, p. 320.

20 Letter to Gibieuf, 19 January 1642 (*Descartes: Philosophical Letters*, p. 124). Cf. *La Logique ou l'Art de Penser*: 'nous ne pouvons juger des choses que par les idées que nous en avons' (p. 389).

21 Letter to Gibieuf, *loc. cit.* The same example was used in the fifth Meditation: see H.R. I, 181.Cf. p. 92 above. Dr Stewart has pointed out to me that *Locke* clearly explains this close connection between abstraction and impossibility: 'The *general Idea* of a *Triangle* . . . must be neither Oblique, nor Rectangle, neither Equilateral, Equicrural, nor Scalenon; but all and none of these at once. In effect, it is something imperfect, that cannot exist' (*Essay* 4, 7, 9).

22 *Principles of Philosophy* I, 63: 'they in truth do not differ but in thought' ('scilicet ab ipsâ ratione tantum diversae sunt': A.T. VIII-I, 31; H.R. I, 246). In the same work, Descartes distinguishes between modal distinctions and distinctions of reason (*Principles of Philosophy* I, 61–2), although he says that earlier, in his Reply to the First Objections to his *Meditations*, he did not make this differentiation. I have tended to gloss over it in this discussion, since Descartes himself clearly does not think it very important. Descartes also discussed the interconceivability of space and matter in the *Regulae* and the *Meditations* (cf. H.R. I, 57–8; H.R. I, 193). Hume probably also knew the criticism of the Cartesian view of space in Lecture X of Isaac Barrow's *The Usefulness of Mathematical Learning Explained and Demonstrated*: this lecture follows the one in which the concept of 'equality' is discussed (see T.46n. for Hume's reference to Barrow on this topic). Barrow himself claimed that space is 'the *mere Power, Capacity, Ponibility* or . . . *Interponibility of Magnitude*' (p. 176). Hume appears to accept Barrow's notion as *experimentally* valid (T.63), although he clearly does *not* accept Barrow's ontological claim that this *potentiality* has 'some sort of Reality' (see pp. 177–8 of Barrow's book). I am indebted to David Raynor for calling my attention to Barrow's discussion.

23 Bayle, 'Zeno of Elea' (*Dictionary*, vol. 5, 615b–16a; Popkin, *Selections*, p. 379).

24 *Ibid.*, italics mine. Charles Hendel has argued that Hume was probably influenced by Leibniz's attack on the Newtonian notion of the vacuum (*Studies in the Philosophy of David Hume*, first edition, chapter 5). Indeed, the words of Hume cited in our next paragraph seem to echo Leibniz's claim that 'space is nothing else but an order of the existence of things' (*The Leibniz–Clarke Correspondence*, ed. H. G. Alexander, p. 63). However, it is important to bear in mind that Leibniz, unlike the Cartesians, does not base this ontological claim on the inconceivability of space without matter; he bases it on his principles of perfection and sufficient reason (see Alexander's introduction to the *Correspondence*, pp. xx–xxii). Hume's discussion, on the other hand, turns entirely on the Cartesian question of conceivability.

25 T.639. The existence of the vacuum was still actively debated by writers on natural philosophy in Scotland in Hume's day. In the same year in which Hume published the words cited here (i.e. the Appendix to *Treatise*), George Martine, a physician of St Andrews, argued against the view that the vacuum is necessary: see his *An Examination of the Newtonian Argument for the Emptiness of Space and of the Resistance of subtile Fluids* (1740). Colin Maclaurin, Professor of Mathematics at the University of Edinburgh, defended the Newtonian view against Martine in his *Account of Sir Isaac Newton's Philosophical Discoveries* (1748). See the discussion in Robert Schofield, *Mechanism and Materialism*, p. 107. Roger Emerson, who has been studying the history of the Edinburgh Philosophical Society (of which Hume later became secretary, §16(*a*)), tells me that he thinks it possible that the dispute between Martine and Maclaurin may have been carried on at the meetings of the society. There is, of course, no evidence that Hume was attending meetings at this early date.

26 'I must here have recourse to it, in order to account for the mistakes that arise from these relations' (T.60). See §7(*c*).

27 Karl Popper, 'Berkeley as Precursor of Mach and Einstein', *British Journal for the Philosophy of Science*, 4 (1953). Reprinted in C. B. Martin and D. M. Armstrong, eds., *Locke and Berkeley*. See pp. 437–8 in the reprint.

28 In his article on 'Zeno of Elea' Bayle says that 'since the same bodies are sweet to some men, and bitter to others, it may reasonably be inferred that they are neither sweet nor bitter in their own nature, and absolutely speaking'. He claims that 'modern philosophers' teach that all the secondary qualities 'are perceptions of our mind, and do not exist in the objects of our senses' (*Dictionary*, vol. 5, 612a; cf. Popkin, *Selections*, pp. 364–5). Hume echoes Bayle's interpretation of modern philosophy in the *Enquiry* when he says that the secondary qualities 'exist not in the objects themselves, but are perceptions of the mind, without any external archetype'

(E.154). It is of some importance to note that the argument which Bayle goes on to give, to show that primary qualities are also in the mind, is *not* that of Hume. Bayle's argument is based on the claim that contrary primary qualities can be observed to exist in the same object: 'the same body appears to us little or great, round or square, according to the place from whence we view it: and certainly, a body which seems to us very little, appears very great to a fly' (*Dictionary*, vol. 5, 612a). Berkeley employs this form of argument at *Principles*, I, 11. However, Hume's argument is drawn from Berkeley's discussion of the analysis of the idea of matter. According to Hume's categories, Bayle's argument is based upon 'causal reasoning', as is the argument for the subjective character of secondary qualities. For Hume, unlike Bayle, there is an asymmetry between the two parts of the argument leading to the conclusion that primary qualities are subjective. The fact that Hume's discussion of the argument for the subjectivity of primary qualities is oriented by Berkeley and not Bayle has been clearly shown in an important unpublished paper by David Raynor entitled 'Hume and Berkeley's *Three Dialogues*'.

29   See *Recherche* I, 147, the section entitled 'Qu'on se trompe de croire que tous les hommes ont les mêmes sensations de mêmes objets'. For Malebranche, sensations are states of mind or modifications of the soul (R. I, 415). In his book *Le Cartésianisme de Malebranche* Alquié writes that 'les états de l'âme ne représentent rien, les modifications, qui appartiennent à son être, et le constituent "d'une telle ou telle façon", sont aveugles' (p. 155). Contrast the quotation from Descartes' *Meditations*, n. 31, below.

30   It is interesting to note that the arguments of Descartes are primarily *conceptual*. At *Principles of Philosophy* II, 4 he suggests a series of conceptual experiments to determine which qualities really belong to bodies: if one can conceive of a body not having a property like hardness then that property cannot be conceived to be essential to body (H.R. I, 256). Descartes stresses the lack of 'intelligible resemblance between the colour which we suppose to exist in objects and what we are conscious of in our senses' (*Principles of Philosophy* I, 70; H.R. I, 249). In both his third and sixth Meditations he notes that our sense perceptions may not resemble external objects (H.R. I, 160 and I, 192).

Locke, too, appears to be suggesting a kind of conceptual experiment at *Essay* 2, 8, 9 (cf. 2, 8, 20) which will determine which qualities are primary. He claims that when we conceive of matter being divided to the point that it becomes insensible, we must still conceive every part of the division as having 'Solidity, Extension, Figure, and Mobility'; then he goes on to present his account of secondary qualities as mere powers depending on the primary qualities of the insensible parts. Later on he *uses* his distinction to *explain* why we feel the same water hot and cold with different hands (2, 8, 21). At 2, 8, 15 Locke claims that the ideas produced in us by the sensible qualities do not resemble those qualities.

31   Locke went so far as to insist upon the *adequacy* of all our simple
     sensible ideas: 'For if Sugar produce in us the *Ideas*, which we call
     Whiteness, and Sweetness, we are sure there is a power in Sugar to
     produce those *Ideas* in our Minds. . . . And so each Sensation
     answering the Power, that operates on any of our Senses, the *Idea* so
     produced, is a real *Idea*, . . . and cannot but be adequate, since it
     ought only to answer to that power' (*Essay* 2, 31, 2). Similarly, in his
     sixth Meditation Descartes wrote: 'I very easily conclude that there
     are in the bodies from which all these diverse sense-perceptions
     proceed certain variations which answer to them, although possibly
     these are not really at all similar to them' (H.R. I, 192). While his
     claim is certainly not as strong as that of Locke, Descartes also
     stressed the objective validity of our sensible ideas. Locke stressed
     that whiteness and sweetness are qualities or powers in the object
     and so distinguished them from their ideas in us.
32   *Siris*, §234, in *The Works of George Berkeley*, vol. 5. But Berkeley also
     stressed the need for a 'mind or spiritual agent' to explain the
     limitations of mechanical explanations (§237). Note also the
     reintroduction of specific medicines which is suggested at §238. For
     a discussion of the distinction between Berkeley's views on
     mechanism and those of Hume see below pp. 145ff.
33   For the importance of this idea in the development of Kant's
     philosophy see Lewis W. Beck, 'A Prussian Hume and a Scottish
     Kant', *McGill Hume Studies*, p. 67. This idea first became central in
     Kant's *Inaugural Dissertation* of 1770.
34   See Kant's *Critique of Pure Reason*, pp. 549ff., and his *Critique of
     Judgment*.
35   See *Critique of Pure Reason*, pp. 630ff., and *Groundwork of the
     Metaphysic of Morals*, chapter three.
36   Kant attempted to distinguish his own view from that of Berkeley
     by saying that the latter interpreted space 'as a property that must
     belong to things in themselves' (*Critique*, p. 244). I find it difficult to
     understand how Kant arrived at this interpretation of Berkeley's
     philosophy: does he mean that space is a formal property of
     Berkeley's God?

FOUR

Causal scepticism and necessary natural powers

§13

All our ideas, or weak perceptions, are derived from our impressions, or strong perceptions. . . . *Father Malebranche* . . . must allow, that however we may compound, and mix, and augment, and diminish our ideas, they are all derived from these sources.

– Hume, *Abstract*, pp. 647–8

By bringing ideas into so clear a light we may reasonably hope to remove all dispute, which may arise, concerning their nature and reality.

– Hume, *Enquiry*, p. 22

§14

The small success . . . has at last oblig'd philosophers to conclude, that the ultimate force and efficacy of nature is perfectly unknown to us, and that 'tis in vain we search for it in all the known qualities of matter. In this opinion they are almost unanimous; and 'tis only in the inference they draw from it, that they discover any difference in their sentiments.

– Hume, *Treatise*, p. 159

§15

Nothing can be more serviceable, than to be once thoroughly convinced of the force of the Pyrrhonian doubt, and of the impossibility, that anything, but the strong power of natural instinct, could free us from it.

– Hume, *Enquiry*, p. 162

§16

He carried in his hand a bundle of essays, of which the coachman was curious enough to inquire the contents. 'These,' replied the gentleman, 'are rhapsodies against the religion of my country.' – 'And how can you expect to come into my coach, after thus choosing the wrong side of the question?' – 'Ay, but I am right,' replied the other, 'and if you give me leave, I shall in a few minutes state the argument.'

– Goldsmith, 'The Fame Machine'

Hume is commonly considered to be the father of twentieth-century positivism.[1] Rudolf Carnap wrote in 1935 that 'the opinion that metaphysical propositions have no sense because they do not concern any facts, has already been expressed by *Hume*'.[2] The analysis of Hume's metaphysical reasonings presented in the last chapter clearly stands in opposition to this positivist interpretation of his philosophy. According to Hume, those propositions which are founded upon the 'establish'd maxim in metaphysics' may well be false but they are not senseless. By applying this maxim to our human ideas we arrive at claims about the nature of reality which are meaningful – even though they oppose our natural and scientific beliefs. Herein lies the essence of the Pyrrhonian scepticism which Hume discusses in the first two parts of Section XII of his *Enquiry Concerning Human Understanding.* Following the arguments (though not the spirit) of Berkeley, Hume goes so far as to assert that metaphysical reasonings can, in principle, undermine our belief in all objective matters of fact. This does not seem possible if, as Carnap says, metaphysical propositions 'do not concern any facts'.

It is of some importance to recognise that metaphysical propositions, such as they are understood by Hume, pass his own test for sense and meaning. In his *Enquiry* Hume expresses that test as follows, as a test to be employed in *doing* metaphysics.

When we entertain ... any suspicion that a philosophical term is employed without any meaning or idea (as is but too frequent), we need but enquire, *from what impression is that supposed idea derived?* ... By bringing ideas into so clear a light we may reasonably hope to remove all dispute, which may arise, concerning their nature and reality.[3]

As we have seen in the previous chapter (p. 92) Hume considers metaphysics to be intimately connected with the process of rational analysis of ideas; the quotation that I have just given calls our attention to the fact that this analysis, as it appears in his philosophy, is based upon ideas which are derived from corresponding sense-impressions. In order to discover the genuine sense or meaning of philosophical terms such as 'space', 'time', or 'external existence', Hume seeks to discover the sense-impressions on the basis of which our rational conception of reality can be based. By analysing the ideas based on such impressions he purports to discover that space and time can be conceived only as the manner or order of existence of objects, not as independent substances in their own right. By using the same principle he argues that extension and solidity, as well as 'secondary qualities', cannot be conceived independently of our minds. As we have seen, these results correspond with ontological conclusions which were drawn respectively by Descartes and Berkeley. Even though Hume rejects these conclusions, it is clear that he holds that the metaphysical reasonings on which they are based make perfect *sense*. For he himself claims to show how they are based upon a correct analysis of ideas which are derived from the impressions of the senses.

One misses the essence of Hume's philosophy if one assumes, as is so often done, that he sought to limit the nature of reality to our ideas.[4] Hume's principle that every idea is derived from a corresponding impression plays an essentially sceptical role in his philosophy; it shows us the limitations of the beliefs which we can found upon our ideas. He believed that the (ontological) conclusions which were derived from the analysis of our ideas by his rationalist predecessors (including Berkeley) stand in opposition to eighteenth-century science and common sense (see §10 and §11). Hume thought that scientific notions like the Newtonian 'absolute space' and 'absolute time', and the Lockean 'primary qualities', are contrary to our clear and distinct ideas. Strictly speaking the terms standing for these notions are 'without meaning or idea'. Nevertheless careful attention to Hume's text reveals that he did not intend to deny that they may refer to something real.

In order to understand Hume's philosophical intentions one needs to consider those other parts of his reasoning which, according to his letter of 26 August 1737 (see Chapter 3, n. 2), have 'so little Dependence on all former systems of Philosophy'. We have seen that Hume sought to show how our beliefs in absolute space and external existence arise in 'irregular reasonings' of the imagination and not in metaphysical reasonings based on clear and distinct ideas. Hume's central aim in the *Treatise* was to explain the non-rational processes upon which 'life and action intirely depend, and which are our guides even in most of our philosophical [i.e., scientific] speculations' (A.647).

Strictly speaking, Hume believed that it is those judgements which are founded in human nature – not metaphysical ones – which lack sense. But this is a rather specialised sense of 'lack sense', since at the same time those *natural* judgements are the basis for all conclusions concerning matter of fact and real existence. As we have seen previously, Hume argued that our belief in external existence is based upon a 'fiction'[5] which results from the fusion of disparate ideas of sense and imagination. Hume uses the technical term 'fiction' here to stress that there is no sense content which corresponds with our judgement of real independent existence. We shall see in the present chapter that Hume also argues that our judgement that there are real causal processes in nature is based upon another sort of fusion of ideas. He argues that empirical science is grounded in judgements which, at a fundamental level, involve a disregard for the sense and meaning of our ideas.

The positivist interpretation of Hume's philosophy is based largely on those passages in the *Enquiry* in which he distinguishes all objects of human reason into relations of ideas and matters of fact – and then goes on to deny that any inquiries into relations of ideas, other than those of quantity and number, constitute knowledge. In the final part of Section XII of the *Enquiry* Hume claims that all books which attempt to extend our idea-based knowledge beyond the bounds of mathematics result in mere 'sophistry and illusion'. Carnap thought that Hume was saying that propositions other than those of mathematics and empirical science 'are without sense'.[6] But the illusions which Hume intends at the end of his *Enquiry* are the metaphysical paradoxes of Berkeley and Malebranche – paradoxes which result from trying to base our conception of reality upon 'meaning or idea'. Hume proposes to counter such claims with his own '*mitigated* scepticism or *academical* philosophy' (E.161). This philosophy is based on what, in our last chapter, I called Hume's objective scepticism. It is based on the recognition of the 'narrow capacity of human understanding'[7] – that is, the *inadequacy* of our human ideas. It is also based on the recognition that nothing can free us from the 'Pyrrhonian doubt' engendered by the analysis of ideas except 'the strong power of natural instinct' (E.162). By means of irregular reasonings, natural instincts cause the formation of substantive judgements concerning the nature of reality which lead us beyond our ideas and impressions.

A great deal of confusion has resulted from the fact that in his *Enquiry* Hume limits the term 'relations of ideas' to those legitimate quantitative relations which (according to him) are the subject matter of knowledge. For Hume clearly believes that most human ideas are such that their analysis does not reveal the real nature of things. In fact, as Kant suggested, there is something entirely arbitrary in Hume's acceptance (in the *Enquiry*) of mathematics as a legitimate form of knowledge.[8] The most important use of idea-analysis in Hume's philosophy is *not* that which leads to those legitimate relations of ideas which form the subject matter of mathematical judgements, but that which leads to Pyrrhonian scepticism.

In this chapter I shall consider, in a systematic way, Hume's claims concerning our lack of knowledge of causality and his account of our actual belief in causal efficacy. I shall show that Hume's arguments presuppose a fundamental belief that there are real causes in nature. In §13 I consider some misunderstandings of Hume's theory of causation which arise from the view that he meant to limit the real nature of things to the contents of our senses. In §14 I consider in detail Hume's use of the metaphysical reasoning concerning causality of his Cartesian predecessors. We shall see that Hume regarded such reasoning as leading to an entirely Pyrrhonian conclusion – the conclusion that there are no real forces in nature. I shall show that the philosophical point of view espoused by Hume himself – mitigated scepticism – is intended as a way of avoiding this paradoxical conclusion. Nevertheless, I shall argue, Hume accepted and modified the basic Cartesian requirement of a 'true' cause, namely, that there must be a necessary connection between cause and effect. In §15 I consider Hume's positive account of our belief in real causes in nature. I argue that the natural instinct which Hume calls 'custom' leads us to *suppose* the existence of those very sorts of necessary causes which we are unable to know on account of the inadequacy of our human ideas. Finally, in §16, I consider how Hume's account of causal judgements was employed in his critique of the theological conception of power or force which underlay Newtonian natural philosophy.

§13   *The senses and causal scepticism*

The most important application of Hume's principle that 'every idea . . . is copied from a similar impression' (E.19) is that which leads to his conclusion that our idea of necessity is derived from a subjective impression which arises from the observation of constant conjunction. After summarising his account of the origin of our idea of necessity in the *Abstract*, Hume notes that his philosophy is 'very sceptical, and tends to give us a notion of the imperfections and narrow limits of human understanding' (A.657). In fact, if we concentrate on Hume's accounts of the contents of our actual impressions of constant conjunction and necessity, we find him stressing only the negative sceptical side of his thought. Nevertheless, the context of these accounts indicates that he himself always assumed that there is more to causation than is contained in the contents of these impressions.

Hume is usually understood as claiming that there is no more to causality than the constant conjunction of similar sequences of impressions. In fact the inseparable connection between the proper name 'Hume' and the claim that 'objective causation is no more than constant conjunction' is, without doubt, the closest thing to a proof of Hume's favourite psychological theory – that of association of ideas – that one can imagine. Every introductory philosophy student is taught that connection when he learns to think philosophically, and the suggestion that Hume may not have held the theory is considered tantamount to an attack on philosophy itself. One influential source of the prevalent view that Hume reduced causality to constant conjunction was Ernst Mach's *Science of Mechanics*, although this interpretation of Hume was not original with Mach. The famous Austrian physicist and philosopher claimed that 'Hume first propounded the question: How can a thing A act on another thing B?' He thought that Hume denied that the question made sense and maintained that there is nothing more to causality than constant conjunction of successive sensations.[9] Essentially the same interpretation of Hume on causality has been adopted by influential twentieth century commentators on Hume, including H. H. Price. Price claimed that Hume reduced 'objective causal sequences' to 'objective *constant conjunctions*', though he recognised that Hume's 'analysis' of causality also included a subjective feeling of necessity. More accurate than Mach, Price acknowledged that the actual *question* which Hume raised concerned the origin of our idea of causality in our sense impressions; Price recognised that it was by pursuing this question that Hume reached the conclusion that the only idea we have of objective causality is that of constant conjunction. But like Mach, Price concluded that Hume believed that there is no more to the objective relation than is contained in our sense-derived idea.[10]

There is no doubt that Hume maintained that the essential feature of objects which makes us ascribe causality to them is their constant conjunction in our experience. This is not in question. It is not even questionable whether we can mean any more by objective causality than constant conjunction of similar and successive objects: for in Hume's special use of the term 'meaning' – where meaning is tied up with our sense-derived ideas[11] – we cannot give any more objective meaning to our notion of causality. What is in question is whether Hume maintained that there is no more to the real nature of causality than is contained in our sense-derived ideas. It seems to me undeniable that one misses the central aim of Hume's sceptical philosophy unless one recognises that he consistently maintained the point of view that there are real powers and forces in nature which are not directly accessible to our senses. Throughout his *Enquiry* discussion of causality he distinguished the 'sensible qualities of body' of which we are aware, from the 'power or force' of the cause which 'is entirely concealed from us' (E.63–4). By assuming this point of view he stressed the cognitive limitations of human beings. And he went on to present his thesis that our fundamental judgement that there are real powers and forces in nature is drawn from another source than our ideas.

Throughout his discussions of causality Hume assumes that no one except a few Cartesian philosophers will ever maintain that objective causality is limited to what can be based solely upon our actual ideas. In fact, as we shall see in §14, Hume explicitly *attacked* the view of a philosopher (namely Malebranche) who, having recognised that the only idea we have of causality in sense-objects is that of their constant conjunction,[12] concluded that there is no more to the causality of the objects themselves.

Hume's claims about causality and constant conjunction need to be placed within the context of his own sceptical philosophy. In his *Treatise* Hume certainly claims that we would not have had any notion of causality unless we had experienced some objects as constantly conjoined:

We have no other notion of cause and effect, but that of certain objects, which have been *always conjoin'd* together, and which in all past instances have been found inseparable. (T.93)

But he does not think that the objective causality *is* the experienced conjunction: in the next sentence he stresses that 'we cannot penetrate into the reason of the conjunction'. This claim refers back to Hume's earlier denial that our observation of constant conjunction, considered as such, provides any basis to draw any inferences about new instances:

even after experience has inform'd us of their *constant conjunction*, 'tis impossible for us to satisfy ourselves by our reason, why we shou'd extend that experience beyond those particular instances, which have fallen under our observation. (T.91)

Since a major aim of Hume's discussion of causation is to explain a relation which we use to reason about objects which are 'beyond our senses', and which 'informs us of existences' which we 'do not see or feel' (T.74), it can hardly be maintained that he thought the observation of constant conjunction, by itself, *is* such a relation. For, in the passage cited, Hume denies that constant conjunction explains 'why we shou'd extend . . . experience beyond . . . particular instances' which have already appeared to our senses.

We need, in a similar way, to consider the context of Hume's often quoted 'philosophical' definition of cause. In his *Enquiry* he says that, given the nature of our experience,

we may define a cause to be *an object, followed by another, and where all the objects similar to the first are followed by objects similar to the second.* (E.76)

This definition is based on our actual sense-experience of objects and shows the limits of the objective 'meaning' we can assign to causality. But, as we have already seen (p. 25 above), in both the *Enquiry* and the *Treatise* Hume stresses that such a definition is drawn from 'something extraneous and foreign' to the cause itself, namely, other instances of similar causal connections. In his *Enquiry* Hume stresses that such a definition is necessary because 'the ideas' we form concerning the relation of causation are '*so imperfect*' (E.76, italics mine). Hume prefaces his whole discussion with the rhetorical question 'What stronger instance can be produced of the surprising ignorance and weakness of the understanding than the present?' (*ibid.*). Paraphrasing him we may ask: 'What stronger instance is there of the surprising distortion and misreading of historical texts than that which interprets his philosophical definition of cause as an attempt to *reduce* the objective relation of causation to the sense-experiences to which our idea of that relation is limited?'! Hume's definition is presented as one which must serve in lieu of insight into real objective causal connection.

Hume clearly believes that there is more to objective causality than constant conjunction. However some readers of Hume, such as H. H. Price, have claimed that his explanation of this 'something more' is exhausted by his account of our idea of necessary connection. For Hume traces this idea to 'an internal impression' which arises in our minds when we have observed a constant conjunction of successive objects. Thus, after we have observed billiard balls knock against one another on a number of different occasions, we not only have an impression of the motion of the first ball, its collision with the second, and the subsequent motion of the second ball – but we also 'feel a determination of the mind to pass' from the one object to the other. This subjective feeling of expectation is the source of our idea of necessary connection (T. 165). But according to Price, by tracing our ideas of necessary connection to this purely subjective impression, Hume has undermined the claim that there is more to objective causality than constant conjunction. He thinks that Hume holds that, except under the influence of some mistaken philosophical belief, we never really assert the existence of something more.[13]

Price is wrong in interpreting Hume as holding that we do not ordinarily ascribe necessity or power to objects, and also in his implication that Hume believes that this tendency arises only from a mistaken philosophy. Hume claims that 'the generality of mankind . . . suppose that . . . they perceive the very force or energy of the cause, by which it is connected with its effect' (E. 69). A major aim of Hume's account of causality is to explain why we naturally think there is this real connection in objects. In fact it is the sort of sceptical philosophical analysis in which Hume himself engages which makes us recognise that we have no genuine idea of power or connection in objects. When he concentrates on the actual content of our belief in necessary connection Hume reaches a purely sceptical conclusion about power and necessity. Taken in and of itself, this philosophical analysis of our idea of necessary connection *would* lead to the conclusion which Price attributes to Hume – the conclusion that there is no real connection and force in objects. But, as we shall see in §15, Hume himself goes beyond such Pyrrhonian arguments to show that our judgement of the existence of necessity and power in objects is not drawn simply from our ideas.

Hume's remarks about our idea of necessary connection, like those about constant conjunction, need to be placed in the context of his own sceptical conclusions. He thinks that by tracing up our idea of necessary connection to a subjective impression he has verified the claim that 'we have no idea of power or agency, separate from the mind, and belonging to causes' (T.223). He is saying that we have no idea of the necessity, power or agency of causes, *not* that there is no necessity, power or agency in the objects themselves. For Hume tells us that he is quite 'ready to allow, that there may be several qualities both in material and immaterial objects, with which we are utterly unacquainted' and which correspond to 'the terms of power and efficacy'.[14]

It is true that Hume states that the 'clear idea' of power and efficacy which we possess 'is incompatible with those objects, to which we apply it' (T.168). He goes so far as to say that it is 'impossible' that necessary connection – he clearly means necessary connection in so far as we have any idea of it – can ever exist in matter (T.223). For our idea is based upon a merely subjective impression which does not arise directly from the qualities of objects themselves and can never be directly related to what does exist in them. Our actual idea of necessary connection has no objective content. Thus at the end of Book I of the *Treatise* Hume concluded that

when we say we desire to know the ultimate and operating principle, as something, which resides in the external object, we either contradict ourselves, or talk without a meaning. (T.267)

We contradict ourselves when we ascribe what has meaning or sense – namely, our internal impression of expectation – to external objects, where it cannot exist. We talk without meaning when we ascribe to the objects a power, necessity, or ultimate operating principle of which we have no idea. But *Hume himself clearly assumes the existence of what is contradictory and meaningless according to our human ideas.* For he goes on, in the sentence after the one which we have just cited, to say that *'we are . . . ignorant of the ultimate principle'* which combines cause and effect. One cannot be ignorant of that which cannot exist! Hume attributes our ignorance to the *'deficiency* in our ideas', and assumes the existence of a real power of which we have no knowledge (in both quotations, the italics are mine).

Price was certainly correct in claiming that Hume did not intend his account of our idea of necessary connection as an account of a genuine property of things. It is true that Hume sometimes made the paradoxical claim that 'necessity is something, that exists in the mind, not in objects' (T.165; cf. E.94n). But, as Price very well recognises, Hume does not really mean to say that we have a genuine idea of a necessity in our own minds. Hume argues against a theory, which could have been derived from Locke (cf. *Essay* 2, 21, 4), which maintains that 'we feel [a real] energy, or power, in our own mind' and that we subsequently transfer the idea of this active power to external objects (T.632; cf. E.64–9). According to this theory, we experience a genuine causation in the act of will whereby we bring about changes in our ideas, or movement of our own bodies. But Hume himself rejects this theory, claiming that we learn the connection of the will with its effects merely by experience. In fact Hume reduces our awareness of our own acts of will to a passive impression which is cognitively equivalent to our awareness of causes outside of us. We do have an internal impression of expectation which results from the constant conjunction of the impression of our own will with the various effects which follow. But this impression is no more veridical in the case of our experience of our will than it is in the case of experience of objects outside of us. We have no awareness of any genuine necessity in the operations of our own minds (T.399ff).

Taken in and of itself, Hume's injunction to trace our ideas back to their corresponding sense-impressions plays a purely sceptical role in his philosophy. By tracing our idea of necessity back to an internal feeling which arises in our own minds when we repeatedly observe causal sequences, Hume wants to convince his reader that he has no real 'insight' into the causal processes themselves (T.400). The discovery of the subjective origin of our idea of power or necessary connection provides evidence that we have no observation at all of 'any real intelligible connexion' of objects (T.168). Hume rejects the 'false philosophy' of the ancients who constantly tried to find such connections in the material world itself. Hume argues that when we come to the realisation that our idea of necessary connection arises from a subjective impression, we should sit down contented and 'keep . . . from ever seeking for this connexion in matter, or causes' (T.223). For we learn that the actual idea we have is not even derived from partial insight into the real causal process, and that it is useless ever to seek it there. Hume's principle that every idea is derived from a corresponding sense-impression – in this case, a purely internal one – provides support for his scepticism concerning human knowledge; it provides one major basis for his claim that we have no intellectual insight into the real operations of nature.

Hume concludes that neither our external nor our internal senses can account for our belief in real causes in nature. This belief is determined not simply from the constant conjunction of successive impressions of external events, nor from the internal impression of expectation which arises after we have experienced such a constant conjunction. We have no objective impression of necessary connection, yet Hume clearly maintains that necessary connection, power, or force is the most important part of the relation of causation.[15] After attacking the 'fantastical system of liberty' (T.404) in Book II of the *Treatise*, Hume writes that, according to his definitions, 'necessity makes an essential part of causation' (T.407). When he speaks of necessity here he does not intend either an internal impression or a constant conjunction of events. He is not referring to anything of which we have any clear idea at all. Consider his words at the beginning of this discussion:

'Tis universally acknowledg'd, that the operations of external bodies are necessary, and that in the communication of their motion, in their attraction, and mutual cohesion, there are not the least traces of indifference or liberty. Every object is determin'd by an absolute fate to a certain degree and direction of its motion. . . . The actions, therefore, of matter are to be regarded as instances of necessary actions. (T.399–400)

But this absolute necessity is entirely unknown:

It has been observ'd already, that in no single instance the ultimate connexion of any objects is discoverable, either by our senses or reason, and that we can never penetrate so far into the essence and construction of bodies, as to perceive the principle, on which their mutual influence depends. (T.400)

Hume holds that we are totally unaware of the necessity which exists in material causation. Of course this does not mean that the actual ideas of constant conjunction and necessity which we have do not play an essential role in the discovery of genuine causation – in so far as we can discover it. But it does mean that neither of these sense-derived ideas themselves constitutes the objective relation of causality which we seek to discover.

§14 *Reason*

(a) *Perceptual distinctions*

It may seem a very slight step from Hume's sceptical claims concerning our lack of knowledge of the power or force in nature to the positivist conclusion that, since we have no idea of this power, it cannot exist. However, when we ascribe this step to Hume we disregard the fact that he himself adopts the view he calls 'mitigated scepticism' as a means of combating Cartesian arguments, based on analysis of ideas, which lead to this and other 'Pyrrhonian' conclusions. It is important to recognise that a major portion of Hume's discussion 'Of the idea of necessary connexion' in both his *Enquiry* and *Treatise* is directed against the contemporary theories which sought 'to rob nature, and all created beings, of every power' (E.71). It has been commonly assumed that Hume attacked only the theological side of the doctrine of Malebranche who, having been led to the conclusion that matter 'is in itself entirely unactive' (T.159), turned around and ascribed all activity to the Deity.[16] But, as we shall see, this interpretation is based upon insufficient attention to the logic of Hume's argument against this view, and a lack of appreciation of the nature of his rejection of the ontological conclusions of his predecessors. Moreover, the positivist interpretation of Hume's philosophy disregards his own response, at various periods of his career, to contemporary philosophical and scientific views about the nature of real causal forces.

We have seen that the 'metaphysical parts' of Hume's reasoning which, in his letter of August 1737, he claimed to derive from his predecessors are those which are based upon the rational analysis of our sense-derived ideas. In §10 and §11 I considered cases in which Hume claimed to show that ideas we naturally tend to believe are distinct – for example, space without matter – are not really so. Analysis of these ideas resulted in the discovery of what, in his *Regulae*, Descartes called necessary connections (H.R. I, 42–3). But the analysis of ideas can also yield a result which is of far greater importance for Hume's philosophy: it can lead to the recognition that ideas we naturally hold to be necessarily connected are not really so. In his philosophical writings Hume frequently stressed the separability of various ideas and argued that whatever objects 'may be conceiv'd as separately existent . . . may exist separately, without any contradiction or absurdity'.[17] It is on the basis of this principle of metaphysical reasoning that Hume denied that we are aware of a necessary connection between objects. In this section we shall see that it played a fundamental role in his causal scepticism. But before considering the exact use which Hume made of this principle we shall find it helpful to consider how his Cartesian predecessors used it to arrive at their own doctrines of causation. We shall find that we can form a clear idea of Hume's own views by examining what he accepted and what he rejected of these doctrines.

(*i*) *The occasionalist theory of causality.* In his sixth Meditation Descartes wrote that we need only have the ability 'to apprehend one thing apart from another clearly and distinctly in order to be certain that the one is different from the other', and that 'they may be made to exist in separation' (H.R. I, 190). In the context of the sixth Meditation this principle is employed to draw a conclusion about the real nature of things from a premise about the nature of our ideas. From the fact that our ideas of mind and body can be distinctly conceived, Descartes concluded that the objects are separable, at least in principle. Descartes also argued from the fact that the moments of an enduring thing 'can be separated from their neighbours' to the conclusion that 'a thing which endures through individual moments can cease to exist'.[18] Thus from the analysis of the idea of time – as divisible into distinct isolated parts – Descartes appears to reach the conclusion that objects cannot even continue to exist from moment to moment by any force of their own. This principle had important application in Descartes' physics.[19]

In his popular account *Doutes sur le système physique des causes occasionelles* (1686), Fontenelle claimed that it was the discovery of the complete distinction of mind and body which 'made Descartes invent [the doctrine of] occasional causes': since he could find no 'necessary connection' between the movements of the body and the thoughts of the mind, Descartes concluded that the former could not be the 'true cause' of the latter. As a result (according to Fontenelle) he drew the conclusion that *God* must imprint a thought on the mind 'on the *occasion* of a movement of the body' (italics mine). Fontenelle claims that, having invented the doctrine of occasional causes to account for the mind–body connection, Descartes employed it again when he discovered that, in the case of transference of motion by impact, 'one does not conceive what constitutes the [necessary] connection between the movement of one body and that of a second body struck (*choqué*) by the first, nor how the movement of the first passes into the second'. In order to solve the problem concerning the lack of necessary connection between the motion of the two hard bodies, Descartes concluded that God is the 'true cause' of all such physical actions.[20]

While the account of Descartes' views given by Fontenelle was influential in later discussions of causation it was probably not very accurate historically.[21] The stress upon 'necessary connection' as a *criterion* for a 'true cause' (a view which Fontenelle had ascribed to Descartes) seems to have derived from Malebranche, whose views Fontenelle was primarily attacking in his *Doutes*. In his *Recherche de la Vérité* Malebranche wrote that 'a true cause is such that the mind can perceive a necessary connection between it and its effect' (R. II, 316). Malebranche connects the notion of 'true cause' with that of 'real power' and claims that there is genuine power only where there is a perceivable necessary connection between cause and effect.

It was by applying this criterion for a 'true cause' that Malebranche reached the conclusion that our will cannot cause any bodily movement:

the will . . . is not capable of moving the smallest body in the world: for it is evident that there is no necessary connection between the will which we have, for example, to move our arm and the [subsequent] movement of our arm. (R. II, 315)

Malebranche says that 'it even seems that there is a contradiction' in the claim that we are true causes of the movements which we appear to produce in our bodies (R. II, 316). For if our wills were true causes we could not will anything without its actual occurrence – something which conflicts with the idea we have of the relation between our will and its effects. More generally, Malebranche seems to believe that no particular finite entity or property can be the cause of any other finite entity or property because we never perceive any necessary connection between them. He claims that 'natural causes are not *true* causes but only *occasional* causes' of their effects (R. II, 312).

While Malebranche's central argument to show that we have no idea of any sort of physical causation is not directly based upon his criterion for a 'true cause', in his *Recherche* he refers to an argument presented in another work which presupposes this criterion (see R. III, 208). In his *Entretiens sur la Métaphysique* Malebranche argues that motion is a mere *mode* or quality of a body and he implies that, like shape, it cannot be transferred from one body to another.[22] This argument, which was central for Cordemoy[23] – an earlier Cartesian writer – appears to depend upon the assumption that in the case where one sees a ball move after it has been struck by another, one is dealing with two *distinct* substances. Malebranche claims that since motion is a mere state of the first ball, and as such cannot be transferred to the second, 'their meeting or their impact is only an occasional cause of the [resulting] distribution of their motion' (*Entretiens*, 162).

According to Malebranche God is the only true cause and source of power in the universe. He argues for this conclusion on the basis of the claim that we can only conceive of a necessary connection between the will of an 'infinitely perfect and therefore all powerful being' and its effects (R. II, 313; cf. R. II, 316). For it is a contradiction that God should will something and it should not be the case. Since a necessary connection can be conceived only between God and all created things, Malebranche concludes that God is the only *locus* of power in the universe and that he acts directly in all finite events. The role that this 'doctrine of the universal and sole efficacy of the Deity' (E.73n.) plays in Malebranche's philosophical system is complex and I cannot pretend to give any extensive analysis of it here. The doctrine is at least partly connected with the idea that things occur according to universal laws: Malebranche goes so far as to claim that since laws themselves 'are efficacious, they act, and bodies cannot act' (R. II, 314). But Malebranche intended to assert only that we have knowledge of a general connection between the divine will and the universal laws by which it acts. Unlike Descartes he did not think that the actual laws of motion could be derived from the principle that God conserves a constant quantity of motion.[24] As a result of developments in seventeenth-century mechanics, and the particular criticisms of Leibniz, Malebranche reached the conclusion that 'in this case one can only discover the truth by experience'. This epistemological claim is closely bound up with Malebranche's principle that the particular effects of the physical world *appear* to depend upon 'a purely arbitrary act of the will of God' (*Oeuvres Complètes*, vol. 17–1, p. 53).

(*ii*) *Hume's adoption of the Cartesian criterion of power.* Unlike earlier British writers such as Locke and Clarke,[25] Hume systematically accepted the Cartesian conceptual criterion for knowledge of true causation and real power. Like Malebranche,[26] Hume insisted that 'we can only define power by [necessary] connexion' (T.248), and that when we lack knowledge of such connection we lack awareness of the power by which the cause produces its effects. Thus Hume claimed that the will 'has no . . . discoverable connexion with its effects' since the 'effect is . . . distinguishable and separable from the cause' (T.632). He argued for this conclusion, for example, on the basis of the fact that a person struck with paralysis can be as conscious of a desire to move a limb as a man in perfect health, and yet the movement will follow the volition in the case of the one and not the other (E.66). Analysis of impressions reveals that we are wrong to suppose that we have any genuine awareness of any power we might have to control the motions of our own bodies or even the ideas of our own minds. From the fact that we can discover no necessary connection between our will and its effects Hume concluded that we have no 'idea of force by consulting our own minds' (T.633). Unlike Locke and Clarke, Hume denied that reflection on the operations of our own minds gives us any awareness of power.

Hume also rejected the Cartesian claim that we are aware of such power through reflection on the notion of a divine will. Yet in so doing he appealed to a modified Cartesian conceptual criterion of true power. Paradoxically, it was through the employment of that criterion that he excluded the one case where the Cartesians themselves thought they were aware of necessary connection. To see this it is important to recognise that Malebranche had only claimed to perceive a connection between two abstract ideas – between the general idea of an infinite will and that of its effects. We have just seen that Malebranche did not claim to have an idea of a deity which would show us what *particular* effects result from his volition. But Hume noted that Malebranche's claim that 'the idea of an infinitely powerful being is connected with that of every effect, which it wills' is a mere tautology which 'gives us no insight into the nature of this power or connexion' with his creation (T.248–9). Hume denies that we can have any general idea of power except that which is abstracted from 'some particular species of it'. We must conceive this power as existing 'in some particular being'. Hume claims that the 'true manner of conceiving a particular power in a particular body' is to 'conceive the connexion betwixt the cause and effect' in such a way that we should 'be able to pronounce, from a simple view of the one, that it must be follow'd or preceded by the other' (T.161). Hume interpreted the Cartesian criterion of necessary connection in such a way that he required that such connections should exist between particular finite objects and their effects.

By employing his own modified criterion of necessary connection Hume reaches the same conclusion as the Cartesians: that we have no idea of causation or real power in the case of purely physical events. Hume constantly stresses the *distinctness* of our ideas of cause and effect. At the beginning of his discussion of causation in the *Enquiry* Hume gives 'the reason why no philosopher, who is rational and modest, has ever pretended . . . to show . . . the action of that power, which produces any single effect in the universe': the reason is that 'every effect is a distinct event from its cause'.[27] In his discussion of physical causation in the *Enquiry* and *Abstract*, Hume employed the example which is used throughout the Cartesian literature on this topic – that of transference of motion through impact. He stresses that when a billiard ball strikes another, the 'motion in the second Billiard-ball is a quite distinct event from motion in the first'.[28] This is a consideration which we also found to be relevant for Malebranche and Cordemoy. Hume notes that 'solidity, extension, motion . . . are all complete in themselves, and never point out any other event which may result from them'. He claims that it is these considerations about the distinctness of our sensible ideas of cause and effect which should convince us that 'we are never able, in a single instance to discover any power or necessary connexion' (E.63).

It is important to recognise the extent to which Hume accepted the Cartesian analysis of our *idea* of matter as totally inactive. In his discussion of the Cartesian theory in the section 'Of the idea of necessary connexion' in his *Treatise*, Hume claimed that 'the *Cartesians* . . . have very naturally inferr'd' from their analysis of our idea of matter 'that 'tis impossible for it of itself to communicate motion' (T.159). When he wrote this passage Hume probably had Malebranche's views in the forefront of his mind. Malebranche wrote that 'the idea we have of bodies . . . gives us knowledge that they cannot move themselves' (R. II, 313). We have seen that in his *Entretiens sur la Métaphysique* Malebranche seems to present the argument concerning distinctness of motion in the cause and effect which later became important for Hume. But it is the argument from Malebranche's *Recherche* which Hume summarises in his discussion of the Cartesian theory. Malebranche wrote:

When I see a ball which knocks against another, my eyes tell me, or seem to tell me, that [the former] is the true cause of the movement which it communicates to [the latter]. But when I examine my reason, I see clearly that bodies, not being capable of moving themselves . . . cannot transfer a power which they do not have. (R. III, 208)

In this passage Malebranche's claim that the first ball cannot transfer motion to the second relies on the premise that we have no idea of any active force in the first ball: it is a 'purely passive substance'.[29] Hume summarises this argument as follows:

As the essence of matter consists in extension, and as extension implies not actual motion, but only mobility; they conclude, that the energy, which produces the motion, cannot lie in the extension. (T.159)

This analysis of our *idea* of matter is not one which Hume ever challenges. As we have seen he also accepts Malebranche's claim that we have no idea of power through reflection on the operation of our own will. Hume summarises his own view by saying that,

if no impression, either of sensation or reflection, implies any force or efficacy, 'tis equally impossible to discover . . . any such active principle in the deity. (T.160)

Hume only rejects Malebranche's claim that we have an idea of force when we consider the idea that we have of God.

(*iii*) *Hume's rejection of Occasionalism.* Thus Hume agreed with Malebranche's analysis of our idea of matter. He agreed that we have no idea of power or force in any natural processes. But Malebranche did not limit himself to this claim about our idea and went on to conclude that matter itself is totally inactive. Malebranche concluded from his analysis of our idea that there are no real causes in nature and that natural processes themselves are no more than constant conjunctions of events.[30] The question arises whether Hume followed Malebranche in drawing this ontological conclusion from the analysis of our idea of matter. The answer to this question is of the utmost importance in any attempt to come to an understanding of Hume's own beliefs about power and force in nature. In fact it is very clear that Hume rejected the conclusion about the nature of reality which Malebranche, in good Cartesian fashion, drew from his premise about the nature of our idea.

At the beginning of his *Treatise* discussion of the Cartesian theory of power Hume notes that, when Cartesian philosophers draw their conclusion that matter 'is endow'd with no efficacy', they assume that 'we are perfectly acquainted with the essence of matter' (T.159). But Hume wishes to challenge this assumption. His central argument *against* Malebranche's theory rests upon his claim that that theory depends upon a more general Cartesian premise which embraces this assumption. It depends upon the premise that we are acquainted with the essence of things through the actual ideas we have of them. For Hume argues that, since our actual ideas reveal no more efficacy in God (or finite minds) than in matter, this Cartesian premise leads to the conclusion that there is no efficacy anywhere in the universe –

neither in God nor in nature. But it should be noted that Hume treats this argument as a *reductio ad absurdum* of Malebranche's theory, a *reductio* whose conclusion is to be *avoided* by rejecting the general Cartesian premise:

> If they estem that opinion absurd and impious, as it really is, I shall tell them how they may avoid it; and that is, by concluding from the very first, that they have *no adequate idea* of power or efficacy in any object . . . *neither in body nor spirit*. . . . (T.160; italics mine)

Hume is saying that *neither* our idea of body *nor* our idea of spirit has sufficient adequacy to allow us to draw ontological conclusions about the real nature of things. By rejecting the Cartesian assumption that our ideas are adequate Hume rejects the Cartesian argument which leads to the conclusion that there is no power or force in material events.

As we saw in our last chapter, when Hume denies that we have *adequate* ideas of objects, he rejects what he considers to be a fundamental condition for knowledge. We saw that, in the *Treatise*, Hume makes the possibility of knowledge contingent upon our possessing adequate ideas. Thus, in denying that we have an adequate idea of matter, Hume is denying that 'the relations, contradictions, and agreements' of our ideas need apply to the objects.[31] In the present context he is denying that the lack of necessary connection between our *ideas* of cause and effect need apply to *objects* which correspond to those ideas. In short, Hume's objective scepticism concerning our idea of matter leads to the possibility that those distinctions which Cartesian conceptual analysis reveals as a feature of our ideas may not represent real distinctions, and that therefore there may be power and necessary connection in reality even though we can never perceive it. The importance of Hume's denial of the *adequacy* of our ideas of cause and effect cannot be underestimated.

Both Malebranche and Hume assume that real causation implies a necessary connection between cause and effect. Both philosophers agree that we never perceive any such connection in the physical world. But while Malebranche draws an ontological conclusion that there is no power or force in the physical world from his Cartesian assumption that our ideas reveal the essence or true nature of things, Hume draws an epistemological conclusion by rejecting the same assumption.

For Malebranche the fact that we cannot conceive of power in body leads to the conclusion that there is no such power; for Hume the same fact leads to the conclusion that we have no intellectual understanding of the power and force which there is.

We may schematise the arguments of the two philosophers in the following way. Malebranche argues as follows:

> P.   Our idea of matter is such that it implies no force or energy;
> Q.   We have knowledge of objects through our ideas – that is, our ideas are adequate representations of material objects;
> ∴R. Material objects have no force or energy.

Malebranche goes on to argue that we have an idea of the power and force of the deity and concludes that God alone has real power. Since Hume comes to reject Malebranche's claim that there is a divine power which is not manifested in particular finite beings, and insists that there must be a power which brings about the changes in the universe, his argument may be set down in the following simplified form:

> P.   Our idea of matter is such that it implies no force or energy;
> ~R.   There must be force or energy in material objects;
> ∴~Q. Our idea of matter is not an adequate representation of objects – that is, we do not have knowledge of objects through our ideas.

Hume's whole argument assumes the existence of force or necessary connection in the material universe.

In spite of the fact that his own conceptions are closely related to those of Malebranche and the Cartesians, it is very likely that it is the conclusions of those authors which he has largely in mind at the end of his *Enquiry* when he seeks to consign volumes 'of divinity or school metaphysics' to the flames (E. 165). For Hume refers forward to this section earlier on when he presents his first 'philosophical confutation' of the Cartesian theory (E. 71–2). This confutation is based upon the philosophical view which, at the end of the *Enquiry*, Hume adopts under the name of 'mitigated scepticism'. As we noted at the beginning of this chapter this view is intimately connected with the recognition of 'the weakness of human reason, and the narrow limits to which it is confined in all its operations' (E. 72; cf. p. 126 above). It may be thought that Hume is here merely expressing the view that our reason is too weak to understand the supposed operations of a deity. But we have just seen that in the *Treatise* Hume implied that, because of the inadequacy of our idea of matter, our reason is too narrowly confined to show us the power and force in material events. By affirming the inadequacy of our idea of matter Hume rejected the Malebranchian claim – based purely upon the rational analysis of our sense-derived ideas – that there is no power or force in the natural world. Hume's mitigated or academical scepticism was intended as a philosophical view which could *avoid* contemporary theories which (in Mach's words) rejected 'causality and recognize[d] only a wonted succession' in the natural world. Quite remarkably, the very theory which has been ascribed to Hume is the one which he sought to reject by means of his own mitigated scepticism.

The centrality in his own thought of the belief in the existence of real forces in nature is obvious from a footnote which forms part of the discussion of the Cartesian theory of causality in the *Enquiry* (E. 73). The note takes the discussion of these topics out of the French context in which they were originally formulated and shows clearly that Hume was opposed to British thinkers who, like Malebranche, denied real force in objects.

The *Enquiry* was probably written during Hume's stay in England in 1745 and 1746.[32] In the original edition of this work, which was published under the name *Philosophical Essays Concerning Human Understanding* (1748), Hume complained about writers who claimed that Sir Isaac Newton meant to 'rob Matter of all force or Energy', and attempted to establish that view 'upon his Authority'. The view which is ascribed to Newton is identical to the Cartesian view which, as we have just seen, Hume sought to oppose with his mitigated scepticism. But Hume claims that Newton himself

had recourse to an etherial active Matter to explain his universal Attraction; tho' he was so cautious and modest as to allow, that it was a mere Hypothesis, not to be insisted on, without more Experiments.[33]

Like many other writers of his day Hume seems to have thought of Newton's aether as a material (though perhaps not wholly mechanical) hypothesis, presented to explain active forces such as gravitation which are a source of motion in the universe.[34] In this passage Hume expressed his approval of the fact, which he alleges, that Newton explained gravitation by means of an 'active Matter' – his aether.

In the same footnote of his *Enquiry* in which Hume extols Newton's aether hypothesis, he also cites with approval the opinions of Locke, Clarke and Cudworth 'that matter has a real . . . power'. He asks why the contrary view has 'become so prevalent among our modern metaphysicians' (E.73). The modern metaphysician who was probably foremost in Hume's mind was George Berkeley, who denied the existence of all material forces, in a book which was published just prior to the time Hume was writing his first *Enquiry* (that is, five years after the appearance of the *Treatise*). In his *Siris* of 1744, Berkeley clearly set forth a view which closely resembles what we have come to regard as the positivist programme in science. For he denies that there is anything more to explanation in science beyond the discovery of general laws and the subsumption of phenomena under such laws:

If the explaining a phenomenon be to assign its proper efficient and final cause . . . , it should seem the mechanical philosophers never explained anything; their province being only to discover the laws of nature, that is, the general rules and methods of motion, and to account for particular phenomena by reducing them under, or shewing their conformity to, such general rules. (§231)

Berkeley admits that 'there is . . . a constancy in things, which is styled the Course of Nature' (§234). But 'what is said of *forces residing in bodies* . . . is to be regarded only as a mathematical hypothesis, and *not as anything really existing in nature*'.[35] In his earlier *De Motu* (1721), Berkeley had ascribed his own view of attraction to Newton himself, denying that the great philosopher considered it to be a 'true physical quality' (§17). In *Siris* he admits the existence of the aether but insists that, like Newton himself, he does not suppose 'real forces to exist in bodies' (§246). The aether is merely 'an instrument or medium . . . by which the real Agent doth operate on grosser bodies' (§221). Hume and Berkeley seem to be in sharp disagreement in their interpretation of Newton, as well as in their beliefs about the basic structure of the things which exist in the natural world.

It seems very likely that the footnote to Hume's discussion of the idea of necessary connection in his *Enquiry* was intended as an answer to the Malebranchian views which he found in Berkeley's *Siris*.

Unlike Berkeley, Hume believes that there is more to science than the discovery of general laws of nature. He clearly accepts the existence of real physical force and believes that science makes progress by postulating such forces *as* physical. In order to understand Hume's own philosophical views on causation one must recognise that he did not question the existence of real forces in nature any more than he questioned the existence of independent external objects themselves. Hume held that the existence of these things must be taken 'for granted in all our reasonings'.

(b) Objective necessary connection
Hume clearly rejects the Cartesian view of natural (occasional) causation as mere law-like succession. However, our recognition that Hume accepted real forces in nature should not make us forget that he retained an ideal of knowledge of true causes which was derived from the Cartesians. We have seen that Hume interpreted the Cartesian criterion of necessary connection in such a way that he demanded that such a connection must hold between particular finite objects and their effects. Hume's serious acceptance of his own modified Cartesian criterion of knowledge of causation is indicated not only by the fact that it provides the basis for his own scepticism but also by the fact that he tends to think of the unknown ontological causation in terms of that criterion. This idea is carefully developed in Part IX of his posthumously published *Dialogues Concerning Natural Religion*. [36] While the theses of the *Dialogues* are put forward tentatively by Hume through the words of his three speakers – Demea, Cleanthes and Philo – it seems significant that he attempts to develop the idea of necessity by means of an exchange that includes the views of all three characters. The idea of an ontological necessary connection in finite objects is seriously considered by both characters who are generally considered as candidates for Hume's own views – namely, Cleanthes and Philo.

At the beginning of Part IX of the *Dialogues* Demea presents an argument for the existence of God which is based on the assumption that God is the necessarily existent being. This argument, known to us as the 'argument from contingency', and to Hume as the 'metaphysical argument *a priori*', is rejected by Cleanthes on the ground that 'whatever we conceive as existent, we can also conceive as non-existent'. We have no knowledge of the necessity of God's existence, according to Cleanthes, since we may always conceive him to be non-existent *'while our faculties remain the same as at present'* (D.189; italics mine). I believe it is important to note that this latter claim of Cleanthes – that we lack knowledge of necessary existence (in this case, of God) – is grounded in a claim about the limitations of our human faculties.

The claim that our inability to know necessity is due to our own limitations leads to another suggestion. Cleanthes notes that according to the notion of necessity proposed by Demea 'the material universe' itself may be 'the necessarily existent Being'. For all we know to the contrary, matter itself may contain the necessity of its own existence. Cleanthes says that

We dare not affirm that we know all the qualities of matter; and for aught we can determine, it may contain some qualities, which, were they known, would make its non-existence appear as great a contradiction as that twice two is five. (D.190)

Taking up an earlier suggestion that the universe may consist of 'an eternal succession of objects', Cleanthes goes on to suggest that what we think of as the necessary cause of the whole universe may be no more than the unlimited sum of the finite necessary causes which make up the individual events.

In judging the seriousness with which Hume sets forth these views of ontological necessity we need to weigh his words carefully – not only in the light of the whole *Dialogues* but also in the light of his whole philosophy. It seems to me clear that in earlier sections of the *Dialogues* Hume has rejected the Epicurean claim that the appearance of order in the universe can arise from *chance*. In Part VI of the *Dialogues* Philo stated that 'Chance has no place, on any hypothesis, sceptical or religious' (D.174). In Part VIII he called the Epicurean view 'the most absurd system, that has yet been proposed', and attempted only to show how even that system can be made to *look* plausible (D.182; cf. D.186). Here Philo's views undoubtedly expressed those of Hume himself who, as early as the *Treatise*, expressed the view that 'chance is nothing real in itself' (T.125; cf. p. 12 above). In his *Enquiry* he wrote that chance 'is universally allowed to have no existence' (E.96). The fact that he can summarily reject chance as an ontological principle may surprise us. But our surprise should help us recognise the distinction between our own philosophical views – nurtured by the claims of modern physicists that there is genuine uncertainty in the realm of subatomic particles – and those philosophical views which were available to a sophisticated eighteenth-century thinker like Hume.

In the *Treatise* Hume expressed his belief that physical processes must arise 'from natural and necessary principles, whatever difficulty we may find in explaining them' (T.401). The theme that ultimate causes are both necessary and inherent in nature is consistently developed by Philo throughout the *Dialogues*. In Part VI of the *Dialogues* Philo states his own preference for a system 'which ascribes an eternal, inherent principle of order to the world'. After rejecting the idea of chance Philo says that 'every thing is surely governed by steady, inviolable laws'. But he does not stop with this suggestion of law-governed regularity. He suggests that the source of this regularity lies in nature itself.

And were the inmost essence of things laid open to us, we should then discover a scene, of which, at present, we can have no idea. Instead of admiring the order of natural beings, we should clearly see, that it was absolutely impossible for them, in the smallest article, ever to admit of any other disposition. (D.174–5)

Philo clearly states his conviction concerning the existence of an inherent necessary principle in nature of which 'we can have no idea'.

In Part IX of the *Dialogues* Philo elaborates on Cleanthes' mathematical notion of the unknown necessity which is inherent in nature. In the first place he claims that if we could 'penetrate into the intimate nature of bodies, we should clearly see why it was absolutely impossible' that the universe could be structured in any other way than the way it is actually structured. He likens the knowledge which we should then have to the knowledge possessed by a 'skilful algebraist' who can discover why, of necessity, the sum of the digits of the products of 9 is equal to 9 or some lesser product of 9. 'To a superficial observer, so wonderful a regularity may be admired as the effect either of chance or design' (D.191). The algebraist penetrates into the nature of number and shows the necessity of the regularity. But in the case of the external world we are all such superficial observers. We lack the knowledge of the nature of matter that the algebraist has of the nature of number. Nevertheless Philo clearly expresses his belief in the possibility of such an inherent necessary principle in the nature of matter itself.

Thus we see that Hume attempts some description of the necessity of which we would be aware *if* our ideas were adequate representations of reality. This gives us some notion of the necessary connection which he, like his rationalist predecessors, identifies with the power or force of the cause. Hume suggests that this necessity is inherent in nature itself. Yet, according to him, the necessity is entirely inconceivable to us. For, as we learn from our metaphysical reasonings, our actual ideas are distinct and separable. Why then do we believe that there is a necessary connection in objects? Why do we believe that physical events are absolutely determined? That is the basic problem with which Hume attempts to deal in his philosophical writings on causation.

§15   *Natural judgement of objective connection*

In the first two sections of this chapter we have seen that Hume argues that the power or force of the cause is inconceivable to us. In the first place he stresses that the actual idea of necessary connection which is the basis of our belief in natural causation is merely subjective and gives us no real insight into the nature of causation itself. Secondly, he argues that comparison of ideas by itself leads to the conclusion that there are no real causes in the world. For such comparison reveals that the ideas of what we call cause and effect are entirely distinct and have no necessary connection between them. Nevertheless Hume claims that 'we suppose that there is some connexion' between those items we call cause and effect. We *suppose* 'some power in the one, by which it infallibly produces the other, and operates with the greatest certainty and strongest necessity' (E.75). In spite of the fact that real causal forces in nature are inconceivable to us, we judge that these forces exist.

The official question which dominates Hume's whole discussion of causation in both the *Treatise* and the *Enquiry* is a question concerning the origin of ideas: 'we must consider the idea of *causation*, and see from what origin it is deriv'd' (T.74). Since a major aim of his work on the understanding is to show how all ideas are derived from impressions, it seems as though Hume's problem will be solved when he can literally point out the impression from which that idea is derived. Thus many commentators regard Hume as searching for a kind of *ostensive definition* of causation. However, we have seen that for Hume such a definition leads to a purely sceptical conclusion. In fact in the course of identifying the impression from which our idea of causation is derived Hume presents a whole theoretical explanation of the operations of that faculty which (in the *Treatise*) he calls imagination, and of the way it supplies the deficiencies of the senses and reason. To understand Hume's answer to his question concerning the origin of our idea of causation we must understand his conception of man as a 'natural' as opposed to a 'reasoning' organism. An understanding of Hume's solution to his problem concerning causation comes, not when we see how he ostensively identifies an impression, but when we understand his claim that nothing 'but the strong power of *natural instinct*' can free us from the Pyrrhonian doubts engendered by mere attention to the ideas themselves (E.162; italics mine). The identification of the impression from which our idea of causation is derived forms *part* of Hume's account of natural instinct. But, as we have already seen, the 'nature and reality' of that impression is such that it would not, by itself, lead us to a belief in real causal forces in nature.

(a) The principles of our natural judgement
Hume's talk of natural instinct in the *Enquiry*, and of principles of human nature and imagination in his *Treatise*, is essentially connected with the idea of an organism which is constructed in such a way that it makes 'natural' responses when confronted by stimuli of certain kinds.[37] Hume's idea is that we are, as it were, *programmed* to suppose the existence of real power when we are confronted with impressions which have the characteristics of constant conjunction, succession and (in the *Treatise*) spatial contiguity. Thus Hume stresses that 'this repetition of similar objects in similar situations' actually *'produces'* the transition of the imagination from one object to another (T.164–5). Custom or habit is the natural instinct which gives rise to this new associational link between our ideas. The 'customary transition' from causes to effects (E.75) actually becomes the source of our supposition that there are real powers and forces in nature.

Hume has two different accounts as to how this associational link comes to be ascribed to the objects themselves. Both are accounts in which he attempts to explain how we naturally become inattentive to the actual character of our ideas. In the *Enquiry* Hume relies solely on the natural instinct which he calls custom, but the account given in the *Treatise* in the section entitled 'Of the idea of necessary connexion' requires him to postulate the existence of a separate principle of the imagination. Let us consider these two accounts independently.

In the *Treatise* Hume stresses that the repetition of sequences of objects 'produces a new impression *in the mind*' which is the source of our idea of necessity. This new impression corresponds to the mechanical 'determination of the mind' or the 'propensity which custom produces, to pass from an object to the idea of its usual attendant' (T.165). As we have seen, Hume goes on to stress that this impression of necessity is really subjective. Thus he needs to postulate a separate externalising principle in order to explain how we come to project this impression on to objects. It is in this context that he speaks of another 'propensity' of the mind 'to spread itself on external objects' (T.167). This latter propensity is expressed as a general associational principle which accounts for the fact that we externalise any internal impression which regularly accompanies an external one. Thus, just as we naturally think of the smell of the orange as being contained externally in the visible orange, so we think of our internal impression of 'determination' as being contained in the motion of the first billiard ball prior to the transfer of that motion to the second. We have a natural tendency to think of our internal impression of necessary connection as being contained in the external objects of our awareness.

The *Enquiry* explanation of our supposition of objective forces dispenses with the need to postulate a separate externalising principle. This account relies solely on that natural instinct which Hume calls 'habit', or (in other words) custom. In the *Enquiry* Hume does not consider 'necessity' as if it were a distinct impression apart from the perceptions of cause and effect themselves: it is merely the connection between them. The repetition of event-sequences gives rise to the fact that one '*feels* these events to be *connected* in his imagination' (E.75–6). We feel the natural relation between the ideas of cause and effect and thus suppose the existence of an objective necessary connection which we never can perceive. In his *Enquiry* Hume claims that habit leads us to treat a subjective associational link between our ideas as if it were an objective philosophical one which is known through the understanding.

These two accounts show clearly that Hume held that natural instinct leads us to conclusions directly opposite to those we reach by attending to the nature of our ideas. The *Treatise* account shows that our natural judgement of causal processes is directly contrary to the actual character of our *impression* of necessity. For we are led to believe that this impression is external, though it is in fact internal. The *Enquiry* account shows that our natural instinct leads us to suppose what is directly contrary to what we discover on the basis of comparison of ideas – on the basis of *reason* alone. Reason leads us to the conclusion that our ideas of cause and effect are distinct. Yet natural instinct leads us to a directly contrary conclusion: namely, that there is an objective necessary connection relating those objects which we experience as constantly conjoined.

The description of the character of our natural judgement of causation presented in the *Enquiry* is fundamental to Hume's philosophical thought. This description is clearly presupposed even in the *Treatise*. In the section entitled 'Of the antient philosophy' Hume claims that

'Tis natural for men . . . to imagine they perceive a connexion betwixt such objects as they have constantly found united together; and because custom has render'd it difficult to separate the ideas, they are apt to fancy such a separation to be in itself impossible and absurd. (T. 223)

In the *Treatise* as well as the *Enquiry* Hume claims that custom causes men to suppose that their ideas are actually inseparable, just as they would be if they were able to perceive a genuine necessary connection between them. Hume claims that men judge that there is 'a natural and perceivable connexion' between the objects of their senses.

Hume's language in the section of the *Treatise* we have just considered seems to be derived from the discussion of custom in Locke's *Essay Concerning Human Understanding*.[38] Locke had distinguished two kinds of connections of ideas: there is a 'natural Connexion' founded on reason and 'another Connexion of *Ideas* wholly owing to Chance or Custom' (*Essay* 2, 33, 5). According to Locke custom causes an apparent inseparability of ideas. He states that it often happens that men 'can no more separate them in their Thoughts, than if they were *but one Idea, and they operate as if they were so'* (*Essay* 2, 33, 18; italics mine). Like Hume later, Locke thought that we treat ideas connected by custom as if there were a genuine connection between them other than the fact that they have been experienced together. However, unlike Hume, Locke only stressed the pathological character of such thinking: for Locke, custom is the source of 'Prejudice' and a 'sort of Madness' to which even the most brilliant men are subject (*Essay* 2, 33, 3). While Hume recognised that custom was the source of such false thinking,[39] he insisted that it was also a necessary basis of all experimental reasoning in science.

Hume holds that the experimental scientist, no less than the common man, derives his notion of causal power from the natural instinct which is called custom. This is the basis of Hume's claim in 'Of the antient philosophy' that 'the true philosophy approaches . . . the sentiments of the vulgar' (T.222–3). For Hume thinks that modern experimental philosophy can be distinguished from the philosophy of the ancients and medievals by the fact that modern scientists found their basic notions in principles of the imagination 'which are permanent, irresistable, and universal; such as the customary transition from causes to effects'.[40] It is on this basis that Hume thought he could establish that all causes are 'efficient' and rejected all notions of 'formal, and material, and exemplary, and final causes' (T.171). Only the notion of efficient causality is based on the 'irresistable' principle which Hume calls custom. The causal notions of the ancients, according to Hume, are based on 'trivial' properties of the fancy which made them project their own feelings on to nature as goals, as in the principle that nature abhors a vacuum (T.224–5).

Hume also attempts to show how, from the character of our basic natural principle, we draw the conclusion that all causes are absolutely necessary. As we have seen, he argues that our idea of necessity has its source in the actual transition of the mind from one object to the idea of another when we are confronted by repeated experience. Hume notes that this transition of the mind either occurs or it does not.[41] When our experience is not entirely consistent (A is usually followed by B, but not always), the 'constancy and force' of belief in the effect B varies; but the transition from which our idea of causation itself is drawn does not. It is like a switch which is either on or off. Our mind either moves to the idea of the effect B or it does not. Hume draws the conclusion that "tis impossible to admit of any medium betwixt chance and an absolute necessity' (T.171) and so rejects the reality of what other philosophers called a moral necessity. (Chance here means an 'indifference' of the *mind*: cf. T.125; p. 166 below.) Hume rejects the idea that there can be any causation which does not absolutely determine its effect (T.171).

Of course Hume did not believe that our scientific notion of power was *merely* derived from natural principles. As we have seen before, he holds that 'philosophical decisions' involve the correction of 'the reflections of common life' (E.162). In the section 'Of the antient philosophy' he speaks of 'the vulgar error' involved in the common-sense ascription of causal forces to objects. Men naturally think they perceive a 'connexion betwixt the several *sensible* qualities ... of matter' (italics mine) – that is, between the perceptions themselves. The falsity of this view is determined by philosophers who 'compare the ideas of objects' and 'discover that there is no *known* connexion' between them (T.223; italics mine). Yet the 'true' philosopher still holds with the common man that the *'constant conjunction of objects determines their causation'* (T.173). He yields to the authority of custom in so far as he acknowledges that constant conjunction is the sign of the existence of a real connection of objects themselves; but he follows reason in so far as he recognises that the connection cannot be perceived through the immediate objects of our senses. The resolution of the conflict between the conclusions of instinct and reason is provided by a mitigated scepticism which recognises the inadequacy of our ideas of objects and yet ascribes causal necessity to the external objects themselves on the basis of the criterion provided by the natural instinct.

(b) The identity of cause and effect
It is important to recognise that the unperceived necessary connections which the true philosopher ascribes to external objects on the basis of repeated experience are in fact those real inherent causal connections which we considered in §14. By asserting that custom makes us suppose a real connection of objects, in spite of the contrary evidence of our ideas, Hume

found a way to undermine the Cartesian claim that there are no real forces in nature. For that claim was based on the assumption that our ideas are adequate and that their distinctness reveals a real distinctness of objects. By rejecting this assumption empirical science is able to give credence to the inconceivable supposition engendered by custom which makes us regard cause and effect as if, to use Locke's words, 'they were but one *Idea*'. In this sense empirical science postulates those very unknown connections which are described by Cleanthes and Philo in Part IX of Hume's *Dialogues*. Custom allows us to postulate real existential connections between objects which appear to us as entirely distinct.

As we saw at the beginning of §14, the Cartesians used their discovery of the distinctness of ideas as a basis for their denial that there can be any natural power operating in the causal relations of mind and body. They also used claims concerning the distinctness of ideas to deny that any genuine natural powers operate in the production of purely physical events. In an important sense Hume reverses these arguments. By yielding to the authority of natural instinct Hume was led to affirm a real power and necessary connection in the relations of mind and body, and also in purely physical events. In a fundamental sense he even seems committed to the view that there is no ultimate ontological distinction between the object corresponding to our idea of cause and that corresponding to our idea of effect. Thus Hume suggests that the possibility of causal connection between some motions in the body and some perceptions favours materialism – the view that there is a kind of identity between the motions and the thoughts. We shall also see that there is a corresponding identity which seems to be implied by Hume's account of our ascription of real necessary connections to the objects of our external senses.

Towards the end of his section 'Of the immateriality of the soul' Hume discusses an argument against the view that there is causal connection between body and mind. This argument is similar to that which Fontenelle attributed to Descartes: since we can perceive no conceptual relation between brain-events and the perceptions with which they are conjoined "'tis concluded to be impossible, that thought can ever be caus'd by matter'.[42] In response to this argument Hume claims that we have no less reason to believe in causation here than in other cases: 'we are never sensible of any connexion betwixt causes and effects, and . . . 'tis only by our experience of their constant conjunction, we can arrive at any knowledge of this relation' (T.247). He claims that 'every one may perceive, that the different dispositions of his body change his thoughts and sentiments' and that we find *by experience* that 'thought and motion . . . are constantly united'. He proposes the *certain conclusion* that 'motion may be, and actually is, the cause of thought and perception' (T.248). Thus far it seems that Hume holds a view which is perfectly compatible with occasionalism, namely the view that there is merely a repeated succession of physical states and perceptions, and that this repeated succession is all we *intend* by ascribing a physical causation.

But Hume goes on to present the following dilemma:

There seems only this dilemma left us in the present case; either to assert, that nothing can be the cause of another, but where the mind can perceive the connexion in its idea of the objects: Or to maintain, that all objects, which we find constantly conjoin'd, are upon that account to be regarded as causes and effects. (T.248)

We have already considered Hume's account of the first horn of this dilemma in connection with his discussion of Cartesianism: he concludes that if we accept this side 'we in reality affirm, that there is no such thing in the universe as a cause or productive principle' (T.248). As we have seen Hume clearly considers this to be an absurd conclusion. 'Thus', he writes, 'we are necessarily reduc'd to the other side of the dilemma' (T.249). Hume seems clearly committed to the view that we should in fact ascribe a 'cause or productive principle' when we experience body states and perceptions as constantly conjoined. But it is his description of the result of accepting this view which should hold our attention. Hume writes that the acceptance of this horn of the dilemma *'evidently gives the advantage to the materialists above their antagonists'* (T.250; italics mine). Since materialism is the view that 'all thought' really is conjoined 'with extension' (T.239) Hume seems left with the conclusion that the causal connection of mental states with material ones implies that there is no substantial distinction between the two. He seems to think that a genuine causation commits one to a kind of mind–body identity, though one must admit that this identity is never perceivable to us. Such a view seems perfectly in accord with Hume's mitigated scepticism and his claims concerning the inadequacy of human ideas. It is true that Hume stresses that our 'unextended' perceptions such as tastes, smells, and emotions (cf. T.234–9) appear without the properties of matter. He concludes that 'all our perceptions are not susceptible of a local union . . . with what is extended' and that 'the question concerning the substance of the soul is absolutely *unintelligible*' (T.250; italics mine). However, he leaves open the possibility that their constant conjunction with material states shows that, in some unintelligible way, passions and other unextended perceptions really are necessarily connected with matter (cf. T.248–50).

If the account I have given of Hume's philosophical ascription of necessity is correct, it would seem that there must also be a kind of identity between purely physical causes and their effects. At first sight this seems entirely paradoxical. Yet if custom makes one attribute a genuine necessary connection between causes and effects, then this would seem to preclude any absolute distinction between the objects. Let us consider the problems with this view and see if we can make some sense of the claim that there is a real identity between the objects of those ideas we call cause and effect.

As we have seen at the beginning of §14 (*a*), the fundamental conceptual basis for Descartes' denial of genuine forces in nature lay in his analysis of time. It seems to have been this analysis which led to his conclusion that a body cannot continue either at rest or in a state of motion by any force of its own. It is important to note that the relevant features of the conceptual analysis of time which led to Descartes' denial of finite natural forces are shared by Hume.

At the outset of his *Treatise* discussion of causality Hume demands that there be a 'PRIORITY of time in the cause before the effect' (T.76). But this demand would seem to lead to the conclusion that there is a genuine discontinuity between cause and effect, and that they are entirely isolated in discrete temporal units which can have no existential connection one with another. For Hume also claims that 'every moment must be distinct' from every other (T.31). If successive moments are distinct, and what we call cause and effect occur successively, then what we call cause and effect must be distinct. Thus all necessary connection and real power must be excluded from finite objects. It seems that the demand for real force and connection in temporally finite objects is absolutely contradictory, just as Malebranche thought.

It is important to underline the fact that this whole argument is derived from the conceptual analysis of time. Consider Hume's argument to show that every moment of time is wholly distinct from every other:

> if each moment, as it succeeds another, were not perfectly single and indivisible, there would be an infinite number of co-existent moments, or parts of time; which I believe will be allow'd to be an arrant contradiction. (T.31)

Once again we should be struck by the fact that Hume employs the rational analysis of ideas to reach an entirely paradoxical conclusion. It is perhaps worth noting that, in an article of the *Dictionary* to which Hume refers us in his letter of 1737, Bayle used this same analysis of time as a series of indivisible moments to revive Zeno's paradoxes concerning the impossibility of motion.[43]

We saw in the previous chapter that Hume began Part II of the *Treatise* with an attempt to argue that time and space, in their real existence, may be composed of discrete minimal parts. Even in his later *Enquiry* he stressed the paradoxes which result from regarding time and space as infinitely divisible, and suggested that such paradoxes could be avoided by recognising that we have ideas of *minima* derived from the senses and imagination. In these discussions he seems to disregard the fact, stressed by Bayle, that analysis of time as composed of discrete parts leads to its own paradoxes. However, Hume should not have been troubled by the suggestion that time itself is composed of continuous successive parts, even though (according to him) our perceptions must be analysed into discrete *minima*. Indeed, he himself claims that in our actual experience, the points which compose our impressions of *space* are entirely 'confounded with each other'.[44] As we have seen, Hume even seems to think we have a *natural propensity*, founded in the imagination, to believe that space is infinitely divisible and hence continuous. We have a natural propensity which opposes the results of our conceptual analysis of space. May not the same be said of time? While Hume produced no such explicit account as to how we naturally think of events as temporally continuous, it seems reasonable to consider such an account as implicit in his description of the origin of our idea of necessary connection in that natural instinct he calls custom or habit. Natural instinct supersedes the conceptual analysis of impressions and ideas which makes us think that events are composed of discrete parts. It makes us suppose a continuity in the objects themselves. In order to allow for the possibility of real forces in nature Hume needs to abandon *completely* the 'establish'd maxim in metaphysics' as a basis for ontological judgements – even those concerning space and time!

Thus we see that by using custom as a basis for the ascription of causal forces Hume seems committed to the view that there is no absolute distinction between the particular objects of our ideas of cause and effect, and yet that they exist successively in time. To see that such a view is not really bizarre it may be helpful to note that the view of ontological causality which we are ascribing to Hume was held by an earlier eighteenth-century writer on causality, Hermann Boerhaave. Boerhaave claimed that 'If we could understand the Nature of Things . . . we should not then use the Name of Cause and Effect, but we should see every thing as existing together'. He thought that there is no 'real Difference betwixt the Cause and the Effect, since the Cause is inseparable from the Effect, and the Effect from the Cause, and differ only with respect to Duration in ourselves'. But Boerhaave did not seem to have in mind a purely logical relationship. In discussing the transference of motion by contact of one elastic ball with another he claimed that if we 'unite all the Particulars' of the process together we will have an idea of the identity of cause and effect. At the moment of contact the balls are 'as it were, one Body'.[45] This analysis of causality is transferred in a fascinating way to his own account of the cause of disease – most significantly to an account of mental disease. Its details cannot concern us here; our aim is merely to point out that there were other major thinkers of Hume's day who regarded real natural causation as involving a continuous process in which there was no objective separation of cause and effect.

To sum up the main results of Hume's discussion of natural instinct and causation: custom leads us to suppose the existence of a causal power which is identical to that of which we would have knowledge *if* Hume's modified rationalist criterion, which we considered in our last section, were ever fulfilled. Custom leads us to suppose the existence of a causal power inherent in the objects of the senses, whether they be the immediate objects (as on the view of common sense), or the independent unperceived external objects (as on the view of the true philosopher). It leads us to ascribe an absolute necessity relating those objects which we call cause and effect. And it leads us to suppose that there is no absolute existential distinction between them.

§16   Hume's rejection of Newtonian 'active powers'

Hume's account of the experimental scientific notion of causation has both an analytic and a synthetic side. While the 'true' scientific thinker rejects the ontological implications of the Cartesian analysis of ideas (i.e., that there are no real causes in nature) he employs this same analysis to conclude that we have no *a priori* knowledge of causation. Thus Hume speaks of a conceptual or 'metaphysical'[46] possibility that 'any thing may produce any thing. Creation, annihilation, motion, reason, volition; all these may arise from one another, or from any other object we can imagine' (T.173). Hume's list does not appear to be entirely arbitrary: one suspects that his contemporaries would have noted that the 'objects' he in fact mentions have particular relevance to theological questions. For example, as we shall see in a moment, the question of whether new motion must arise from volition was of particular importance for the natural theology of Hume's day. But Hume does not limit himself to the merely negative claim that we have no *a priori* conception of any causal links. He formulates certain rules which, according to him, make it possible for us to 'know' which of these things 'really are' the causes of other things.[47] Ultimately these rules are based on the belief that invariant conjunction really does give us *evidence* of a causal connection. While Hume clearly thinks we lack knowledge of ultimate causation owing to the inadequacy of our human ideas, he believes that by systematically applying the criterion of causation derived from natural instinct we can approach such knowledge. The analytic and synthetic sides of Hume's account of causation combine to form a powerful tool which he uses to attack the voluntaristic cosmology which was closely connected with Newtonian science in the first half of the eighteenth century.

(a) Hume's dispute with John Stewart

In §14 we saw that Hume expressed approval of the fact that major English writers, unlike the Cartesians, had ascribed real power to matter. Hume especially praised Newton who, he claimed, had postulated the existence of an 'etherial active Matter to explain his universal Attraction'. We have seen that Hume took issue with Berkeley, who had maintained that Newton really held the theory that God was the only source of power in the universe. But Hume's own interpretation of Newton was itself challenged by a contemporary physicist – John Stewart, who was Professor of Natural Philosophy at the University of Edinburgh – and this attack led Hume to make a change in his text.

In 1754, Stewart submitted a paper to the Philosophical Society of Edinburgh in which he expressly attacked Hume's claim that Newton intended 'to ascribe activity to matter'.[48] Stewart's paper was in direct response to one presented by Henry Home (Lord Kames) entitled 'Of the Laws of Motion': Kames' aim was to argue against the doctrine 'maintained by the bulk of our philosophers, that matter is altogether incapable of active powers'.[49] Stewart insisted that Hume and Kames had misunderstood a fundamental dualism in Newton's philosophy between the passive inertial power of matter and the active power attributed to gravity. To ascribe activity to matter is 'a manifest contradiction to the primary laws of motion, delivered by [Newton] in the beginning of his *Principia*' (p. 130). In a letter to Stewart, Hume admitted that he (Stewart) had shown that 'Lord Kames is mistaken in his Argument'.[50] On the first opportunity Hume withdrew his own claim that Newton had ascribed activity to matter itself. In his 1756 edition of the *Philosophical Essays Concerning Human Understanding* Hume maintained only that the Newtonian aether was an 'active *fluid*' and that Newton did not intend 'to rob *second causes* of all force or energy'.[51]

However the real significance of this dispute lay in Stewart's recognition that Hume's own philosophy (as well as that of Kames) threatened basic theological notions underlying the Newtonian concept of force or active power. Hume, who as secretary to the Philosophical Society of Edinburgh edited the volume in which the papers of Stewart and Kames appeared,[52] complained of 'so many Insinuations of Irreligion' in Stewart's paper 'to which Lord Kames's Paper gave not the least Occasion'.[53] But Stewart was only following Clarke and Newton in insisting that 'the genuine characteristic of an active being, is a power of beginning motion either in itself or another, without the means of preceeding motion'.[54] For a Newtonian like Stewart 'a power of beginning motion seems *necessarily* to infer a power of thinking' (p. 114; italics mine). Thus, unlike Hume, Stewart could not ascribe activity to the aether itself: the aether is only 'a more general mechanical cause' used to account for gravity as well as 'the attraction of cohesion and refraction of light, &c.' (p. 129). The real activity must belong to an intelligent being. Moreover, the fact that the aetherial fluid produces great 'variety and regularity' in the motions of attracted bodies shows that such motions '*must* consequently be regarded as the continual effects of thought and design' (p. 130; italics mine). Pretty clearly Stewart thought he had some *a priori* insight into the kind of cause which is ultimately required to bring motion and order into existence. The Newtonians, no less than the Cartesians, assumed that they had some *a priori* conception of what sorts of things require a non-material cause.

It has recently been argued that the contrast between deterministic mechanical causation on the one hand and 'active powers' on the other lay at the foundation of the Newtonian concept of force.[55] This contrast is clearly developed in Query 31 of Newton's *Opticks*, as well as in the Clarke–Newton side of the correspondence with Leibniz.[56] In the correspondence Clarke refers to 'mechanical communications of motion' as involving a kind of causation which 'gives no new motion or impression to matter' (p. 51). He considers such causation to involve 'mere passiveness', and he also says that it entails 'mere fate and necessity'. Yet unlike the Cartesians and Leibniz, Newton and Clarke think that such mechanical principles are not entirely self-sufficient in the natural world: mechanical motion is 'always upon the Decay', due to the 'Tenacity of Fluids, and Attrition of their Parts, and the Weakness of Elasticity in Solids' (*Opticks*, p. 398). Thus Newton writes,

Seeing therefore the variety of Motion which we find in the World is always decreasing, there is a necessity of conserving and recruiting it by *active Principles*, such as are the cause of Gravity, by which . . . Bodies acquire great Motion in falling; and the cause of Fermentation, by which the Heart and Blood of Animals are kept in perpetual Motion and Heat. (*ibid.*, p. 399; italics mine)

The nature of these principles is clearly indicated by Clarke, who defines action as 'the beginning of motion where there was none before, from a principle of life or activity' (*Correspondence*, p. 110). In the *Opticks* Newton clearly thinks that these principles are second causes which can operate independently of God's direct guidance: once God has formed the world by means of such active principles 'it may continue . . . for many Ages'. Yet he stresses that the original creation of the world by means of such principles and their re-introduction when it 'wants a Reformation' requires the guiding 'Counsel of an *intelligent Agent*' who acts with *'Choice'*. This is clearly indicated, according to Newton, by the 'wonderful Uniformity' one finds in certain parts of nature such as the 'Planetary System' and 'the Bodies of Animals' (*Opticks*, p. 402; italics mine). The Newtonian cosmology seems to involve a dichotomy between active, freely chosen, ordering powers on the one hand; and passive, determined, decaying ones on the other.

Hume tried to undermine this Newtonian cosmological system by showing that there is no experimental basis for the *a priori* assumptions underlying its root notion of active power.[57] These assumptions are twofold and we can somewhat arbitrarily separate them: addition of motion requires a voluntary free agent; 'order' requires an intelligent one. The first assumption seems to be most closely connected with the notion of active power developed by John Locke; the second with the notion that is to be found in Ralph Cudworth. Hume's critique of the notion of 'active power' is most immediately directed against the ideas of these authors. But in attacking their views Hume struck at the heart of the Newtonian conception of power or force.

(b) Do we know an active cause through human volition?
In his *Essay Concerning Human Understanding* Locke claimed that we have an idea of what he called 'active Power' through 'reflection on the Operations of our Minds'. By an active power Locke meant one which could bring about a 'beginning of Motion' where there was none before. Like Newton and Clarke later, he contrasted active power with mechanical transference of

motion by impulse (i.e., 'passive Power', where the impelling body as well as body impelled has 'received' the motion 'from another'). Locke claimed that

The *Idea* of the beginning of motion, we have only from reflection on what passes in our selves, where we find by Experience, that barely by willing it, barely by a thought of the Mind, we can move the parts of our Bodies, which were before at rest. (*Essay* 2, 21, 4)

He may be taken to be implying that we actually have some insight how motion originates when we reflect on our own acts of will. Locke connected this idea of active power in thinking beings with liberty, and claimed that a man is free in so far as his action follows from his own choice or 'Volition'. He also said that those motions of one's body which one cannot choose not to perform are done by 'Necessity and Constraint' (*Essay* 2, 21, 8 & 9).

In his discussion 'Of the idea of necessary connexion' in both the *Treatise* and *Enquiry* Hume rejects Locke's theory that we can derive an idea of power by considering 'the operations of our own minds' (E.64). As we saw earlier (p. 139 above), Hume's argument in the *Treatise* derives directly from that of Malebranche, who denied that there is any necessary connection between our acts of will and the motions of our body. Hume's arguments in the *Enquiry* are more complex, but the denial that we have any idea of our own power rests basically on the same conceptual considerations. Fundamentally, Hume is claiming that we have no idea of any *a priori* connection between a *beginning of motion* and *volition*. Thus Hume implies that it is no 'more difficult to conceive that motion may arise from impulse than that it may arise from volition' (E.73). While Locke certainly does not deny the former possibility,[58] he *does* suggest that there is some conceptual connection between the notions of mind and active power. For he states that 'the active power of Moving. . . is much clearer in Spirit than Body', and he thinks it is possible that this power of adding motion to the universe may be 'the proper attribute of Spirits' (*Essay* 2, 23, 28). Hume brings out the implications of his own view in the *Dialogues* when he writes that 'the beginning of motion in matter itself is as conceivable *a priori* as its communication from mind and intelligence' (D.183).

Unlike Malebranche, Hume did not deny that we have a genuine power to bring about motions in our bodies through our own acts of volition. Our proof of the existence of this power is derived from the constant conjunction of our volition and the motions of our body. This conjunction indicates a necessity in so far as it is regular; though the facts about paralysis to which he appeals (see p. 139) suggest that we are far from directly observing the actual causal mechanisms. But Hume stresses that acts of will are themselves subject to other factors whose connection with them is determined by constant conjunction. We have 'a *false sensation or experience* . . . of the liberty of indifference' when we find that our will moves 'easily every way' (T. 408). An external observer can often see why we choose one action or another, or even why we have the desire to convince ourselves that we are free. He

can commonly infer our actions from our motives and character; and even where he cannot, he concludes in general, that he might, were he perfectly acquainted with . . . the most secret springs of our complexion and disposition. (T. 408–9)

In short,

there is no known circumstance, that enters into the connexion and production of the actions of matter, that is not to be found in all the operations of the mind; and consequently we cannot, without a manifest absurdity, attribute necessity to the one, and refuse it to the other. (T. 404)

For Hume, our acts of will are as necessary as the actions involved in any physical causal process.

That there may be a special causal link between active principles and volition was, as we have seen, suggested by Locke. On the other hand, by appealing to the analysis of ideas Hume noted that there is no more *a priori* reason to assume a causal link between the origin of motion and volition than between the origin of motion and matter. Constant conjunction alone will tell us what is the cause of what. The Newtonians, Hume would say, appear to discover active principles in matter – for example, gravity. Following Locke's suggestion they have gone on to conclude that there must be some volition underlying such principles. But this, according to Hume, is the wrong conclusion. By means of experience (i.e., constant conjunction) we discover that there are apparently a number of causes of activity in the universe, including purely material ones. Given that experience, one might as well conclude that volition is performed by gravity as that gravity is performed by volition! Thus, in the *Dialogues* Hume puts the following speech into the mouth of Philo:

Motion, in many instances, from gravity, from elasticity, from electricity, begins in matter, without any known voluntary agent; and to suppose always, in these cases, an unknown voluntary agent, is mere hypothesis; and hypothesis attended with no advantages. (D.182–3)

There is no advantage for the theist because we have as much reason to say the actions of our will are determined as to say that of the actions of matter itself. Hume's attack on the notion of human freedom, like that of Anthony Collins before him,[59] struck at the heart of the Newtonian theological system.

(c) The cause of order

In Query 31 of the *Opticks* Newton stressed the close connection between the existence of order in certain parts of the universe and the choice of a divine intelligent being (p. 402). At this point in his argument, Newton's conceptions seem very close to those of Ralph Cudworth who, in opposition to the Cartesians, maintained that there are second causes in nature. In his *True Intellectual System of the Universe* (1678) Cudworth claimed, with the ancients, that there is an 'active power' in the universe which has 'the Power of Moving Matter, whether by express Consciousness or no' (p. 27). This power has 'self activity or life'. Cudworth characterises this power in the following way:

there is a *Plastick Nature* under [God] which as an Inferior and Subordinate Instrument, doth Drudgingly Execute that Part of his Providence, which consists in the *Regular and Orderly* Motion of Matter: yet so as that there is also besides this, a Higher Providence to be acknowledged, which presiding over it, doth often supply the Defects of it, and sometimes Overrule it. (p. 150; italics mine)

The essential feature of Cudworth's active power or plastic nature is that it maintains order in the universe. Yet Cudworth insisted that such power ultimately derives from God.

In his *Enquiry* Hume expressed approval of the fact that Cudworth, along with other English authors, believed that there is such an ordering power in the universe – though Hume somewhat misleadingly suggested that Cudworth ascribed such power to matter itself. Yet Hume acknowledged that the power which was ascribed to nature by these philosophers is 'subordinate and derived'.[60] In fact, following Bayle, Hume went on to argue that Cudworth's plastic nature dispensed altogether with the need for a deity outside of nature.

In some manuscript notes which have been preserved in the Royal Society of Edinburgh Hume wrote:

Strato's Atheism the most dangerous of the Antient, holding the Origin of the World from Nature, or *a Matter endu'd with Activity*. Baile thinks there are none but the Cartesians can refute this Atheism.

A Stratonician cou'd retort the Arguments of all the Sects of Philosophy. . . . The same Question, Why the Parts or Ideas of God had that particular Arrangement? is as difficult as why the World had.[61]

Hume's note seems to refer directly to a chapter of Bayle's *Continuations des Pensées Diverses* (1704) entitled *'That it is important to teach that matter is devoid of activity'*.[62] In this section Bayle claimed to be supporting a version of the 'Cartesian' principle that it is a contradiction to say that order can arise directly from anything but a being which has knowledge of the order which it bestows. Bayle argues that the admission of 'second causes' in nature which act without consciousness leads to the hylozoic atheism espoused by the third century B.C. Peripatetic philosopher Strato.[63] In this passage Bayle considers such causes to be 'active' in the sense that they transfer order to other parts of nature. Thus, he writes, philosophers think that a pear rather than an apple results from a pear tree because of the *action* of the pear tree (p. 340). Bayle has his Stratonician atheist argue that once one admits the existence of such active principles in nature one can dispense with the need for a mind or consciousness to create such order: 'if this order exists once without consciousness, it will last as such eternally: the most difficult thing to do is [already] done'.[64] Elsewhere he specifically notes that Cudworth is open to the objections of the Stratonician. Bayle says that Cudworth's plastic natures are *'active principles which execute the plan of God'* almost like workmen who 'execute the plan of an engineer'. But unlike the workmen the active principles of Cudworth 'produce plants and animals without having consciousness of their own act'.[65] Hence even Cudworth, who argued for the existence of God on the basis of 'the order and symmetry of the world', had in fact dispensed with the need for such an intelligent being.[66]

As Kemp Smith has shown, Hume took up major themes of Bayle's Stratonician atheism and developed them in the *Dialogues*. Kemp Smith showed that Hume's early notes tie in closely with Philo's claim that there is 'an eternal, inherent principle of order in the world' (D.36). Yet I think it is also important to recognise that, by applying his own two-sided account of causality, Hume has systematically developed the implications of Cudworth's account of active principles. In so doing Hume reached his own rather distinctive conception of the first cause. In the following pages I shall take it for granted that Kemp Smith has correctly identified Hume's own conclusions with those of Philo.[67]

From the beginning of the *Dialogues* Hume appears to have little sympathy with the 'Cartesian' (i.e. Malebranchian) view which Bayle himself claims to espouse – the view that it is a necessary truth that order must arise from a knowing being. In Part II of this work Cleanthes and Philo agree to assume the truth of the proposition that 'for aught we can know *a priori*, matter may contain the source or spring of order originally, within itself, as well as mind does' (D.146). This proposition follows directly from what, on page 161 above, I called Hume's analytic principle of scientific causation. At one point in the *Dialogues*, the third character, Demea, does repeat Bayle's Cartesian claim. He asks: 'how can order spring from any thing, which perceives not that order which it bestows?' (D.179). Yet, even he, speaking earlier in the *Dialogues*, shows that the essential link which Cartesianism maintains between order and the Deity is not really a link between order and *consciousness*. Citing Malebranche, Demea claims that we ought not 'to imagine, that the Spirit of God has human ideas, or bears *any* resemblance to our spirit'.[68] Later on Demea states that God has no 'shadow of distinction or diversity' and is 'without any new judgment, sentiment, or operation'. Cleanthes draws the obvious implication that such an immutable mind has 'no thought, no reason, no will, no sentiment, no love, no hatred; or in a word, is no mind at all' (D.159). It seems clear that Malebranche and Demea have excluded all properties necessary for consciousness from the mind of God.

The fundamental question of Hume's *Dialogues* is: What can

experience tell us about the source of order in the universe? For the whole argument proceeds upon the proposition that 'experience alone can point out . . . the true cause of any phenomenon' (D.146). All characters agree that order is sometimes experienced as deriving from mind. Philo states that mind is 'an active cause, by which some particular parts of nature . . . produce alterations on other parts' (D.147). But he insists that there are others, and this is where Bayle's criticism of Cudworth's views becomes relevant to Hume's discussion. For Philo notes that 'vegetation' and 'animal generation', like 'mind', are words we use to mark 'certain powers and energies in nature' which result in order in the world (D.178). He observes that:

A tree bestows order and organization on that tree which springs from it, without knowing the order: an animal, in the same manner, on its offspring . . . And instances of this kind are even more frequent in the world, than those of order, which arise from reason and contrivance. (D.179)

What *experience* shows us is that none of these principles, more than another, has any 'privilege for being made a standard to the whole of nature' (D.178). All these sources of order, including mind, may well derive from 'original unknown principles' which 'belong to matter' (D.179). In fact this seems the most probable hypothesis since, as Philo points out, the material active principle of generation has a priority in experience to that of mind: 'For we see every day the latter arise from the former, never the former from the latter' (D.180). Thus generation appears to experience to be a more basic ordering principle than mind. Moreover, since nature as a whole resembles an animal or a plant even more than it does the products of human artifice (D.172), its cause or causes must more closely resemble generation and vegetation. Thus in Part XII of the *Dialogues* Philo concludes that one should base one's cosmology on 'energies that probably bear some remote analogy to each other' such as 'the rotting of a turnip, the generation of an animal, and the structure of human thought' (D.218).

When Hume argues that vegetation and generation provide good models for the first principles of the universe, his ideas appear to be close to those of the Stratonician or hylozoic atheist. Cudworth described Strato's God as being no other than 'a Life of Nature in Matter, as was both devoid of Sense and consciousness'.[69] Philo seems to be repeating the first part of this view when he claims that we should not look for a source of order outside of the 'material world' and that 'supposing it to contain the principle of its order within itself, we really assert it to be God' (D.162). Strictly speaking, Philo avoids hylozoism by claiming that *'the cause or causes of order in the universe probably bear some remote analogy to human intelligence'* (D.227). But it is difficult to read the *Dialogues* with care and not become convinced that this analogy is so remote as to be almost irrelevant. Having dispensed with Cudworth's God, Philo is left with Cudworth's plastic natures as the ultimate source of order in the universe. Philo's claim in Part XII of the *Dialogues* that the dispute between the theist and the atheist is merely verbal (D.217–18) echoes Cudworth's own claim that the 'Controversie whether the Energy of the Plastick Nature, be Cogitation, or no, seems to be but a Logomachy, or Contention about Words'. The issue for Cudworth hangs on the question of whether a being without 'Self-perception or Self-Injoyment' can be called conscious.[70] Philo asks Cudworth's verbal question, not of a second cause but of the very first principle or principles of the universe itself.

From this point of view the *Dialogues* seem to present a secularised version of the more-than-mechanist cosmology developed by Cudworth, Newton and Clarke. Such a cosmology would contain both active principles which tend to generate order and motion in the universe, and passive ones which tend to decrease those phenomena. Such a secularised view of 'nature as a perpetual worker' was becoming popular in Hume's own day, and the sections of Hume's *Dialogues* discussing these active principles may be seen as looking forward to the theory of the earth as a living being which was later developed in the work of his compatriot James Hutton.[71]

(d) Humean mechanism
On the other hand, there is good reason to think that Hume would not have been satisfied with active principles in the sense of Cudworth and Newton – even when these principles are conceived as inherent in nature. In Part VIII of the *Dialogues*, where Hume presents an account of the origin of forms from purely material processes, 'active force' is interpreted purely in

terms of the perpetual agitation of matter.[72] Here Philo sets aside the possibility of Newtonian active powers in favour of a purely mechanistic hypothesis:

why may not motion have been propagated by impulse through all eternity, and the same stock of it, or nearly the same, be still upheld in the universe? As much as is lost by the composition of motion, as much is gained by its resolution. (D.183)

He goes on to employ this hypothesis in accounting for the origin of worlds in an infinite time with a finite matter.[73] As I mentioned earlier, Philo rejects this modified Epicurean account at the end of Part VIII of the *Dialogues*. At the same time, what Philo (and Hume himself) finds absurd in the Epicurean system is the suggestion that the world is formed by chance. But there is no reason to think that Hume would have been unhappy with the modified Epicurean cosmology suggested by Descartes in the fifth part of his *Discourse on Method*. While Descartes proposed that matter began in chaos, he thought that by means of concurrence of the Deity and the 'laws of nature' established in matter 'all things which are purely material might in the course of time have become such as we observe them to be at present' (H.R. I, 109). Unlike Descartes, Hume would only insist that the action of the Deity is inherent in matter itself.

It is important to note that Hume's criticism of the idea that there is an original source of motion and order in mind seems to undermine the central idea of *all* active powers. We have seen that Hume insists against Locke that all acts of volition are rigidly determined by prior causes. In the *Dialogues* Philo insists that 'a mental world or universe of ideas requires a cause as much as does a material world or universe of objects . . . ' (D.160). Our limited experience certainly shows that the order of ideas depends upon prior causes:

A difference of age, of the disposition of his body, of weather, of food, of company, of books, of passions; any of these particulars or others more minute, are sufficient to alter the curious machinery of thought, and communicate to it very different movements and operations. (D.161)

Such arguments should apply *mutatis mutandis* to the other active principles which Philo and Cleanthes discuss in the *Dialogues*. Generation and vegetation should, at least in principle, be traceable to prior causes – especially those which are 'more minute'. Hume's analysis of human volition appears to preclude the existence of *any* original sources of motion and order in the universe. Was John Stewart so very far from the mark in 1754 when he likened Hume's own view of active matter to that of Spinoza who, according to Stewart, believed that 'there is a progression of causes and effects, *in infinitum* all acting blindly, without intelligence and design'?[74] Hume's views are entirely compatible with the idea that order is eternally present in matter.

The question concerning Hume's beliefs about the ultimate nature of the power and force of nature is difficult to resolve. Certainly Hume was willing to allow, with his Newtonian contemporaries, that the actual *phenomena* of the world were not capable of being reduced to mere mechanism. In his *History of England* Hume praised Newton for showing the 'imperfections of the mechanical philosophy' and for restoring nature's 'ultimate secrets to that obscurity in which they ever did and ever will remain'.[75] In his *Enquiry* Hume placed 'active principles' on an equal footing with mechanical ones from the point of view of our experience: 'elasticity, gravity, cohesion of parts, communication of motion by impulse . . . are probably the ultimate causes and principles which we shall ever *discover* in nature' (E.30; italics mine).

However, both Hume and Newton did speculate on the nature of the 'ultimate springs and principles' which are 'totally shut up from human curiosity and enquiry'.[76] In spite of the claims of both philosophers to limit themselves to the phenomena, they went on to make speculative claims about what really exists beyond our experience. As we have seen, Hume praised one of Newton's most important hypotheses, that of the aether: he praised Newton for postulating the existence of an active aetherial matter. But, in fact, *Newton* did not intend the aether as an ultimate material principle. He insisted that without some other principles than those which belong to matter 'there never could have been any Motion in the World' (*Opticks*, p. 397). According to him the 'very first Cause . . . certainly is not mechanical' (*Opticks*, p. 369). The ultimate cause postulated by Newton was that of a providential being who corrects the decaying operations of brute matter; the 'wonderful Uniformity in the Planetary System must be allowed the Effect of Choice' (*Opticks*, p. 402). Newton insisted on the existence of a benevolent God who has 'dominion' as well as power, and hence voluntarily chooses the order which we find in the world.[77] But the ultimate principle which *Hume* recommended was entirely different. He clearly rejected the view that there is a principle of volition over and above the natural operations of matter. Motion is inherent in matter itself and does not need to be superadded by any non-material being. Hume's own faith that the mechanical laws of motion can account for the complex operations of nature was clearly expressed at the beginning of his *Natural History of Religion* in 1757:

Could men anatomize nature, according to the most probable, at least the most intelligible philosophy, they would find, that [the unknown causes of their hopes and fears] are nothing but the particular fabric and structure of the minute parts of their own bodies and of external objects; and that, by a regular and constant machinery, all the events are produced, about which they are so much concerned. (G.G. IV, 316)

This statement indicates a faith in the all-pervasive application of mechanical laws. Even if Hume entertained a vitalistic hypothesis in his later *Dialogues*, his statement of 1757 goes back to the real mechanist roots of his own philosophy. According to Hume, the mechanical powers which determine human life are mostly hidden; but he believed that they are inherent in matter itself.

§17   *Conclusion*

In the last section of his *Enquiry*, Hume appears to recommend us to withhold our instinctual belief in causality in so far as it leads us to draw conclusions in natural theology:

While we cannot give a satisfactory reason, why we believe, after a thousand experiments, that a stone will fall, or fire burn; can we ever satisfy ourselves concerning any determination, which we may form, with regard to the origin of worlds, and the situation of nature, from, and to eternity? (E.162)

In this passage Hume embraces, in a limited sphere, the Pyrrhonism which results from the application of conceptual or metaphysical analysis to our actual sense-derived ideas. For it is Hume's application of such an analysis which leads him to the conclusion that we can give no 'satisfactory reason' for the acceptance of a belief in causal connection. However, if the interpretation we have given in the last section is correct, Hume ultimately succumbs to natural instinct even in theological matters. In his *Dialogues*, Hume adopts the instinctually grounded belief that constant conjunction of successive events can provide a basis for an understanding of causal connections. Certainly the passage from the *Enquiry* which we have just cited represents the viewpoint espoused by Philo right at the beginning of the *Dialogues*. Yet in the argument of Parts XI and XII of that work Philo clearly adopts Cleanthes' principle that experience can point out the true cause of any phenomenon. For it is by consistently adhering to that principle that Philo reaches the conclusions that the original source of all things is entirely indifferent to all human conceptions of good and evil (D.212) and that it bears only the remotest analogy to human intelligence (D.217). These conclusions appear to represent those of Hume himself.

More accurately, we can distinguish three distinct stages in Hume's public statements about the *design argument* – the argument which was the basis for eighteenth-century natural theology. In his *A Letter from a Gentleman to his Friend in Edinburgh*, written in 1745, Hume suggests that his view that experience is the only foundation for belief in causality provides support for the argument:

tho' all Inferences concerning Matter of Fact be thus resolved into Experience, these Inferences are noway weakned by such an Assertion. . . . Wherever I see Order, I infer from Experience that *there*, there hath been Design and Contrivance . . . . The same Principle obliges me to infer an infinitely perfect Architect, from the infinite Art and Contrivance which is display'd in the whole Fabrick of the Universe. (pp. 25–6)

Here Hume purports to be sympathetic to the teleological argument for the existence of a Deity which was espoused by the Newtonian writers of his day. In contrast, in the *Enquiry*, written shortly thereafter, he implies that his analysis of causation supports a Pyrrhonian suspense of judgement on the whole question. Finally, in the concluding sections of the *Dialogues*, Hume again allows an inference to the first cause, but is careful to consider the exact form of conclusion which we can draw. He allows an inference based on experience, but acknowledges that the inference leads to a very attenuated form of deism.

Although Hume certainly puts his faith in experience as the

basis for the determination of true causes, it is important to recognise that *experience* is never for him a simple unproblematic source of belief. Hume never thinks that our success in employing regularity as a basis for the determination of causation is a rational ground for that employment. For, by itself, our past success provides no basis for the belief that similar cases in future will disclose the same causal powers. Thus, for Hume, the real foundation for our conclusions from experience lies in a natural instinct. As we have shown in §15 of this chapter, Hume held that this instinct takes us beyond our perceptions and leads us to ascribe a genuine necessary connection to their objects. In so far as Hume thinks there is any justification for this assumption, it lies in his belief that the assumption is based upon the 'more establish'd properties of the imagination' (T.267). In Hume's philosophy it is the established properties of the imagination rather than the established maxim of metaphysics which provide the clue to the role of experience in the determination of causal principles. Hume's aim in the *Treatise* was to understand the central principles of the human imagination and the way they provide the basis for empirical science and civilised human behaviour. In the final chapter, I shall attempt to reach some general understanding of Hume's original conception of that faculty and its operations.

Notes

1   Perhaps the most systematic attempt to support such an interpretation is to be found in Farhang Zabeeh, *Hume, Precursor of Modern Empiricism*. But the essential features of the interpretation are presented in the majority of twentieth-century commentaries on Hume which were published before 1975. It is remarkable how often these writers on Hume's philosophy tell us that he really does not mean what he says when he tells us that we lack knowledge of reality. See Chapter 1.
2   Rudolf Carnap, *Philosophy and Logical Syntax*, p. 35.
3   E.22. Cf. A.648–9.
4   In the discussion of his 'empiricist' principle in his *Enquiry* Hume writes: 'It is readily allowed, that other beings may possess many senses of which we can have no conception; because the ideas of

them have never been introduced to us in the only manner by which an idea can have access to the mind, to wit, by the actual feeling and sensation' (E.20). Contrast here A. Pap, *Semantics and Necessary Truth*, p. 80: 'It would be impossible, on Hume's theory, that there should exist in the universe colors which nobody has ever seen.' Hume certainly does not want to limit ideas to those possessed by human beings. For the importance of Hume's claim, see p. 132, below.

5   Cf. pp. 65–6 and 104 above. It is of some importance to recognise that this was a technical term in seventeenth- and eighteenth-century philosophy, closely tied up with abstraction. For example, in the reply to the fourth set of objections to his *Meditations* Descartes spoke of 'a fiction or intellectual abstraction' ('fictionem, vel abstractionem intellectûs': A.T. VII, 229). In the *Recherche* (III, 207), right after a passage paraphrased by Hume at T.158, Malebranche says that 'the power attributed to created beings' is 'a fiction of the mind of which we naturally have no idea'.

6   *Philosophy and Logical Syntax*, p. 36.

7   E.162. Hume also speaks of the 'infirmities of human understanding' (E.161) and 'the imperfection of [our] faculties . . . , their narrow reach, and their inaccurate operations' (E.162).

8   Hume believes that the validity of mathematics rests upon the thesis that 'the component parts of quantity and number are entirely similar' (E.163). But earlier in the *Enquiry* he acknowledged that there are legitimate arguments undermining our notions of finite quantity (E.155–9). Rather defensively, in a footnote, he returns to the *Treatise* view that we have legitimate sense-derived ideas of *minima* (E.158). Hume himself seems to have been led to believe that his own ideas on the foundations of mathematics were inadequate: see H.L. II, 253; E. C. Mossner, *The Life of David Hume*, pp. 321–2; and A. Flew, *Hume's Philosophy of Belief*, pp. 64ff.

9   *The Science of Mechanics*, p. 580.

10 'The permanent significance of Hume's philosophy', pp. 16–17.

11 However it is important to note that Hume had another 'intentional' conception of meaning: see T.168 where he speaks of 'meaning . . . unknown qualities'.

12 In his *Méditations Chrétiennes et Métaphysiques* (in *Oeuvres Complètes de Malebranche*, vol. 10, p. 48) Malebranche wrote: 'you imagine that bodies move one another because a body is never struck without being moved'. This passage is referred to by Malebranche in a section of the *Recherche de la Vérité* which Hume certainly read with some care. See R. III, 208: the passage of Malebranche which Hume paraphrases at T.158 is from this section. In *A Study in the Philosophy of Malebranche*, pp. 93ff., R. W. Church argued that Malebranche (as well as Cordemoy) held the essentials of the view that we believe in natural causation because we experience a constant conjunction of events. Cordemoy even attributed this belief to 'custom' (see *Oeuvres Philosophiques*, p. 137).

13 H. H. Price, 'The permanent significance of Hume's philosophy', pp. 13–14.

14 T.168. Compare here the quotation from the *Enquiry* in n. 4 above.

15 T.77. At T.157 Hume identifies the terms *'efficacy, agency, power, force, energy, necessity, connexion* and *productive quality'*. And at T.90 (cf. E.67–8) he says that 'the idea of *production* is the same with that of *causation'*.

16 See, for example, D. Radner, *Malebranche, a Study of a Cartesian System*, p. 40: 'Instead of restoring efficacy to creatures, Hume denies it to God.' For another recent expression of this view see Jean Theau, 'La critique de la causalité chez Malebranche et chez Hume', *Dialogue* 15 (1976), p. 549: 'Le seul tort de Malebranche aux yeux de Hume serait donc de ne pas être allé assez loin.' Theau writes that Hume, 'theoricien de la contingence absolue dans l'ordre ontologique, est aussi le theoricien du déterminisme absolu dans l'ordre phenomenal' (p. 553n.). But in my view Hume always supposes an ontological determinism, even though he recognises that things are contingent from the point of view of phenomena. Professor Theau comes closer to my own view later in his article when he writes that 'Hume concentre toute son analyse sur la question épistémologique' (p. 554; cf. pp. 142ff. below).

17 T.634. Cf. T.80 where Hume designates this rationalist principle, somewhat confusedly, a principle of the imagination. At T.10 it is introduced as a principle which expresses *'the liberty of the imagination to transpose and change its ideas'*. At this point Hume intended to contrast this principle with the associational principles of the imagination which result in the natural linkage of our ideas. But it should be noted that Hume always assumes that the natural or imaginative separation of our ideas results in a genuine conceptual (or metaphysical) distinction between them. This is made clear in his later formulations of the principle.

18 H.R. II, 219; cf. H.R. I, 168. See also N. Kemp Smith, *New Studies in the Philosophy of Descartes*, pp. 202ff.

19 In formulating his second law of motion, Descartes claimed that a body continues to move in a straight line without regard to its movement 'a little time before' (*Principles of Philosophy*, II, 39: A.T. VIII-1, 63–4; cf. A.T. VIII-2, 86). The fundamental idea is that the 'inertial' force exerted in curvilinear motion continues to act in a straight line even though, in the previous moment, the actual movement of the body was curved. Such passages seem to indicate that 'inertial' force, for Descartes, was non-material and derived from God. For a recent interpretation of Descartes as an occasionalist see the fascinating article of Gary Hatfield, 'Force (God) in Descartes' physics', *Studies in the History and Philosophy of Science*, 10 (1979). In his *New Studies in the Philosophy of Descartes* N. Kemp Smith argued against this occasionalist reading of Descartes. Kemp Smith stressed the fact that the proof of body in the sixth Meditation depends upon the existence of real force in nature. This

seems to me to be an important argument against reading Descartes as an occasionalist. I have assumed the correctness of Kemp Smith's account of Meditation VI on p. 61. *Hume's* view was that *'Des Cartes* insinuated that doctrine of the universal and sole efficacy of the Deity, without insisting on it' (E.73n.). I have considered the relevance of the analysis of time to Hume's philosophical notion of causation on p. 158 below. Hume's analysis of the causal relation between mind and body is given on pp. 155–8.

20 G. B. Depping, ed., *Fontenelle, Oeuvres Complètes*, vol. 1, p. 617.

21 See T. M. Lennon, 'Occasionalism and the Cartesian metaphysic of motion', *Canadian Journal of Philosophy*, supplementary vol. 1, part 1 (1974). For Lennon's own views concerning the direction of Malebranche's occasionalism and its relevance for later thought see his 'Philosophical Commentary' to N. Malebranche, *The Search after Truth*, pp. 809ff.

22 'The moving force of a body ... is by no means a quality which belongs to this body. Nothing belongs to it apart from its modes; and modes are inseparable from their substances' (*Entretiens sur la Métaphysique*, in *Oeuvres Complètes de Malebranche*, vol. 12, p. 162). Descartes, who had already said that motion is a mere mode of matter (*Principles* II, 25: H.R. I, 266), seems to be ambiguous on the question of whether this doctrine has the implications which Malebranche and Cordemoy draw from it. See W. E. Anderson, 'Cartesian motion', in P. Machamer and R. G. Turnbull, eds., *Motion and Time, Space and Matter*, esp. pp. 218–19.

23 Cordemoy writes that 'quand on dit que B étoit mû, si l'on n'a pas pensé à ce qui le faisoit mouvoir, on a entendu, qu'il étoit en un certain état; & en ce sens, on n'a pas dû croire, qu'il pût communiquer son mouvement à C: *car l'état d'un corps ne passe point dans un autre*' (*Oeuvres Philosophiques*, p. 138; italics mine). While Cordemoy was certainly considered a Cartesian (*op. cit.*, pp. 26ff.), he broke with the orthodox Cartesianism of the day by denying the infinite divisibility of matter and espousing atomism (*op. cit.*, pp. 39ff.). However, it is important to recognise that Descartes' own theory, while not atomistic, clearly recognised the division of matter into parts: he argued from the fact that he can conceive 'the two halves of a part of matter ... as two complete substances' to the conclusion 'that they really are divisible' (A. Kenny, *Descartes: Philosophical Letters*, p. 124).

24 For Descartes' views see the article by G. Hatfield referred to in n. 19 above. Malebranche's criticism of Descartes is given in the 'Lois générales de la communication des mouvemens' which were appended to the fifth edition of the *Recherche*. See *Pièces Jointes, Ecrits Divers*, in *Oeuvres Complètes de Malebranche*, vol. 17–1, p. 55. A discussion of the development of Malebranche's views is given in T. Lennon's 'Philosophical Commentary' to *The Search After Truth*, pp. 809ff. See also P. Mouy, *Le Développement de la Physique Cartésienne*, pp. 282ff.

25   Locke draws a fundamental distinction between mechanical 'passive' power and another kind of power – 'active power' – which we are aware of through reflection on the operations of our own minds (*Essay* 2, 21, 2ff.). Necessary connection seems an essential feature of Locke's conception of mechanical power (*Essay* 4, 3, 13), though he may not be absolutely consistent on this (see R. M. Mattern, 'Locke on active power . . . ', *Studies in the History and Philosophy of Science*, 11 (1980), esp. p. 50). But necessary connection does not appear to be part of Locke's conception of *active* power. Clarke's contrast of mechanical necessity and action seems close to that of Locke: see 4th Reply, §§ 32–3, in H. G. Alexander, ed., *The Leibniz–Clarke Correspondence*, p. 51. Locke's views on active power are discussed on pp. 164ff. below.

26   The influence of Malebranche on Hume's views on causation is well established. Hume refers directly to Malebranche twice in the *Treatise* (T.158 and T.249), both times in relation to the discussion of causation. At T.158 Hume paraphrases a passage from the XVth Eclaircissement of the *Recherche* (R. III, 205). A good comparison of Hume's and Malebranche's texts has been made by R. W. Church in 'Malebranche and Hume', *Revue Internationale de Philosophie*, 1 (1938), esp. pp. 149ff. While I disagree with a major contention of Church (that for Hume 'nothing in existence is connected by logical necessity with anything else' (p. 158), I agree with his claim that the fundamental nature of Hume's debt to Malebranche lay in his adoption of 'Malebranche's definition of the causal relation' (p. 159). I should only add that Hume has applied that definition directly to show that we have no awareness of any power through our own will. The relation of Hume's account of physical causation to that of Malebranche is far more complex.

27   E.30. Compare T.79 where Hume claims that we have no 'distinct idea of a cause or productive principle' on the ground that 'all distinct ideas are separable from each other, and . . . the ideas of cause and effect are evidently distinct'.

28   E.29; cf. A.649ff. Hume does not employ this example in the *Treatise* itself.

29   Malebranche writes that 'no bodies, great or small, have the force to move themselves. A mountain, a house, a stone, a grain of sand – in short, the smallest or the largest bodies of which we can conceive – have not the force to move themselves' (R. II, 312–13).

30   See Chapter 4, n. 12 above.

31   See pp. 88–9 above.

32   See E. C. Mossner, *The Life of David Hume*, pp. 174–5.

33   I have used the second edition of this work (1750). The discussion of Newton's aether appears in a note to p. 119. A revised version of this note appears at E.73. See Chapter 4, nn. 50, 51, below, for the history of revisions to this passage.

   The importance of this note for the interpretation of Hume's philosophy has been recognised by G. Buchdahl in *Metaphysics and the Philosophy of Science*, pp. 330ff. See also P. M. Heimann, 'Voluntarism and immanence: conceptions of nature in eighteenth-century thought', *Journal of the History of Ideas*, 39 (1978), 277–8 (however, neither Buchdahl nor Heimann has noted changes in Hume's text). Buchdahl thinks that Hume's concerns about the aether relate to worries about gravity acting at a distance. I agree with Buchdahl that Hume would probably have regarded the aether as operating by mechanical means: that was the idea favoured by Scottish Newtonians such as Colin Maclaurin (see his *An Account of Sir Isaac Newton's Philosophical Discoveries*, 1748, pp. 388–9) and John Stewart (see pp. 162–3 below). Maclaurin stresses that the aether operates according to the mechanical law of 'the equality of action and reaction' (p. 388). Moreover, when another Newtonian – George Cheyne – became a critic of the aether theory in 1740, he likened the aether to *'Descartes's* and *Leibnitz's Vortices, Hugen's* [sic] and *Fatio's* infinitely rare, rapid, subtil Matter' (*Essay on Regimen*, 1740, p. 148–9): Cheyne clearly regards the aether as a mechanical hypothesis. In his *Treatise* Hume himself clearly states his belief that causes do not operate at a distance (T.173, Rule 1). But Heimann is undoubtedly right in thinking that Hume's greatest concern here is with the notion of activity. I believe that when he originally wrote his note, Hume saw no incompatibility between mechanism and activity. Yet, as we shall see shortly, he was later led to admit that there was an incompatibility.

34   See the post-1740 writers discussed by R. Schofield, *Mechanism and Materialism*, esp. pp. 115ff.; also P. M. Heimann, ' "Nature is a perpetual worker": Newton's aether and eighteenth-century natural philosophy', *Ambix*, 20 (1973), esp. pp. 10ff. There was a revival of interest in Newton's aether-hypothesis in the 1740s due to the publication in 1744 of a letter from Newton to Boyle which indicated Newton's early interest in such speculations (see Schofield, pp. 105–6). In the 'General Scholium' which was added to the 1713 edition of the *Principia* Newton spoke of 'a certain most subtle spirit . . . by the force and action of which spirit the particles of bodies attract one another at near distances, and cohere, if contiguous' (*Sir Isaac Newton's Mathematical Principles of Natural Philosophy*, vol. 2, p. 547). The aether was introduced under that name in the 1717 edition of the *Opticks*. In Query 21 it was used to explain the process of gravitation. In Query 18 Newton referred to the aether as active; but the clearest ideas of activity were developed earlier, quite independently of the aether-hypothesis, in Query 23 of the 1706 *Opticks* (later Query 31). When Hume and others thought of Newton's aether as an active matter they may well have been combining two divergent and incompatible elements in his philosophy of nature. That Hume's interpretation of Newton is not completely implausible seems clear from a recent discussion of the latter's ideas on the aether in E. McMullin, *Newton on Matter and Activity*, pp. 96–101.

35 *Ibid.*; italics mine. I have not wanted to suggest that Berkeley's occasionalism was any more pronounced in *Siris* than in *De Motu* and other early works – only that the exact nature of Berkeley's views was probably brought home to Hume by the publication of the former work in 1744. Hume's note at E.155 suggests that he previously thought of Berkeley as a sceptic like himself. It is clear that, by the time he wrote his *Enquiry*, Hume realised that occasionalism was taken seriously in Britain, especially by Berkeley.

Occasionalism was a popular view in Scotland for much of the eighteenth century. Hume's critic Thomas Reid wrote in 1780: 'By the cause of a phenomenon, nothing is meant but the law of nature, of which that phenomenon is an instance. . . . Gravity is not an efficient cause, but a general law, that obtains in nature, of which law the fall of this body is a particular instance' (cited in A. L. Donovan, *Philosophical Chemistry in the Scottish Enlightenment*, p. 58; Donovan mistakenly attributes the same view to Hume). It is important to recognise that Reid's views were part of a more general theological outlook. See his *Essays on the Active Powers of Man*, in *The Works of Thomas Reid, D.D.*, vol. 2, pp. 522–5.

36 The importance of this discussion for interpreting Hume's notion of necessity has been shown by R. F. Anderson, *Hume's First Principles*, pp. 154ff. and Donald Livingston, 'Hume on ultimate causation', *American Philosophical Quarterly*, 8 (1971).

37 On p. 218 below I discuss the psychophysiological account (derived from Locke) which probably underlay Hume's account of the natural instinct which he called custom.

38 What Hume calls a 'natural and perceivable connexion' at T.223 is what he normally calls a '*philosophical* relation' (T.14). By a '*natural* relation' he normally intends a *mere* associational connection of ideas (e.g., T.94).

39 See especially the discussion of prejudice at T.146ff.

40 T.225. For a discussion of Hume's use of this principle see chapter IX of John Yolton's forthcoming book *Perceptual Acquaintance from Descartes to Reid*.

41 It seems to me important to note that such a principle may be true of the Cartesian psychophysiological model of association favoured by Hume (T.60–1) but not of the vibrational Newtonian model of association favoured by David Hartley. On the Cartesian account, the spirits either pass or do not pass from one corporeal idea to another; but the vibrational account seems to lend itself more easily to an infinite gradation of connections. Cf. p. 190 below.

42 T.246–7: 'Now as these different shocks, and variations, and mixtures are the only changes, of which matter is susceptible, and as these never afford us any idea of thought or perception, 'tis concluded to be impossible, that thought can ever be caus'd by matter'. Hume's discussion in this passage seems to be modelled on Bayle's discussion of these issues in his article on Dicaearchus in the *Dictionary*.

43 'If you once grant that the present time is indivisible, you will be obliged unavoidedly to admit Zeno's objection' (*Dictionary*, 5, 609a; cf. Popkin, *Selections*, 354).

44 T.45; cf. p. 97 above. Hume's claims concerning the confounding of the points of space were pointed out to me in conversation by Professor Robert McRae.

45 *Dr Boerhaave's Academical Lectures*, vol. 5, pp. 373–4. Boerhaave's views on causality are discussed in L. S. King, *The Philosophy of Medicine*, pp. 222ff.

46 At A.650 Hume writes: 'The mind can always *conceive* . . . any event to follow upon another; whatever we *conceive* is possible, at least in a *metaphysical* sense' (the italics on the word 'metaphysical' are mine). One cannot overstress the importance of the equivalence, in Hume's writing, of metaphysical possibility or impossibility with conceptual possibility or impossibility (cf. T.172).

47 T.173; my italics. Obviously Hume is caught in a verbal inconsistency in speaking of *knowledge* in this context. Strictly speaking we are here dealing with what at T.124 he called *proofs* – claims which are more certain than probabilities and yet do not attain the absolute certainty of knowledge. Nevertheless Hume clearly thought that causal reasonings approach knowledge.

48 'Some remarks on the laws of motion and the inertia of matter', *Essays and Observations, Physical and Literary, Read before a Society in Edinburgh, and published by them*, p. 130. Stewart refers to p. 119 of Hume's *Philosophical Essays* and was apparently using the second edition, to which I referred above. For a recent account of the history of the society see Roger L. Emerson's papers on 'The Philosophical Society of Edinburgh', *British Journal for the History of Science*, 12 (1979) and 14 (1981). Emerson's second paper discusses what is known of Hume's role in the society.

49 *Essays and Observations*, p. 10.

50 H.L. I, 186. In his letter Hume does not answer Stewart's charge that he has misinterpreted Newton. Instead, Hume defends himself against another claim in Stewart's essay, that in the *Treatise* he had maintained 'that something may begin to exist, or start into being without a cause . . . ' ('Some remarks . . . ', pp. 116–17). Hume's denial of Stewart's charge has been discussed by Kemp Smith in *The Philosophy of David Hume*, pp. 408ff. Kemp Smith is undoubtedly correct in claiming that Hume never denied that causes were absolutely necessary for every event. But it is also important to note that Stewart probably never seriously thought that he did. In his essay Stewart assimilates Hume's presumed denial of universal causation with the view he ascribes to Lord Kames that motion can arise from 'an internal inanimate principle' ('Some remarks . . . ', p. 116). Stewart's remark should probably come under the heading of 'raillery' (see Hume's letter, p. 186); elsewhere in the essay (e.g., p. 101) he shows a good understanding of Hume's philosophy.

51 *Op. cit.*, p. 116; italics mine. The footnote appears in the version I

have cited p. 145 above, in volume 2 of the *Essays and Treatises on Several Subjects*, published in 1753; this is still referred to as the second edition. David Norton tells me that he thinks that the 1751 and 1753 editions of the *Philosophical Essays Concerning Human Understanding* are probably the 1750 edition with a new title page. The earlier version of the footnote still appears in the French translation of the *Philosophical Essays* in volume 1 of *Oeuvres Philosophiques de Mr D. Hume,* 1758 (p. 190). Hume changed the name to *An Enquiry Concerning Human Understanding* in the English edition of 1758; but the old name still appears in the French translation of the same year. The interpretation of the significance of Hume's textual modifications which I present in the next paragraph is, I believe, given additional support if we examine a text which is the forerunner to the footnote in the *Philosophical Essays* – namely, *A Letter from a Gentleman to his Friend in Edinburgh.* In this letter of 1745, in which Hume is trying to defend himself from the charge of atheism, there is no talk of active matter; Hume merely insists that Newton rejected the Cartesian hypothesis of occasional causes 'by substituting the Hypothesis of an Aetheral Fluid, not the immediate Volition of the Deity, as the Cause of Attraction' (*Letter,* pp. 28–9). It seems reasonable to conclude that it was only when he thought he could be less defensive of his own views, in re-writing the passage for the *Philosophical Essays,* that Hume let slip his belief that Newton supposed the existence of an active matter.

52   See E. C. Mossner, *The Life of David Hume,* pp. 257–8. The essays were edited by Hume along with the other secretary of the society, Alexander Munro, *secundus.* I agree with Mossner that Hume probably wrote the preface to the volume, but a contrary view is held by Roger Emerson (see n. 48 above).

53   H.L. I, 186.

54   'Some remarks . . . ', p. 86.

55   J. E. McGuire, 'Force, active principles, and Newton's invisible realm', *Ambix,* 15 (1968) and Ernan McMullin, *Newton on Matter and Activity,* chapter 2, esp. pp. 54–6. McGuire writes: 'Newton did not . . . deny the existence of mechanical forces. He was, however, concerned to maintain the existence of other sorts of forces' (p. 182).

56   See H. G. Alexander, ed., *The Leibniz–Clarke Correspondence.* Clarke is Newton's spokesman in this debate. But Newton also took an active role in the actual formulation of Clarke's position. See Marie Boas and A. R. Hall, 'Clarke and Newton', *Isis* 52 (1961), pp. 583–5; and I. B. Cohen and A. Koyré, 'Newton and the Leibniz–Clarke correspondence', *Archives Internationales d'Histoire des Sciences,* 15 (1962).

57   The intellectual roots of the Newtonian notion of active power are complex. The relation of this notion to the idea of active power in Cudworth has been stressed by J. E. McGuire in 'Force, active principles . . . ' (esp. p. 204), and a more recent article entitled 'Neoplatonism and active principles: Newton and the Corpus

Hermeticum' in R. S. Westman and J. E. McGuire, *Hermeticism and the Scientific Revolution*. But Newton may also have had alchemical sources for this notion: see B. J. T. Dobbs, *The Foundations of Newton's Alchemy*, e.g., pp. 204ff. I have no independent evidence for the connection I see between the Newton–Clarke theological idea of force and the Lockean notion of agency except the texts compared in the present chapter. I believe that the stress on active powers as motion-originating principles is far more explicit in Locke than in Cudworth, although the notion seems to be *implicit* in Cudworth's idea of *'Autochinesie* or *Self-Activity'*: see *The True Intellectual System of the Universe*, p. 844.

58   Locke writes that 'the increase of Motion by impulse, which is observed or believed sometimes to happen, is yet harder to be understood' than how our minds move our bodies (*Essay* 2, 23, 28).

59   See his *A Philosophical Inquiry Concerning Human Liberty*, and the discussion of J. P. Ferguson, *Dr Samuel Clarke, An Eighteenth Century Heretic*, pp. 112ff. Hume's ideas bear a strong resemblance to those of Collins (e.g., cf. pp. 12–14 of Collins' book and Hume's discussion of the liberty of indifference at T.408). Collins may also have influenced some other details in Hume's philosophy, e.g. his analysis of personal identity.

60   E.73n. I believe that much work needs to be done relating Hume's theological writings to those of Cudworth. On p. 171 below, I have suggested one passage in the *Dialogues* in which Hume seems to be directly influenced by Cudworth. In Hume's 'Early memoranda' the following note occurs: 'Four kinds of Atheists according to Cudworth, the Democritic or Atomical, the Anaximandrian or Hylopathian, the Stratonic or Hylozoic, the Stoic or Cosmo-plastic. To which he might have added the Pyrrhonian or Sceptic. And the Spinozist or Metaphysical. One might perhaps add the . . . Anaxagorian or Chymical' (see E. C. Mossner, ed., 'Hume's early memoranda, 1729–1740', *Journal of the History of Ideas*, 9 (1948), p. 503).

61   Mossner, 'Hume's early memoranda . . . ', p. 501.

62   *Op. cit.*, §111, in P. Bayle, *Oeuvres Diverses*, vol. 3, p. 340. In his edition of the *Dialogues* Kemp Smith has translated §106 of this work (pp. 81–6).

63   p. 341. Strato is identified and discussed on p. 107 of Cudworth's *True Intellectual System of the Universe*.

64   §106, p. 336; cf. D.86.

65   See *Oeuvres Diverses*, vol. 4, pp. 182–3. This passage occurs in a 'Mémoire' which appeared in *L'Histoire des Ouvrages des Savans* in December of 1704 and is in response to an article of Jean LeClerc in the fifth volume of the *Bibliothèque Choisie*.

66   *Ibid.*, p. 163; cf. p. 181. Cf. also *Continuations des Pensées Diverses*, §11: *Oeuvres Diverses*, vol. 3, pp. 216–17.

67   See the introduction to his edition of the *Dialogues*, esp. pp. 57ff.

68   D.142. There is a close connection between the views of

Malebranche and those espoused by Demea throughout the *Dialogues*. Apparently it has commonly been believed that Demea's views represent those of Clarke (see, for example, R. Hurlbutt, *Hume, Newton, and the Design Argument*, p. 137). There is an acknowledged borrowing from Clarke in Part IX; but when Demea invites a mechanist explanation of vegetation and generation at the bottom of D.177, he clearly reflects the views of Malebranche and not those of Clarke. (It is interesting to note that Malebranche himself repeated Bayle's objections to Cudworth in the sixth edition (1712) of the *Recherche* (R. II, 310)).)

69   *The True Intellectual System of the Universe*, p. 107.
70   *Op. cit.*, p. 159.
71   See P. M. Heimann, ' "Nature is a perpetual worker" . . .', pp. 17ff. Also F. Ellenberger, 'La thèse de doctorat de James Hutton et la rénovation perpétuelle du monde', *Annales Guébhard*, 49 (1973). The interpretation of Hume's *Dialogues* presented in this paragraph is that accepted by N. Kemp Smith: see p. 33 of his edition of the *Dialogues*.
72   Philo says he has supposed 'motion and active force' to be inherent in matter (D.184). But the meaning of 'active force' here must be taken from the characterisation of the hypothesis on the previous page.
73   The account of the origin of the worlds which Hume gives in Part VIII of the *Dialogues* is remarkably similar to that given by Denis Diderot in his *Lettre sur les Aveugles*, first published in 1749. See *Oeuvres Philosophiques de Diderot*, p. 123: 'Combien de mondes estropiés, manqués, se sont dissipés, se reforment et se dissipent peut-être à chaque instant dans des espaces éloignés . . . où vous ne voyez pas, mais où le mouvement continue et continuera de combiner des amas de matière, jusqu'à ce qu'ils aient obtenu quelque arrangement dans lequel ils puissent persévérer. . . . Qu'est-ce que ce monde . . . ? Un composé sujet à des révolutions, qui toutes indiquent une tendance continuelle à la destruction; une succession rapide d'êtres qui s'entre-suivent, se poussent et disparaissent; une symétrie passagère; un ordre momentané. . . .' It is highly unlikely that Hume would not know Diderot's book, which appeared just prior to the time he began work on his *Dialogues*.
74   *Essays and Observations*, pp. 130–1.
75   *History of England*, p. 381.
76   E.30. Newton, unlike Hume, denied that the causes of any phenomena were 'uncapable of being discovered and made manifest' (*Opticks*, p. 401). But Hume's own claims are seldom as dogmatic as these words suggest.
77   'General Scholium' to *Sir Isaac Newton's Mathematical Principles of Natural Philosophy*, vol. 2, pp. 544–5. Cf. *The Leibniz–Clarke Correspondence*, p. 14.

FIVE

Hume's science of human nature

§18

If, in examining several phaenomena, we find that they resolve themselves into one common principle, and can trace this principle into another, we shall at last arrive at those few simple principles, on which all the rest depend. . . . This seems to have been the aim of our late philosophers, and, among the rest, of this author. He proposes to anatomize human nature in a regular manner, and promises to draw no conclusions but where he is authorized by experience.

– Hume, *Abstract*, p. 646

We find by the comparing their ideas, that thought and motion are different from each other, and by experience, that they are constantly united; which being all the circumstances, that enter into the idea of cause and effect, when apply'd to the operations of matter, we may certainly conclude, that motion may be, and actually is, the cause of thought and perception.

– Hume, *Treatise*, p. 248

§19

The vividness of the first conception diffuses itself along the relations, and is convey'd, as by so many pipes or canals, to every idea that has any communication with the primary one.

– Hume, *Treatise*, p. 122

§20

The science of man is the only solid foundation for the other sciences.

– Hume, *Treatise*, p. xvi

I must distinguish in the imagination betwixt the principles which are permanent, irresistable, and universal; such as the customary transition from causes to effects, and from effects to causes: And the principles, which are changeable, weak, and irregular. . . . The former are the foundation of all our thoughts and actions, so that upon their removal human nature must immediately perish and go to ruin.

– Hume, *Treatise*, p. 225

In the Introduction to Hume's *Treatise* two central themes are discussed, one concerned with the basic project of that work, the other with the method by which that project is to be carried out. Hume claims to be providing a foundation for the other sciences on that of human nature, and he claims that 'the only solid foundation we can give to this science itself must be laid on experience and observation'. These two themes are often confused by commentators on Hume's philosophy, but he himself clearly distinguishes them.[1] Hume uses his methodological pronouncements to place his book in the context of an English experimental philosophy stemming from the writings of Francis Bacon (T.xvii; cf. A.646). But he does not claim any great novelty for his method. Hume notes that, in applying the experimental method to the science of man, he is continuing the tradition established by 'some late philosophers in *England*' including Locke, Shaftesbury, Mandeville, Hutcheson and Butler. On the other hand, he does claim some novelty for his project of founding the other sciences on human nature: in so doing he claims to be employing the science of man in a new way:

In pretending therefore to explain the principles of human nature, we in effect propose a compleat system of the sciences, *built on a foundation almost entirely new,* and the only one upon which they can stand with any security. (T.xvi; italics added)

The central aim of my fifth and final chapter is to explain the nature of Hume's foundational science and show how he thought he could base the other sciences on it. Hume's attempt to employ an 'experimental method' – which many commentators regard as a complete failure[2] – will then be seen in the context of his own fascinating philosophical project.

Throughout this study we have seen the central role in Hume's science of human nature which is played by the faculty which he calls 'imagination'. Indeed, in Part IV of Book I of the *Treatise* Hume claims that the imagination is 'the ultimate judge of all systems of philosophy' (T.225). This statement indicates Hume's belief that imagination is the source of our fundamental conceptions of reality and our scientific reasoning processes. In §15(*a*), for example, we saw how Hume attempted to base our scientific judgement of necessity on certain properties of the imagination.

But what is that faculty itself? Much has been written on 'imagination' in Hume, but I believe that the basic nature of the faculty has been misunderstood.[3] As a result the philosophical significance of his constant appeal to the imagination is missed. When contemporaries of Hume opened up their copy of Chambers' *Cyclopaedia* – a standard scientific reference book of the day – to the entry 'Imagination' they read the following definition:

A Power or Faculty of the Soul, by which it conceives, and forms Ideas of Things, by means of certain Traces and Impressions that had been before made in the Fibres of the Brain by Sensation.

They would have gone on to read about how the 'Fibres of the Brain' are generally 'much more agitated by the Impression of Objects, than by the Course of the animal Spirits', and how this explains the fact that we normally judge objects to be present only when we are affected by such impressions. They would, in fact, have read a general account of the psychophysiological factors which account for 'all the different Characters which appear in the Minds of Men'.[4] The theory of imagination presented by Chambers was the standard account of this faculty accepted by most philosophers in the first half of the eighteenth century. There is, I would suggest, absolutely no reason to think that Hume did not accept its basic outlines, though he certainly did attempt to modify its details. There is every reason to think that the discussion of impressions and ideas in the opening pages of the *Treatise* would have been understood by Hume and his readers in the context of the basic theory laid down by Chambers.[5]

One does not have to look very far to discover the source of Chambers' views on the imagination. At the end of his entry Chambers writes: 'See Father *Malebranch* Recher. de la Verité, lib. 2'. In fact, most of Chambers' entry is simply a loose translation of passages in the opening chapter of Book II of Malebranche's *Recherche*. The importance of the Cartesian account of the imagination in the thought of early eighteenth-century writers in psychology cannot be exaggerated.[6] From a modern point of view we may say that it provided a psychophysical metaphor through which they understood and explained human thought and behaviour. But in its own day it probably represented, however roughly, the basis for a genuine 'scientific' account of human psychology.

This does not mean that the general psychophysiological theory of the imagination laid out by Malebranche and others went unchallenged. A central part of the theory involved the postulation of the existence of 'animal spirits' – the nervous fluids which played a dynamic role in changing the structures of the brain on which thought and action were supposed to depend. The main challenge to the existence of animal spirits in the early eighteenth century came from Newtonians like Henry Pemberton and George Cheyne, who supported an entirely different theory of nervous vibrations through a subtle aether.[7] This latter theory reached its culmination in David Hartley's *Observations on Man*, published in 1749. Yet the animal spirit theory was still supported later in the century by the foremost physiologist of the period, Albrecht von Haller.[8] It continued to be the established theory throughout most of the eighteenth century.

It is easy for a modern reader to miss the significance of the frequent references to 'the spirits' which occur throughout Hume's *Treatise*. In the Cartesian theory, which Hume appears to assume, these spirits are supposed to act in a purely physical way, according to the laws of fluid dynamics.[9] Hume's own attitude to the existence and function of the animal spirits may have been determined by his own reading of Bernard de Mandeville's *A Treatise of the Hypochondriack and Hysterick Diseases* (1730). Mandeville's attitude to the theory is of particular interest because Hume's analysis of his own early psychosomatic illness as a 'waste' of 'spirits' is based on that which is presented in Mandeville's book,[10] and because Mandeville is cited by Hume as one of the authors who has introduced the experimental method of reasoning into English moral philosophy. In the first edition of this work (1711), Mandeville assumed the existence of animal spirits (that they are the 'intermediate Officers between the Soul and the grosser parts of the Body no Man denies') and argued *from experience* that those spirits responsible for thinking and digestion are of the smallest kind.[11] He believed that they operate purely mechanically although, because of their 'Minute and Volatile' character, we cannot 'enter into the Mechanism of them'.[12] In the 1730 edition, Mandeville seems aware that there is *some* doubt about the existence of animal spirits but he still claims to be able to establish their existence *'a Posteriori'*.[13] At one point, however, he claims that he is using the term without 'pretending to determine what is the cause' of motion and feeling. The term 'animal spirits' only refers to 'the Instruments of Motion and Sense', whatever be their exact nature (p. 163). Mandeville seems to have some awareness that the physical model he employs may not be entirely accurate. But he is still convinced that there is some physical system of the nerves similar to the one he describes, which accounts for the psychosomatic symptoms he seeks to explain.

Hume, too, may have had some doubts about the real existence of animal spirits. But, like Mandeville, he thought and interpreted experience in terms of the general psychophysiological model of his predecessors. In §19 we shall see that this model is embedded in Hume's use of terms like 'impression' and 'force and vivacity'. We shall see that it is essential for an understanding of the central unifying thesis of Hume's science of man, a thesis which concerns the subservience of the passions to the imagination. I should probably add that I do not believe that Hume's use of such a model in any way detracts from his achievements: on the contrary, it provides the perspective in which they can be properly measured. Hume works within the context of an established psychophysiological theory *and* attempts to modify it in terms of experience. But like any good theory, it 'interacts' with the data, and provides a perspective in which they are observed.[14] We can do little more here than hint at the significance of this interaction and the role it plays in Hume's social and economic doctrines.

In §18 of this chapter I shall discuss the significance of 'experimental method' in Hume's philosophy. We shall see that Hume's claims to found the sciences of man on experimental method cannot be given a narrow positivistic interpretation. In the first part of this section I shall place Hume's methodological claims in the context of those of other writers of his day. In the second part I shall examine Hume's actual use of inductive techniques at the beginning of his book on the passions: this will take us beyond Hume's slogans into an examination of his actual practice.

While in §19 of this chapter I shall examine the nature of Hume's foundational science of man, in §20 I shall show how he thought it provided a foundation for the other sciences. We shall see that Hume took up and modified the Cartesian conception of 'natural judgements'. We shall discover that both mechanism and biological adaptation played a basic role in Hume's conception of these psychological processes. However, in the conclusion I show that, in his discussions of the foundation of society, Hume claimed that the mechanisms of the human mind lead us into non-adaptive behaviour. He argued that the processes of human nature must be replaced by those of reason and artifice.

§18   *Experimental method*

(a) Pronouncements

It is commonly asserted that Hume's science of human nature is based on a pure description of the immediate contents of our own minds. For example, John Passmore speaks of 'Hume's attempt to work out a phenomenalist "psychology of knowledge" which would give an account of the traditional "mental acts" . . . without making any reference to independent existence, or to anything except "perceptions" ':

To pass beyond 'perceptions' is to leave knowledge for conjectures; if the science of man is to be judged superior to physical science it must be able to complete its work . . . without venturing beyond the security of our immediate perceptions.[15]

Passmore's assurance that Hume sought to establish such a self-evident science of mind is puzzling in the light of his assertion elsewhere that the method which Hume proposes at the beginning of the *Treatise* is 'experimental; it rests upon experience, not upon self-evident propositions'.[16] Does not Hume's claim to found his science of human nature on experimental method belie the claim that he sought a purely non-conjectural descriptive science of immediate contents of our awareness?

Nowhere in the Introduction to the *Treatise* does one find the claim that the investigator in the science of man has more access to his object than does the physical scientist. In justifying his employment of experimental method, Hume notes that 'the essence of the mind' is 'equally unknown to us with that of external bodies'. The use of 'careful and exact experiments' is connected with the 'observation' of the 'effects' of mind, not with the observation of the mind itself. The goal of the moral scientist is to explain these effects 'from the simplest and fewest causes' (T.xvii). These explanatory causes are the operations of the mind itself. However, the effects are described as 'men's behaviour in company, in affairs, and in their pleasures' (T.xix). Hume's experimental method is described as one in which the principles of the human mind are inferred from the observation of human *behaviour*.

Hume even appears to believe that the moral scientist has *less* direct access to the principles which he seeks to discover than does the physical scientist. In order to see this we need only consider the reason which Hume gives for denying that one can carry out anything like a laboratory experiment in the sciences of man. On Hume's view the principles which the moral scientist seeks to discover are the 'natural principles' of the mind. But, according to him, 'reflection and premeditation would so disturb the operation of my natural principles, as must render it impossible to form any just conclusion from the phaenomenon' (T.xix). In rejecting introspective experimentation as a means of proceeding in the science of man Hume appears to deny the usefulness of any direct observation of the causes which he seeks to discover.

However, in spite of these difficulties, Hume thought that experimentation in the sciences of man was not essentially different from experimentation in the physical sciences. He thought that by carefully choosing one's *in vivo* observations one can vary certain circumstances and leave others constant. As we saw in Chapter 1, Hume believed that in science one can 'attain the knowledge of a particular cause merely by one experiment . . . after a careful removal of all foreign and superfluous circumstances' (T.104). In Book II of the *Treatise* he attempts to show how such experiments can be performed in the sciences of man, when he employs them to verify his hypothesis of the origins of the passions of pride, humility, love and hatred. The circumstances which Hume varies include the pleasantness or unpleasantness of some object in one's environment, and its relationship to oneself or to another. By observing what passions (if any) arise when some of these factors are present and others are absent, Hume claims to be able to verify his account of their causes. But the observations which he makes can be made by anyone in the course of social life. This is clearly where he wants us to look for confirmation of what he says (T.332ff.).

When Hume speaks of the experimental method of reasoning he seems to have in mind a method of discovery even more than a method of confirmation. He claims to be able to arrive at his principles through a careful induction from the phenomena. But when we come to examine his application of this method (in the second part of this section) we shall find that the principles at which he arrives lie a long way from the evidence which he provides in support of them. In the *Abstract* Hume describes his method of analysis or *resolution* in the following way:

If, in examining several phaenomena, we find that they resolve themselves into one common principle, and can trace this principle into another, we shall at last arrive at those few simple principles, on which all the rest depend. (A.646)

We should not assume at the outset that Hume's process of resolution is a simple process of generalisation. The 'common principle' which unites the different phenomena may well be a principle which, while it can account for them, is not a phenomenon in the same sense. If we examine Hume's writings with care, we find that he is dealing with principles at different theoretical levels. These principles are adapted from general theories, such as Malebranche's theory of imagination and Aquinas' theory of reminiscence,[17] which Hume seeks to modify in terms of the phenomena. The scientific enterprise which Hume attempted in the *Treatise* was of a highly theoretical nature.

Hume's earliest work in the sciences of man is most distinctively characterised by his goal to explain the phenomena of human life by the *simplest* possible principles. This goal of simplicity is stressed both in the Introduction to the *Treatise* and in the *Abstract*. At the beginning of Book II of the *Treatise* Hume claims that the goal of the skilled 'naturalist' is to find the 'few and simple' principles which account for many effects (T.282). Later on in the same book he speaks of 'simplicity' as the 'principal force and beauty' of his 'system' (T.367). In fact, it is remarkable how far Hume did succeed in reducing human psychology to a few operations of a single faculty – that of *imagination*. His explicit methodology here has seldom been recognised by commentators on Hume's philosophy – mainly because the nature of that faculty has been misunderstood. Hume presented a simple explanatory model of the forces which account for complex human thought and behaviour.

Of course, it is true that Hume attempted to balance his demand for simplicity with the stipulation that 'we cannot go beyond experience'. He claimed to reject 'any hypothesis, that pretends to discover the ultimate original qualities of human nature' (T.xvii). Hume clearly believed that one must stop short in one's search after causes. In Part I of the *Treatise* he notes that the causes of his own central principle of association of ideas 'are mostly unknown' (T.13). He appears to want to draw an analogy between his own procedure and that of Newton, who, in the Preface to his *Principia*, claimed that the forces which cause the attraction and repulsion of bodies were still unknown. Yet it is clear that, in his Introduction, *Hume* disapproves only of 'conjectures and hypotheses' which are put forward as 'most certain principles'.[18] We have already seen that he approves of hypotheses when they are put forward with caution. Not only does he approve of (what he takes to be) Newton's materialistic explanation of gravity (see §§14(a) and 16(a)), but he also puts forward his own mechanical hypothesis to explain the association of ideas (see §7(c)). In fact, throughout the *Treatise* Hume speaks of his own highest principle, which concerns the dependence of the passions on the association of ideas, as an hypothesis.[19] In his *Enquiry* he says that this principle is founded on 'speculations, which, however accurate, may still retain a degree of doubt and uncertainty' (E.47). Hume considers his hypothesis to be legitimate in so far as it is based on experience and espoused undogmatically.

Yet did Hume not claim, like Newton, to be able to distinguish hypothetical causes from the phenomena which they explain? Concerning his own explanation of the fact that we tend to mistake ideas which are closely related to each other, Hume wrote:

we must distinguish exactly betwixt the phaenomenon itself, and the causes, which I shall assign for it; and must not imagine from any uncertainty in the latter, that the former is also uncertain. The phaenomenon may be real, tho' my explication be chimerical. The falsehood of the one is no consequence of that of the other. (T.60)

Of course it is very questionable whether the particular phenomenon which Hume sought to explain – mistaking the idea of a full space for that of an empty space – is any more real than his proposed explanation.[20] But it is most important to recognise that what he attempts to isolate *as* the phenomenon is not described in bare observational terms without any theoretical overlay. In this context Hume describes the phenomenon he seeks to explain using the terms 'relations' and 'ideas', two theoretical terms in his philosophy. Similarly, in Book II of the *Treatise*, where Hume attempts to distinguish his hypothetical explanation of sympathy from the 'phaenomena', he still describes the latter in the language of the *'conversion* of an *idea* into an *impression'* (T.319–20; italics mine). It is a mistake to think that Hume attempted to describe experience in some sort of non-theoretical observation-language. *What he attempted to do was to distinguish those parts of his theory which were uncertain from those which were not.* Hume thought that he could be certain about the general nature of the causes which he was describing, though the particular explanation which he attempted to give for them was only 'specious and plausible'.[21]

In this respect we must admit that Hume's goals resemble those of Newton – even if we argue that his successes do not. Few historians of science nowadays think that Newton's aim was merely to discover functional relationships between phenomena which were directly observable. Rather, Newton sought to discover their 'true and sufficient causes'. While in his dispute with Hooke about the nature of light, Newton refused to decide among a number of competing mechanical hypotheses, he clearly did think he had gone some distance in explaining the nature of light. He thought that his prism experiment showed that different colours are *rays* with different properties and that those rays are *substances.* Newton thought that he could reach *some* absolutely certain conclusions about the *causes* of his observations.[22] Hume himself seems to have thought that, as a result of Newton's experiments, 'light is in reality anatomized' (D.136).

Hume's methods in the science of man have often been compared to those of Newton in the physical sciences. It is commonly said that Hume sought to become 'the Newton of the moral sciences'.[23] At the end of the *Opticks* Newton had suggested that 'if natural Philosophy in all its Parts, by pursuing this [experimental] Method, shall at length be perfected, the Bounds of Moral Philosophy will also be enlarged' (p. 405). It has been assumed that the subtitle to the *Treatise* – 'An Attempt to Introduce the Experimental Method of Reasoning into Moral Subjects' – announces Hume's aim to realise the Newtonian experimental programme in the moral sciences.

This claim must be treated with some caution. In the first place it is important to realise that Newton is never referred to in the *Treatise*.[24] The Newtonian philosophy is explicitly discussed only in the Appendix in relation to the theory of empty space. 'Experimental method' as Hume understands it was applied to physics long before the time of Newton: Hume identifies Bacon – not Newton – as the 'father of experimental physicks' (A.646; cf. T.xvi-xvii). In the second place, what one modern scholar, Henry Guerlac, regards as the two most distinctive features of Newton's methods have no application in Hume's science of man:

In two ways Newton's method must be distinguished from that of the majority of his predecessors and nearly all his contemporaries. He insisted upon the cogency of a single, well-contrived experiment to answer a specific question, as opposed to the Baconian procedure of collecting and comparing innumerable 'instances' of a phenomenon. Perhaps even more significant, Newton's experiments, whenever it is possible, are quantitative.[25]

The model of the 'single well-contrived experiment' for eighteenth-century scientists was the famous prism experiment of the *Opticks*. However, as we have seen, Hume denies the possibility of performing experiments in this sense in the science of man. Moreover, he never even considered the possibility of applying quantitative methods in psychology. Finally, it should be recognised that when Newton referred to 'moral' philosophy at the end of the *Opticks* he had in mind a much narrower subject than that which is the concern of Hume's book. Newton refers only to 'our Duty towards [God], as well as that towards one another' (*Opticks*, p. 405); whereas for Hume, 'morality' in this narrow sense is only one small part of moral philosophy.

On the other hand, there is some reason to think that in his stress on simplicity as a scientific ideal, Hume was following Newton rather than Bacon. In his Preface to the second edition of the *Principia* Roger Cotes wrote that those who pursue the experimental method 'derive the causes of all things from the most simple principles possible'.[26] In his own Preface to the first edition Newton appeared to express the hope that the principles of attraction and repulsion could be applied to explain 'the rest of the phenomena of Nature' (p. xviii). It is interesting to note that Hume was probably first called a moral Newtonian because of his desire to found the sciences of man on a few simple principles. Referring to Hume and other eighteenth-century forerunners of Bentham, Elie Halévy wrote of a 'moral Newtonianism' in which 'the principle of the association of ideas and the principle of utility take the place of the principle of universal attraction'.[27] Hume himself seems to have identified Newtonian methodology with the generalisation of a principle established in one area to new areas of discourse. In his *Enquiry Concerning the Principles of Morals* he appeals to what he calls Newton's 'chief rule of philosophizing' – the third rule laid down at the beginning of Book III of the *Principia* – in order to justify his own belief in the widespread application of the principle of utility: where 'any principle has been found to have a great force and energy in one instance' we should 'ascribe to it a like energy in all similar instances'.[28]

Since the time of Halévy the claim that Hume aimed to be the Newton of the moral sciences has commonly been used to buttress the belief that Hume rejected all hypotheses in science. But writers on Hume need to take as much care in interpreting his strictures against speculation as scholars have come to take with those of Newton. It is now generally conceded that hypotheses played a very important role in Newtonian science. I. B. Cohen has written:

Newton's speculations on the nature of matter, light, the aether, and the mode of action of the gravitational force eventually took him far beyond the rigid limits of mathematical deduction or even direct observation of nature. His brilliant imagination produced a series of physical concepts which were a continual source of inspiration to the experimental scientists of the eighteenth century. . . . The rise of electrical theory . . . can be written largely in terms of the mechanisms of gross and subtle matter in imitation, contradiction, extension, or revision of Newton's ideas.[29]

In his book *Atoms and Powers* Arnold Thackray has shown the importance of the Newtonian principles of attraction and repulsion in the development of eighteenth-century chemistry. It seems to me that Cohen, Thackray and others have shown us that we must not judge the theoretical constructs of the eighteenth century by those current in the twentieth century. Rather, we must enter into an imaginative appreciation of the role which such theories played in the scientific life of their own day.

It is important to remember that the claim to espouse the experimental method and avoid hypotheses was standard in scientific books in Hume's day – yet those books were often of a highly speculative character. A recent writer on eighteenth-century Newtonian natural philosophy goes so far as to remark that the claim to avoid hypotheses and base one's conclusions on a 'cautious and full induction' should always be taken as 'a signal to look for some concealed theoretical structure'.[30]

One contemporary who clearly recognised the theoretical nature of Hume's primary psychological terms was Thomas Reid. It is well known that Reid thought that Hume's scepticism resulted from his postulation of sets of entities called impressions and ideas.[31] What is less well known is the fact that Reid thought that Hume and others were led to postulate the existence of these entities by their desire to explain mental operations on analogy with physical ones:

There is a disposition in men to materialize everything . . . ; that is, to apply the notions we have of material objects to things of another nature. Thought is considered as analogous to motion in a body; and as bodies are put in motion by impulses, and by impressions made upon them by contiguous objects, we are apt to conclude that the mind is made to think by impressions made upon it, and that there must be some kind of contiguity between it and the objects of thought. Hence the theories of ideas and impressions have so generally prevailed.[32]

Reid himself thought that it was a philosophical error to conceive of mental processes such as perception in physical terms. I think that, whether or not one approves of Reid's own philosophical principles (Hume clearly did not), one should recognise that he has identified a central theoretical assumption which underlies terms like 'impression' – at least as they were used by Hume. This will become clear in §19.

Reid's application of 'experimental method' led him to very different conclusions from those of Hume. L. L. Laudan has argued that Reid was the first British moral philosopher to understand the epistemological implications of Newton's methodological pronouncements.[33] But while Reid normally commends (what he takes to be) Newtonian methodology, he sometimes takes issue with the master's practice. For example, Reid opposes Newton's suggestion in the Preface to the *Principia* that 'all the phaenomena of the material world are produced by attracting or repelling forces'.[34] Reid thinks that even Newton was misled by the love of simplicity. In general,

Men are often led to error by the *love of simplicity, which disposes us to reduce things to a few principles, and to conceive a greater simplicity in nature than there really is.* (p. 470)

In contrast to Hume, Reid opposes the Newtonian hypothesis of the aether, for he claims that it lacks direct evidence. He is especially opposed to the extension of this hypothesis to the explanation of nervous action – an application first proposed by Newton and then embraced by David Hartley in his *Observations on Man*.[35] It should be noted that Reid's opposition to this hypothesis is based on his belief that it tends to 'make all the operations of mind mere mechanism, dependent on the laws of matter and motion' (p. 249). This is not the place to discuss Reid's own theoretical commitments: these were clearly very different from those of either Hume or Hartley.

(b) Practice

It is generally conceded that Hume's clearest attempt to apply the experimental method of reasoning to moral subjects occurs in Book II of the *Treatise* where he sets out to explain the origins of the passions of pride and humility. Yet if we follow Hume's account with some care we shall see that he employs that method within the context of a certain theoretical framework. Even before attempting to introduce any sort of inductive procedures Hume sets out the general theory – that of the double relations of ideas and impressions (T. 282–4) – which he is going to use to explain the origin of these passions. The upshot of this theory lies in the claim that an associational relation of ideas furthers a transfer of related feelings. I shall argue that this theory must be understood in terms of the basic psychophysiological theory of the imagination and passions current in Hume's own day.

Before applying and adapting his general theory to the

explanation of the passions of pride and humility, Hume seeks to discover the features which are common to all the objects which cause those passions in us. He makes it clear at the outset that he is assuming that there is not a unique property, different in each item in which we take pride:

'Tis absurd, therefore, to imagine, that each of these was foreseen and provided for by nature, and that every new production of art, which causes pride or humility; instead of adapting itself to the passion by partaking of some general quality, that naturally operates on the mind; is itself the object of an original principle, which till then lay conceal'd in the soul, and is only by accident at last brought to light. (T.281)

Hume thinks that the sources of pride are too varied to make it likely that each was provided for by such an 'original principle'[36] of human nature. Thus he regards himself as the *Copernicus* of the moral sciences: 'moral philosophy', he tells us, 'is in the same condition as natural, with regard to astronomy before the time of *Copernicus.*' Hume is going to find some qualities common to all the sources of pride and all the sources of humility which will allow us to explain their origin by some simple principles (T.282).

Hume applies simple inductive procedures to find the qualities common to the stimuli in our environment which produce pride and humility. He claims, in the first place, to discover that many of those stimuli 'concur in producing the sensation of pain and pleasure' (T.285): those objects which produce pride are pleasurable, and those which produce humility make us uneasy. Hume does not hold that these are sufficient conditions for the production of these passions. An object may produce pleasure without producing pride; an object may produce pain without producing humility. Nevertheless, Hume generalises from the properties which he finds common to the objects which produce pride and humility:

What I discover to be true in some instances, I *suppose* to be so in all; and take it for granted at present, without any farther proof, that every cause of pride, by its peculiar qualities produces a separate pleasure, and of humility a separate uneasiness. (T.285)

In making this generalisation Hume is applying the fourth and sixth methodological rules which he cited earlier in the *Treatise* (T.173–4). Similarly, Hume generalises from another property which he finds common to 'many obvious instances' – that of *relation to self.* Men are proud of the good effects of their own actions, of their own personal appearance, and of the objects which they possess. A pleasurable object which lacks a relation to the self does not produce pride; a painful object which lacks this relation does not produce humility. Hume forms the *'supposition'* that the sources of *both* pride and humility 'are either parts of ourselves, or something nearly related to us' (T.285).

Having formed a generalisation about the properties common to the stimuli or occasioning causes of pride and humility, Hume turns to a consideration of 'the passions themselves' in order to discover something in them which corresponds to these properties. Here, Hume really does seem to appeal to direct inspection. He claims to discover that pride and humility are connected with the idea of oneself: when one is stimulated by either of these passions one's ideas turn to self. Hume considers the idea of the passion and the idea of self to be conceptually distinct; however, he claims that there is an innate connection between them, a relation due to 'the primary constitution of the mind' (T.286; cf. T.277). Hume *also* discovers that pride itself is 'a pleasant sensation, and humility a painful' one (T.286). He seems to consider pleasure an *intrinsic part* of our conception of pride; it seems to be distinguished from pride only by what he earlier called a 'distinction of reason' (T.25).

The final stage in Hume's method of discovering the origin of pride and humility derives from a *comparison* of the qualities of the sources of these passions with the properties of the passions themselves. It is from this process of reason or comparison that Hume claims to derive the principles which explain the phenomena. At this point he says that 'the true system breaks in upon me with an irresistible evidence' (T.286). But here the consideration of the phenomena takes him well beyond any sort of direct evidence. For he is no longer talking about the stimulating causes and passions themselves (which can be directly observed), but of the cause which produces the latter from the former. Hume is moving to the level of what, in his *Dissertation on the Passions*, he called 'the real, efficient causes of the passion' (G.G. IV, 146). Hume's assignment of this cause is connected with his *supposition* 'that nature has given to the organs of the human mind, a certain disposition fitted to produce a peculiar impression or emotion, which we call *pride*', a disposition which requires the stimulus of some external object in order to operate (T.287).

According to Hume, the key to the origin of pride and humility lies in an association of ideas which makes possible an association of impressions. When we are confronted with a stimulus-object which is related to the self, our mind moves from the idea of that object to that of the self. The principles of the transition of ideas which were previously postulated by Hume were resemblance, contiguity, and causation: we tend to associate objects in our minds which have these relations. But in the present context Hume gives these relations a particular interpretation.[37] We tend to associate ourselves with our fellow countrymen, or with those of the same religious or professional group: these persons are related to us (respectively) by contiguity and resemblance. We tend to associate ourselves with our blood relatives: they are related to us by causation. We also tend to associate ourselves with inanimate objects which are our property: this, too, Hume regards as a relation of causation, since property implies that we have power over the object. As these relations become closer, so the transition from the idea of the object to that of ourselves will become easier. These associations of ideas allow a feeling to be transferred from the idea of the stimulus-object to that of ourselves. But in the course of this transference, the nature of the feeling becomes changed. For according to Hume there is also an association of impressions or feelings: the feelings tend to be transformed into resembling ones. Thus if the object which is related to us is pleasant, the pleasurable feeling associated with the object becomes transformed into that pleasurable feeling particularly connected with the idea of self – namely, pride. When the observation of some person or thing which is closely related to us is unpleasant, we come to feel the unpleasant emotion of shame or humility. The unpleasant feeling of the stimulus-object comes to be transformed into that unpleasant feeling which is innately connected with the idea of self – namely, shame or humility (T.287–9).

This, then, is Hume's account of the primary mechanisms which enter into the formation of our passions of pride and humility. It seems clear that in postulating these mechanisms Hume has gone well beyond the evidence of his senses. He himself calls his explanatory account an 'hypothesis' (T.289). But in order to understand his use of this term I think we need to raise the question of whether we should read his account as one which is supposed to be concerned with purely mental processes, or whether we should regard Hume as attempting some sort of reduction of mental to physical processes according to the theories which were available to him in his own day. I would suggest that unless we regard Hume as setting out a theory of this second kind we will not really understand his explanation of the origin of pride and humility.

Hume writes that when he considers 'the nature of *relation*' he cannot doubt that it is the principle which 'bestows motion on those organs' which are 'naturally dispos'd to produce' these passions (T.288). The relations which control the production of pride and humility do not appear to be abstract relations of ideas, but rather *natural* relations which control the transfer of motions in the brain. I think that this becomes clearer when Hume likens his hypothesis of the mechanisms involved in the formation of pride and humility to those involved in his account of the causes of belief. Hume reminds us that in the earlier account he had shown that belief required

a present impression, and a related idea; and that the present impression gives a vivacity to the fancy, and the relation conveys this vivacity, by an easy transition, to the related idea. Without the present impression, the attention is not fix'd, nor the spirits excited. Without the relation, this attention rests on its first object, and has no farther consequence. (T.290)

In this earlier discussion Hume had conceived of the relation of ideas as a means by which the excitation of the animal spirits (which is correlated with emotion or feeling) comes to be transferred from the impression of the cause to the idea of the effect. The relation allows what Hume calls an 'easy transition' of the nervous energy from one idea to another. This explains why we form a belief in the existence of the object corresponding to the idea. (Hume's account of belief will be explained in detail in the next section of this chapter.) Similarly, in the formation of the indirect passions, the *transfusion of feeling* from the idea of the object to that of the self depends upon a relation; namely, that of the object and the self. This relation should be understood as a natural one which regulates the transfer of motion from the idea of the object to that of the self. At the beginning of Book I of the *Treatise* Hume defines a natural relation as 'that quality by which two ideas are connected together *in the imagination*' whereby 'the one naturally introduces the other' (T.13; italics mine). If, as I have suggested, Hume and his contemporaries understood the italicised words in a Cartesian sense, as referring to an extended portion of the brain in which ideas were located, then would it not have been clear that the connections which he was talking about were connections between brain-traces? Would this not be the way they *conceived* of such relations?[38] A natural relation is a characteristic of the objects which 'produces an union among our ideas' (T.94) – that is, among our ideas as they are 'plac'd' in a certain 'region of the brain' (T.61).

I believe that the general account of relation which Hume presupposed was that set down in Chapter Five of the first part of Malebranche's 'Of the Imagination' (Book II of the *Recherche*). In this chapter Malebranche discussed a number of different kinds of relations or connections (French '*liaisons*'). The one which is of most concern to us here is 'the reciprocal connection which exists between [brain-] traces' (R. I, 212). For, according to Malebranche, the stimulation of these traces 'awakens ideas in the mind' and thus the connection of the brain-traces one with another corresponds with a connection of ideas. Just as the ideas are directly correlated with the brain-traces, the 'passions of the will' are directly correlated with 'movements' which are 'excited in the animal spirits'. Since the connections between the traces 'are followed by the movements of the animal spirits', there is a corresponding transfer of a passion from one trace to another, or (in phenomenal terms) from one idea to another (R. I, 214). Malebranche gives the following example:

the trace of a large body which is about to fall on us and crush us is . . . linked naturally with that which represents death to us, and with the motion of the spirits which disposes us towards flight and towards the desire to flee. (R. I, 223)

The passion of fear is an agitation particularly related to the brain-trace which corresponds to the idea of our own death; there is a natural connection between the trace which corresponds to the idea of the dangerous object and that which corresponds to the idea of our death; thus the excitation of the spirits which corresponds to fear of death gets transferred to the idea of the 'large object which is ready to fall on us'. The transition of the imagination results in transmission of feelings.

Malebranche also discusses various *causes* which determine the existence of connections between brain-traces in the imagination. For example, he claims that connections are formed between traces whose objects appear to us *at the same time* (see below, p. 218). I shall show the importance of Malebranche's accounts of the causes of connections in §§19 and 20. For present purposes it is more relevant to consider Malebranche's statement concerning the *effects* of these connections:

the mutual connection of [brain-] traces and consequently of ideas one with another is not only the foundation of all the figures of rhetoric, but also of an infinity of other things of greater importance in morals, in politics and generally in all the sciences which have any relation to man, and consequently in many things which we shall discuss in the sequel. (R. I, 222–3)

Malebranche considered the connection between brain-traces and their corresponding ideas to be important in criticism, morals and politics – in short, in those sciences which in Hume's words 'intimately concern human life' (T.xvi). An understanding of the psychophysiological basis of human thought and action is essential in founding the sciences of man.

This discussion of 'the nature of relation' appears to have taken us far from Hume's account of 'experimental method'. Yet it has, I believe, given us a clearer understanding of the basic theory which Hume attempted to establish and modify in terms of that method. Hume's simplest principle, the principle which he sought to establish by induction, concerns the control of *relations* over feelings. But, if I am right in seeing Malebranche's theory in the background of that of Hume, the relations he is talking about are those which determine the connections of ideas in the corporeal imagination.

Whether or not one accepts the claim that the Cartesian psychophysiological theory is essential for an understanding of Hume's highest and simplest principle, one must recognise that that principle does stand at the roots of his own foundation of the sciences of man. Hume claims that his method has led him to a single unified principle of human psychology. This principle is given its clearest expression in Book II of the *Treatise*:

This easy or difficult transition of the imagination operates upon the passions, and facilitates or retards their transition; which is a clear proof, that these two faculties of the passions and imagination are connected together, and that the relations of ideas have an influence upon the affections. (T.340)

This can be illustrated by a brief consideration of the central role which this principle plays in Hume's own theories of criticism, and morals and politics.

In all the editions of the *Enquiry* which appeared in Hume's lifetime, he illustrated his theory of association of ideas with a long discussion of critical theory which illustrated what he called 'the sympathy between the passions and imagination':

we observe that the affections, excited by one object, pass easily to another connected with it; but transfuse themselves with difficulty, or not at all, along different objects, which have no manner of connexion together.[39]

This principle may also play a central role in the theory of tragedy in the dissertation on that subject which Hume published in *Four Dissertations* in 1757.[40] In fact, it is possible that Hume's principle was first suggested to him in connection with its application to critical theory. For its rudiments are to be found in Joseph Addison's *Spectator* papers on 'The Pleasures of the Imagination': Hume cites a passage from these papers at the beginning of Book II of the *Treatise* in order to illustrate his theory of the mutual association of ideas and passions.[41] In this passage Addison describes how the pleasures of one idea get transferred to another when their objects are related in experience. It is of interest to note that in another passage, which Hume does not quote, Addison presents his own 'Cartesian' explanation of the cause of the phenomena. He speaks of the way 'pleasure traces' tend to reinforce each other because of their connection in the imagination.[42] As with Hume, Addison's model closely follows that of Malebranche (cf. R. I, 275, and §7(*c*) above). I would suggest that even though neither Hume nor Addison stresses the physiological model of the imagination to the extent that Malebranche did, it does provide the metaphor in which they understand the nature of the faculty and the way it interacts with the passions.

Hume's principle of the interaction of imagination and the passions becomes central to his discussions of morals and politics through his analysis of *sympathy*. This principle is first presented by Hume as one which modifies his basic model for the production of pride and humility. It explains why we are especially proud or ashamed of objects which are 'very discernible and obvious' to other people (T. 292). Later on in Book II of the *Treatise*, Hume gives the following mechanism of sympathy: the process begins with the idea which we form of the feelings of others by 'those external signs' in their 'countenance and conversation'. This *idea* of a feeling in another person becomes converted into the actual feeling (or impression) by means of our *relation* to the person. For, according to Hume, our 'consciousness gives us so lively a conception of our own person' that 'whatever object . . . is related to ourselves must be conceived with a like vivacity' (T. 317). To some extent this sympathy will occur between any human beings because of the 'general resemblance of our natures', but it becomes stronger as the relationship gets closer: 'the more easily does the imagination make the transition, and convey . . . the vivacity of [the] conception' of ourselves to that of the other person, and so to the idea which we have of his feelings (T. 318). Thus, for example, the enjoyment which others take in our possessions comes to heighten our own enjoyment of these possessions; this, in turn, increases our pride. But this effect will be much greater if the other person is closely related to us – if he is a brother or neighbour, rather than a complete stranger. The parallel between this mechanism and those we discussed earlier will be very obvious. The easy *transition* of the imagination which allows a transfer of feeling depends on the strength of the connection between the ideas and their corresponding brain-traces. I shall discuss the significance of this mechanism for Hume's moral and political theory in the conclusion to this chapter.

In his discussion of the origin of pride and humility Hume takes note of other principles which modify the strength of feeling associated with an object, and which further or retard the transition of the imagination. A detailed examination of these principles would take us too far from our present concerns. However, we should recognise that Hume presents these principles in order to bring his basic model into accord with *experience*. Yet this model itself provides the core conception of human nature on the basis of which Hume seeks to explain his observations of human behaviour.

In his book *The Philosophy of David Hume* Norman Kemp Smith argued that Hume's philosophy could be distinguished from that of his predecessors and contemporaries by the fact that *feeling* or *passion* took over the role normally ascribed to *reason*. According to Kemp Smith, Hume adopted the essential insight of the theory of moral sense (as espoused by Hutcheson and others) and sought to use it to explain the nature of our commerce with reality: just as we have an *immediate awareness* of the distinction between vice and virtue through a moral sense, so we have an immediate *feeling* of belief which distinguishes reality from unreality. According to Kemp Smith, what is distinctive in Hume's philosophy arises from his principle that 'reason is, and ought only to be the slave of the passions'.[43]

Hume's own judgement of his achievement in the *Treatise* was very different. Looking back on that achievement in the *Abstract* Hume wrote:

if any thing can intitle the author to so glorious a name as that of an *inventor*, 'tis the use he makes of the principle of the association of ideas, which enters into most of his philosophy. (A.661–2)

Hume goes on to stress that the association of ideas is the only means by which our thoughts are connected one with another and that 'it is by means of thought only that any thing operates upon our passions.' Reason is the slave of the passions; but Hume clearly also believes that the passions are themselves the servant of the imagination. The theory of association of ideas plays a fundamental role in the account of the origin of the social passions in Book II of the *Treatise*. As we have seen, the analogy which Hume himself finds between his account of the origin of the passions and his theory of belief is based on the role of association in accounting for a transfer of feeling from one idea to another. It is the synthetic *imagination* which, on Hume's theory, *controls feeling*. Indeed, *pace* Kemp Smith, what is most distinctive and original in Hume's theory of belief is not the claim that our sense of reality comes through feeling: what is distinctive is his account of the way association regulates the transfer of the feeling from an impression to an idea. According to Hume the principles of association 'are really *to us* the cement of the universe': by controlling the transfer of psychic energy in an orderly way they determine our sense of reality (A.662).

In his book Kemp Smith attempted to play down the importance in Hume's philosophy of what he called the 'statics and dynamics' of the mind, that is to say, the mechanistic model related to Hume's theory of the association of ideas (p. 75). Kemp Smith noted that Hume sought to 'get behind both sympathy and belief . . . to account for them in a mechanistic manner' (p. 59n.). This mechanism, according to Kemp Smith, 'is modelled on the pattern of the Newtonian physics'. However, 'it exercises a disturbing influence on the argument of the first two books of the *Treatise*' (p. 71). It works in opposition to the positive influence of Hutcheson's philosophy, which leads Hume to recognise that 'the processes of mind . . . are adaptive, not mechanical in character'. According to Kemp Smith, in the final analysis, it is 'biological not physical analogies' which play the decisive role in Hume's conception of human nature (p. 76).

To anyone versed in eighteenth-century biology the absolute *distinction* between mechanistic and adaptive analogies must appear rather artificial. This is readily apparent if we correct Kemp Smith's transparent error about the origins of Hume's 'statics and dynamics of the mind'.[44] Even the Cartesian tradition, which officially eschewed the role of final causes in the study of physical nature, reintroduced them in its description of the animal machine.[45] Descartes clearly described his animal machine as one which is constructed in such a way that it performs adaptive responses to environmental stimuli. In §20 I shall examine the relevance of the Cartesian conception of human nature to the development of Hume's own psychology. I shall note the close correlation of mechanism and adaptation in Hume's analysis of custom in Book I of the *Treatise*. Yet in the final analysis, in Hume's account of the formation of human society, the mechanisms of human nature dominate and must be artificially corrected by reason. Hume had a clear idea of these mechanisms independent of their adaptive role, and in fact was willing to allow that they operate even when human beings are led to self-defeating behaviour. We are getting ahead of our story. But, at the outset, we must recognise that it is important to consider Hume's account of the mechanisms of the mind carefully before passing judgement on their irrelevance to his central philosophical doctrines.

I think that it is not at all unlikely that Kemp Smith was led to a rather 'Whiggish' historiography of ideas[46] as a result of his own sympathy with idealist philosophy which stressed the importance of feeling and value in giving us our sense of reality.[47] But if we consider the whole role of *feeling* in Hume's own philosophy, we shall discover that his analysis is closely bound up with his attempts to explain psychological processes in physical terms.

Hume believed that our mental processes and contents have mechanical causes. As we saw in §15, at the end of the *Treatise* section 'Of the immateriality of the soul', Hume claimed that there are some clear cases where 'motion . . . actually is the cause of thought and perception'. He even claimed that we discover this 'by experience' (T.248). Did Hume think that he was establishing a correlation between motion and thought in the *Treatise* itself? Given the crudeness of Hume's mechanical models this interpretation may seem far-fetched. Yet I would suggest that if we attempt to think ourselves imaginatively into the ideas of Hume's own day, then we can at least appreciate his aims, even if we are not entirely able to appreciate his claims to have achieved them. Even in his *Dissertation of the Passions*, which was published many years after the *Treatise*, Hume retained the goal of showing that thought has its origin in motion. Hume claimed that it would be sufficient for his purpose if he had made it appear that

in the production and conduct of the passions, there is a *certain regular mechanism*, which is susceptible of as accurate a disquisition, as the laws of motion, optics, hydrostatics, or any part of natural philosophy.[48]

Clearly, Hume continued to aim at the goal expressed in the *Treatise* – even if he was less dogmatic in his claim to have achieved that goal.

(a) Impressions

Many accounts of Hume's philosophical principles begin with the claim that while he employs the term 'impression' to represent one of the two main contents of our awareness, he strips this word of the physiological connotations which it had for his contemporaries. It is said that while Locke, for example, spoke interchangeably of 'an *Impression* or *Motion*, made in some part of the Body, as produces some Perception in the Understanding',

Hume employed the word in an entirely different way.[49] The main evidence put forward for this view is a footnote to the second page of the *Treatise*:

By the term of impression I would not be understood to express the manner, in which our lively perceptions are produced in the soul, but merely the perceptions themselves; for which there is no particular name either in the *English* or any other language, that I know of.

It is said that in identifying an impression as a *perception* Hume was rejecting all the physical connotations of the term and using it to refer only to our awareness itself. But this will only be so if he expected his reader to understand the term 'perception' in a purely phenomenalistic way. However, on the previous page of the *Treatise* Hume speaks of perceptions themselves as if they were physical motions in the brain as well as objects of our awareness: he describes how they 'strike upon the mind, and make their way into our thought or consciousness'. The difference between impressions and ideas is said to lie in their 'degrees of force and liveliness' (T.1). After introducing his distinction between impressions and ideas in his *Enquiry* Hume speaks of the former as 'sensations or movements' (E.18). In Hume's own day this disjunction was not philosophically insignificant.

In order to understand what Hume means when he says that he is not using the term 'impression' to refer to 'the manner, in which our lively perceptions are produced in the soul', it is important to consider the precise way in which the term was employed by his predecessors. In the section we quoted in the last paragraph Locke spoke of 'Impressions made on our Senses by outward Objects' (*Essay* 2, 1, 23). At the beginning of Book II of the *Recherche* Malebranche discusses 'the impression which objects make on the exterior surface of the fibres of our nerves and which is communicated to the brain' (R. I, 191). In both these cases the term is clearly used to represent those neural motions which arise from the external senses. Following Malebranche, Ephraim Chambers contrasts impressions with motions of the brain which are caused by the 'Course of the animal Spirits, or in *some other manner*'.[50] It seems clear that in his footnote Hume reads his predecessors as if they have limited impressions to those caused by natural objects. He himself does not limit the term 'impression' to an agitation which arises *in a certain manner* – namely from the outer senses. For, he notes, he is using it to refer to *all* our lively perceptions, our 'passions and emotions' *as well as* images which arise from external objects.[51] But there is no reason to think that Hume rejects his predecessors' definition of the passions in terms of the forceful motions of animal spirits.[52] Why, then, should we deny that he uses the term 'impressions' in a general way to refer to any forceful motions in the brain?

Malebranche used the term 'impression' for a mere *occasional* cause of the contents of our awareness. But, as we have seen, Hume rejected Malebranche's theory of occasional causation and held that there is a real (though unknown) necessary connection between cause and effect. Hence, it does not seem likely, as John Laird claimed, that Hume adopted the physiological term of his contemporaries to stand for a *mere* content of awareness. It is much more likely that he used it to stand for *both* a mental content *and* the cause which is immediately connected with that content. We should therefore expect to find the physiological conceptions of his contemporaries implicit in Hume's use of terms like 'impression'.

'Impressions', according to Hume, are the perceptions which strike the mind with the most force and liveliness. This characteristic of impressions is intimately connected with what he calls *feeling*. For the central claim which he wants to make in the opening pages of the *Treatise* is that 'feeling and thinking' lie on a continuum – that is, that impressions and ideas differ only in degree.[53] Yet in making this claim Hume was merely echoing Malebranche, who stressed, at the beginning of Book II of the *Recherche*, that there is no absolute distinction between the faculties of sense and imagination: they differ only as 'the greater from the less'.[54] Hume wrote that 'in sleep, in a fever, in madness, or in any very violent emotions of soul, our ideas may approach to our impressions' (T.2). Similarly, Malebranche had claimed earlier that in the case of 'a hot fever' or 'violent passion' people 'sense what they ought only to imagine' (R. I, 192). Sensation, for Malebranche, is tied up with a 'natural judgment' that external objects are present and 'capable of making [the soul] feel pleasure and pain'. Like Hume, Malebranche relates sensation to feeling: we are, he claims, ordinarily more 'affected' (*touchée*) by external objects than by motions which arise from internal sources.[55]

Malebranche's doctrine of the continuity of sense and imagination was explicitly physiological, and it was only rather artificially that, in the previous paragraph, I have attempted to isolate the purely psychological aspects of his theory. For Malebranche, our natural judgement of external existence is directly correlated with the forceful agitation of the fibres in the centre of the brain. The doctrine that sense and imagination differ only in degree is related to the claim that while ordinarily 'the fibres of the brain are much more agitated by the impression of objects than by the course of the animal spirits', this influence may sometimes be reversed in the case of the strong feelings which accompany a violent agitation of these spirits (R. I, 192). Moreover, earlier on, Malebranche had claimed that our 'strong and lively sensations' such as pain and pleasure are themselves 'accompanied not only by the traces of the brain but also by some movement of the spirits . . . appropriate to change the position of the body and excite the passions' (R. I, 138).

I would suggest that, while Hume does not explicitly lay out all this physiology in the opening pages of the *Treatise*, he does assume that an account such as that given by Malebranche is true. The essence of the theories of both authors lies in the claim that forceful motions in the brain, whatever their source, give the soul a sense of the *presence* of objects. It feels them and hence ascribes a reality to them. But, even for Hume, this feeling is understood as closely correlated with a neurological event. In Book II of the *Treatise* Hume wrote that 'no object is presented to the senses, nor image form'd in the fancy, but what is accompany'd with some *emotion or movement of spirits* proportion'd to it' (T.373; italics mine). In this passage he clearly identifies feeling with a motion of the animal spirits which accompanies the images formed in the imagination.

(b) Beliefs

Strictly speaking, Hume's 'theory of belief' has to do with his claim that *ideas* themselves can obtain a force and vivacity which is sufficient to make us believe that their objects exist, even when those objects have not ever been present to our senses. However, this theory is clearly an extension of the doctrine laid out in the opening pages of the *Treatise* that feeling and thought lie on a continuum. Once again our sense of reality is described as a certain *feeling*, and this feeling is explained 'by calling it a superior *force*, or *vivacity*, or *solidity*, or *firmness*, or *steadiness*'. This manner of conceiving our ideas causes them to 'appear of greater importance; infixes them in the mind; and renders them the governing principles of all our actions' (T.629; cf. E.49–50).

The outlines of Hume's theory of belief – at least the part of it which we considered in the last paragraph – are clearly foreshadowed in a discussion of 'strong imaginations' in Part III of Book II of the *Recherche*.[56] Once again a central difference between Hume's account and that of Malebranche lies in the fact that Malebranche always makes his psychophysiology fully explicit. Malebranche describes how people are persuaded by others who cause them to form 'very lively and sensible images' in their minds (R. I, 329). While such lively images do not make them 'believe that they [actually] see absent objects before their eyes' these images do make people approach that state. Malebranche explained the forcefulness of conception in the following way:

To the degree which the [brain-] traces become larger and deeper, the soul also judges that the object becomes greater and more important, that it approaches nearer and nearer us, and finally that it is capable of affecting and harming us. (R. I, 326)

Apart from his explicit stress on the physiology, Malebranche's account of the nature of belief is identical to that of Hume. Much of Malebranche's discussion in Book II of the *Recherche* is taken up with a description of the various factors which determine the size of the brain-traces, and so condition human belief. One of these factors, repetition of stimuli, seems to be of particular relevance to Hume's later discussion. Malebranche wrote:

we imagine things more strongly to the degree that these [brain-] traces are deeper and better engraved, and the animal spirits pass there more often and with greater violence. . . . When the spirits have passed that way several times they enter with greater facility.[57]

Malebranche believed that repetition of impressions is one of the factors which result in the deepening of brain-traces and that the deepening of these traces is correlated with the stronger and more distinct imagination of objects. For, given the laws of fluid dynamics, the animal spirits will enter such traces more easily than others where they will meet with more resistance.

We have already seen that Hume refers back to his own physiological conceptions of belief in his discussion of the origin of pride and humility at the beginning of Book II of the *Treatise*. He first presented these conceptions in the section of the *Treatise* entitled 'Of the causes of belief' (T.98ff.). It is in this section that he puts forward what he afterwards refers to as his 'new hypothesis' about the origins of belief (T.107). In order to understand Hume's account one must be aware of his general view that a belief in the existence of an object is connected with the 'force and vivacity' of the conception; but one must also understand that this force and vivacity depends on the degree of nervous energy involved in that conception – that is, on whether 'the spirits are more or less elevated'. A 'new object' always causes an increase in nervous energy; it changes what Hume calls the 'disposition' of the animal spirits. But it also gives them 'a new direction'. Thus,

when the mind is once inliven'd by a present impression, it proceeds to form a more lively idea of the related objects, by a natural transition of the disposition from the one to the other. (T.99)

It is likely that Hume expects his reader to understand this 'natural transition' of the animal spirits to the related idea according to the fluid dynamic model of the brain which he himself had set out a few pages earlier (T.60–1; see pp. 68ff. above). Later on, in Part III of Book I of the *Treatise* Hume writes:

The vividness of the first conception diffuses itself along the relations, and is convey'd, as by so many pipes or canals, to every idea that has any communication with the primary one. (T.122)

The excitation caused by an impression gets transferred in a purely physical way to the ideas of related objects, and so makes us believe in their existence. Hume's new hypothesis of belief has to do with the factors which condition the natural transition of the elevated animal spirits from the impression to the idea.

Hume does not merely seek to explain the general phenomenon of belief; he aims to show why we form, in a systematic way, beliefs in certain objects and not others. According to Hume, the relations of 'resemblance and contiguity' are not sufficient by themselves to make us believe in the existence of an object: they do not allow a sufficient transfer of force and vivacity from the impression of one object to a particular idea of another. 'The relation of cause and effect is requisite to persuade us of any real existence' and give force to these other relations (T.109). It is the natural transfer of force and energy to the ideas of objects which are causally related to those which we have sensed which makes us form a natural judgement of their existence. In this way we come to form a belief in particular objects which we never have sensed: 'each impression draws along with it a precise idea, which takes its place in the imagination, as something solid and real, certain and invariable' (T.110). Thus Hume speaks of the ideas of causally related items as forming a 'system' of realities which is related to that other system which is formed by the 'impressions or ideas of the memory' (T.108).

Hume's belief in the psychological strength of the causal relation appears to be based on his account of its origin. As we have seen, Hume thinks that we come to believe in causal relations as a result of *custom* – that is, as a result of the constant repetition of stimuli. Custom actually *produces* the propensity of the mind to pass from the impression of one object to the idea of another which has been constantly conjoined with it (see p. 151 above). The belief in the second object varies according to the strength of the habit. It increases with the number of instances in which we experience two objects conjoined:

As the habit, which produces the association, arises from the frequent conjunction of objects, it must arrive at its perfection by degrees, and must acquire new force from each instance, that falls under our observation. . . . 'Tis by these slow steps, that our judgment arrives at a full assurance. (T.130)

The increase in the forcefulness of conception is a result of increase in 'the *impulse* or tendency to the transition' from the impression to the idea (T.130; italics mine). Why would this *impulse* grow stronger as a result of the constant repetition of the stimuli?

We saw earlier that, in the *Enquiry*, Hume identified custom as a 'mechanical tendency' (E.55) or 'mechanical power' (E.108). It does not seem likely that Hume's use of this word would have been accidental, especially since the mechanical theory of custom was under attack by at least one important writer in Scotland in his own day.[58] Hume is clearly taking a stand on the mechanical nature of the involuntary operations of the mind. Further, the language of Cartesian psychophysiology which is used throughout the discussions in the *Treatise* should certainly have led Hume's readers to recognise that he presupposed a mechanical account of custom. The basic physiological model for the acquisition of connections of ideas was laid out by Malebranche. Certain connections result from

the identity of time in which they were imprinted in the brain, for it suffices that several traces have been produced at the same time, in order that they can only be reawakened together. For the animal spirits, finding the pathways of all the traces which are made at the same time open, continue their way through them because they can pass there more easily than through other places in the brain. (R. I, 222–3)

But the clearest mechanical account of custom as a cause of association of ideas was given by Locke. In the chapter of his *Essay* entitled 'Of the Association of Ideas' Locke put forward the following hypothesis which, he said, 'may help us a little to conceive of Intellectual Habits, and of the tying together of *Ideas*':

Custom settles habits of Thinking in the Understanding, as well as of Determining in the Will, and of Motions in the Body; all which seems to be but Trains of Motion in the Animal Spirits, which once set a going continue on in the same steps they have been used to, which by often treading are worn into a smooth path, and the Motion in it becomes easy and as it were Natural. (*Essay* 2, 33, 6)

Following Malebranche and Descartes (see p. 215 above) Locke gives a description of how the nervous fluids engrave traces in the brain as a result of repeated experience. But Locke clearly adopts the Cartesian physiology in order to explain the strength of the *connection* of ideas which results from custom and the resulting *easy* movement of the animal spirits from one idea to another.[59] Did not Hume presuppose the Lockian account when, in order to explain the cause of belief, he asked his reader to consider 'the nature of relation, and that facility of transition, which is essential to it' (T. 99)?

Hume's theory of belief is a theory about the transfer of feeling from an impression to an idea; but he understands feeling as a nervous energy which is correlated with an excitation of the animal spirits. The transfer of feeling depends upon an association of ideas; but there is good reason to think that, like Locke and Malebranche, Hume conceived of this association as directly correlated with a connection of brain-traces. It seems that Hume held that this latter connection comes to be widened as a result of repeated experience and so allows an easier transmission of nervous energy from an impression to a related idea. Hume is presupposing the mechanistic theories of *belief* and *custom* laid out by his predecessors. Yet we must recognise that he synthesised these theories in a new way. The explicit theory that the 'easy transition' formed by custom actually allows the enlivening of ideas seems to be original with Hume. Moreover, he employed this theory in a new way to explain the lack of influence of reason and reflection on our natural beliefs: for it is one's 'natural propensity, and the course of my animal spirits and passions' which force one to accept a 'belief in the general maxims of the world' in spite of all 'reasoning and philosophy' (T.269).

(c) Ideas

Hume claimed that impressions are the 'causes' of their corresponding ideas (T.5). This amounts to the claim that our more forceful perceptions – whether from outer or from inner sources – are the cause of our less forceful ones. But how exactly would Hume and his contemporaries have conceived of the causation which he is talking about? We saw at the beginning of this chapter that Chambers defined imagination as the power by which the soul 'forms Ideas of Things, by means of certain Traces and Impressions that had been before made in the Fibres of the Brain by Sensation' (see p. 189). Does this definition not help us to understand how impressions might cause ideas?

In his *Treatise of Man* Descartes described how, after leaving the central part of the brain where they 'have received the impression of some idea', the animal spirits pass to another part where they 'have the force to enlarge [certain pores or] spaces a little, and to bend and displace the small fibres which they meet in their path in various ways according to the diverse ways they move'.[60] In this work Descartes treated ideas themselves as purely corporeal; he conceived of them as what T. S. Hall has called 'patterned flows of spirits'.[61] The changes which the forceful motions of the animal spirits originally make in the fibres of the brain become the templet for the formation of new excitations which constitute the ideas of memory: 'these figures . . . are conserved in such a way that by their means the ideas . . . can be formed anew long afterwards, without the presence of the objects.'[62]

We have seen that Hume himself explained recollection by noting that 'these spirits always excite the idea, when they run precisely into the proper traces, and rummage that cell, which belongs to the idea' (T.61). Consider Hume's corroborating evidence for the claim that impressions cause ideas:

where-ever by any accident the faculties, which give rise to any impressions, are obstructed in their operations, as when one is born blind or deaf; not only the impressions are lost, but also their correspondent ideas; so that there never appear in the mind the least *traces* of either of them. (T.5; my italics)

We have some reason to think that Hume conceived of these traces as templets in the brain which allow the formation of ideas. Without the original impressions (or forceful motions) the patterns in the brain and in the animal spirits can never be properly formed.

Hume has very little to say about how the stimuli of external objects come to be the source of their corresponding ideas. His main concern is with ideas like 'necessity' which, he argues, are derived from *internal* impressions which do not have any external archetypes. He stresses that 'necessity is something, that exists in the mind, not in objects' (T.165). But in what sense does it *exist* in the mind? Hume describes the idea as 'that determination of the thought to pass from causes to effects' (T.166). The impression from which the idea is derived is described as 'that propensity, which custom produces, to pass from an object to the idea of its usual attendant' (T.165). But we have seen that Hume's predecessors conceived of the effects of custom in terms of the formation of a pathway between brain-traces which allows an easy movement of the animal spirits. It seems likely that Hume and his contemporaries would have conceived of the propensity of the mind literally as a movement of spirits which is made possible by the formation of such a pathway.[63] The pathway itself is the templet which is the source of our idea of necessary connection. It has its origin in a change in brain-structure which does not arise directly from any archetype in the external world.

In this section we have seen that when we interpret terms like 'impression', 'belief', and 'idea' in the light of theories current in Hume's own day, we can understand his suggestion that thought has its origin in motion. There is no reason to think that Hume's originality lay in the rejection of these theories, or in an attempt to interpret them in purely mentalistic terms. Hume sought to adapt and modify contemporary theories of mental operation by appeal to experience. He employed them to explain human thought and behaviour.

In the first part of this section we noted that Malebranche considered the forcefulness of the impressions of external objects to be the source of a legitimate *natural judgement* that there are external objects independent of us. However his account of the enlivening of the *ideas* of the imagination is an account of the source of *false* beliefs and *false* judgements. Similarly, both Malebranche and Locke considered association of ideas to be the source of false ideas and false judgements. Hume, on the other hand, employs these mechanisms to explain how, quite spontaneously, we come to form legitimate natural judgements of the existence of objects which we never have experienced. These mechanisms operate – to borrow Kemp Smith's term – in an *adaptive* way: they make us form natural judgements which orient us to our environment. However, Hume had a far more direct source for his account of natural judgements than that which is given by Kemp Smith. In the final main section of this book I shall consider Hume's modification of the Cartesian theory of natural judgement.

§20 *Natural judgements*

The central project of Hume's *Treatise* was to provide a 'foundation for the other sciences' in a 'science of man' which consisted of 'principles of human nature' (T.xvi). I have been arguing that Hume attempted to put forward a mechanistic conception of human nature and that his principles of human nature are, at bottom, psychophysiological. But one central part of Hume's science of man includes *logic*. Hume says that 'the sole end of logic is to explain the principles and operations of our reasoning faculty, and the nature of our ideas' (T.xv). But is not logic a *normative* science? Does it not explain the source of *correct* principles of reasoning? The question arises how the mechanistic principles of mind which Hume describes can provide a *normative foundation* for scientific reasoning. In order to answer this question we must reconsider the epistemological conceptions which lie at the root of the mechanical philosophy.

The project announced at the beginning of the *Treatise* invites comparison with that of Descartes' *Meditations on First Philosophy* – the fourth book which Hume mentioned in his August 1737 letter from Tours. In that work Descartes had claimed to 'build anew from the foundation' in order to establish a 'firm and permanent structure in the sciences'. As with Hume, the image of rebuilding from the *foundation* was central in Descartes' description of his own scientific project.[64] Moreover, like Hume, Descartes sought to found the sciences on *nature*. Yet in the *Meditations* Descartes made a distinction between two different senses in which nature teaches me things. By nature we may mean 'a certain spontaneous inclination which impels me to believe' something; or we may mean 'a natural light which makes me recognise' what is true (H.R. I, 160). It is on 'nature' in this second sense that Descartes sought to found the sciences. For Descartes believed that he could find in himself ideas 'which possess natures which are true and immutable' (H.R. I, 180). He thought that he could found the sciences upon an analysis of the nature or essence of our ideas – especially those of mathematical objects. It is only by basing belief upon *nature* in this sense that we can determine the structure of reality as it exists in itself.

The analysis of Hume's philosophy given in Chapters Three and Four has shown that, in the *Treatise*, he came to reject completely Descartes' claim that the sciences can be founded on a consideration of the nature of our ideas. Hume argued that if we examine our actual sense-derived ideas according to a proper application of Cartesian principles, we shall find that we have no rational basis for any of our fundamental beliefs. If we attempt to found our beliefs on the analysis of such ideas we shall be led to absurd conclusions such as the conclusion that there are no causes in reality, a conclusion which is opposed to common sense and science. As Malebranche and Berkeley have shown us, reasoning based upon 'the nature of our ideas' can undermine our basic scientific conception of reality. According to Hume, the part of *logic* which deals with analysis of ideas arrives at purely negative ontological conclusions.

(a) The teachings of human nature: Descartes' theory

However, in spite of his stress on the natural light of reason, Descartes left an important role in his philosophic system for *nature* in his other sense – the natural inclination to believe things. Descartes' account of natural belief is developed in Meditation VI and other writings where he explains how 'the nature of man' as constituted by the substantial union of mind and body teaches me things about external objects which surround me.[65] This theory forms part of a wider theory which includes an account of sense-experience, of human behaviour, and of natural signs. Descartes developed a seminal theory of human nature which was taken up by a number of subsequent seventeenth- and eighteenth-century writers on this topic.[66]

Before turning to Descartes' actual account of natural belief it is useful to consider briefly the theories of sensation and natural human behaviour which are closely related to it. In Meditation VI Descartes describes how in a healthy human body external objects cause certain motions in the nerves which are transferred to the part of the brain in which 'the mind immediately receives [its] impression'. This impression causes a 'sentiment' or sensible perception in the mind which is, of all possible sensible perceptions, the one which under normal circumstances is 'ordinarily the most useful for the conservation of the human body'.[67] For we have a natural tendency to seek out those objects which make us feel pleasure and shun those objects which are unpleasant. In his *Passions of the Soul* Descartes claims that sensible perceptions are linked up with certain passions which 'dispose the soul to desire those things which nature tells us are of use' (Art. 52, H.R. I, 358). Each motion of the pineal gland is linked 'by nature' with certain thoughts in our mind and certain neurologically based passions.[68] These latter are tied to specific responses of the human organism which are beneficial for its survival.

Underlying Descartes' conception of human nature as teacher is the idea of an organism which is constructed in such a way that it naturally makes an adaptive response to stimuli presented by external objects. Our sensible perceptions are conscious signs which correspond to this response – signs which can be interpreted by the rational mind. But the original sign can be determined by natural relations which are established in the imagination of the organism. In *La Dioptrique* Descartes stressed that we do not see objects directly, but 'only through the mediation of the brain'.[69] He described a 'natural geometry', a kind of automatic calculating process through which the distance of objects is determined on the basis of certain data – namely, the distance between our two eyes and the size of the angles formed by focusing both eyes on a single point on the object. He claims that this occurs by means of 'an action of thought which, although it is only a simple act of the imagination, nevertheless in itself contains a reasoning quite like that employed by surveyors' (pp. 137–8). Descartes may be assuming that the actual reasoning process takes place in the corporeal imagination without our being aware of anything but the perceived distance of the object – though this is certainly not entirely clear. In any case, the resulting awareness of distance makes it possible for us to react in appropriate ways to the objects in our environment.

In Meditation VI, Descartes claims that 'in all things which nature teaches me there is some truth contained' (H.R. I, 192). Our sensible perceptions teach us which objects to seek out and which to avoid. Descartes holds that when we examine our sensible perceptions by reason, we can determine truths about particular bodies surrounding our own. We can conclude, for example, that different sensible qualities of objects arise from 'certain variations' in the objects 'which answer to them, although possibly these are not really at all similar to them' (H.R. I, 192; cf. p. 109 above). This belief arises from human nature – that is, from the mind–body union. On the other hand, the false belief, that something really resembling the colours actually exists in the objects, is formed 'in my mind by a certain habit which I have of forming inconsiderate judgments on things'.[70]

Descartes could not dispense with the teachings of human nature, even in questions which relate to the foundations of science. For he appealed to our 'very great inclination to believe' that our sensations derive from other 'corporeal objects' as part of his proof that such objects exist (H.R. I, 191). The appeal to natural inclination was, as we have seen, important in the subsequent discussions of belief in the external world in Malebranche and Hume. What is distinctive in Descartes' discussion is the claim that our natural belief, taken in itself, contains no error.

(b) Hume's adoption of Malebranche's theory of natural judgement

In his development of Descartes' doctrine of the teachings of human nature in his *Recherche de la Vérité*, Malebranche maintained that such teachings may be partially false.[71] We have examined the close connection between Malebranche's account of natural judgement of external existence and that of Hume.[72] It seems clear that Malebranche provides the link between the views of Descartes and Hume. Both Hume and Malebranche assume that through reason we may discover the partial falsity of our natural or instinctive judgement. For both believe that nature teaches us that our sensible perceptions exist while unperceived. However, like Descartes, Malebranche and Hume hold that in what nature teaches us there is *some* truth contained. While human nature deceives us about the exact nature of external objects it does teach us the general truth that there are things which exist outside our own minds (cf. pp. 55–6 and 74–5 above).

When he first developed his doctrine of natural judgement from the conception of 'natural geometry' which he found in Descartes' *Optics*, Malebranche seems to have assumed that we ourselves form such judgements.[73] However, in later editions of his *Recherche* he insists that they are formed 'in ourselves, independently of ourselves, and even in spite of ourselves'. This, he writes, is why he calls them 'natural' (R. I, 119; cf. R. I, 99). These themes are also connected with the notion of natural judging or reasoning as it appears in Hume's writings. (Following Malebranche, Hume considered natural *'conception, judgment* and *reasoning'* to be equivalent mental operations.)[74] Hume tells us that we cannot withhold belief in probability because 'nature . . . has determin'd us to judge as well as to breathe and feel' (T. 183). And as we saw earlier he followed Malebranche in stressing the unconscious and mechanical character of our judgement of external existence.

While Malebranche held that our natural judgements are partially deceptive he stressed their importance for the survival of the human organism. This theme is also present in Hume's discussions. Our judgement of external existence is 'of too great importance to be trusted to our uncertain reasonings and speculations' (T. 187). In his *Enquiry* Hume asks his reader to reflect on the way our natural reasoning processes make possible the adjustment of 'means to ends' and 'the producing of good, or avoiding of evil'. Such reflections, he notes, should give pleasure to 'those, who delight in the discovery and contemplation of *final causes*' (E.55).

Hume clearly accepted the Cartesian principle that we respond in unconscious and adaptive ways to environmental stimuli. Like the Cartesians he considers our natural judgements to be cognitive correlates to this natural response. In Book I of the *Treatise* Hume set as a major task the attempt to show that the foundations of eighteenth-century science lay in such natural judging and inferring processes. In fact, he attempted to show how judgements built on such a foundation could replace the metaphysical judgements which the Cartesians themselves sought to found on an analysis of our ideas. Hume vastly extended the scope of Cartesian 'natural judgements'.

(c) Hume's revisionary conception of human nature as teacher

Can we then conclude that Hume sought to found the sciences on a Cartesian conception of human nature? There is, it seems to me, nothing in Hume's account of our natural judgement of external existence which requires any basic modification of that conception. The principle of association of ideas by resemblance which is derived from Malebranche does play a fundamental role in Hume's explanatory account. But both Descartes and Malebranche readily accepted the role of the mechanisms of association in the formation of our natural inferences. However, when we turn to Hume's account of that principle of human nature which he calls custom or habit, we *do* find a fundamental modification of the Cartesian conception. Hume's major change in the Cartesian theory of human nature lay in his insistence that 'habit is nothing but one of the principles of nature, and derives all its force from that origin' (T.179).

In order to appreciate the revisionist character of Hume's conception of custom we must recognise that his predecessors made a fundamental distinction between natural thought and thought which is derived from custom or habit. In his *Passions of the Soul* Descartes writes that

although each movement of the [pineal] gland seems to have been joined by nature to each one of our thoughts from the beginning of our life, we may at the same time join them to others by means of custom.

Descartes stresses that just as we can employ this latter principle to change the motions of the brain 'in animals deprived of reason' and thus control their behaviour, so we can use it to acquire an absolute control over our own behaviour (Art. 50; H.R. I, 356–7). However, in so far as he speaks of associations which are formed from natural stimuli, Descartes considers them to be purely harmful. He discusses various aversions and phobias which are formed as a result of traumatic experiences. On Descartes' view, customary associations formed apart from the conscious control of human reason appear to play no positive role in human life.[75]

Malebranche makes an even clearer distinction between two different kinds of connections between the traces of ideas – those which are 'natural or proper to the nature of man' and those which are 'acquired'. Borrowing an example from Descartes, Malebranche illustrates the difference between these two kinds of connections with an analogy from dog nature: one can train (*accoûtume*) a dog not to run after a partridge even though 'he is disposed' to do so by his 'natural traces'. (Malebranche calls the connections themselves 'traces' in this passage.) However, the natural traces can never be entirely effaced, and their action will come to predominate unless the acquired ones are constantly reinforced (R. I, 249–50). These acquired traces, unlike the natural ones, are not 'necessary for the preservation of life' (R. I, 223). Thus, they are not essential to dog (or human) nature.

Locke also adopted a distinction between natural associations of ideas and those which are formed by custom, although, unlike the Cartesians, he stressed that the latter are often so strong that they are confused with the former. The first sort of connections are 'truly Natural' since they 'depend upon our original Constitution, and are born with us' (*Essay* 2, 33, 7). The second sort, the customary associations, can be formed 'either voluntarily, or by chance'. As we have seen, Locke believed that these customary associations could become very strong – 'as it were Natural' (*Essay* 2, 33, 6). Like Descartes, Locke noted the irrational 'Antipathies' which result from the chance associations (*Essay* 2, 33, 7). However, he also pointed out that harmful associations result from human volition:

The *Ideas* of *Goblines* and *Sprights* have really no more to do with Darkness than Light; yet let but a foolish Maid inculcate these often on the Mind of a Child, and raise them there together, possibly he shall never be able to separate them again so long as he lives, but Darkness shall ever afterwards bring with it those frightful *Ideas*. (*Essay* 2, 33, 10)

Even more than the Cartesians, Locke was concerned with the harmful intellectual habits which result from the operations of custom or habit.

Like these earlier thinkers Hume recognises that there are *'original'* connections of ideas and passions:

Unless nature had given some original qualities to the mind, it cou'd never have any secondary ones; because in that case it wou'd have no foundation for action, nor cou'd ever begin to exert itself. (T.280)

He considers the connection between the passion of pride and the idea of self to be a non-necessary connection which 'is determin'd by an original and natural instinct' (T.286). However, unlike his predecessors, Hume does not limit the term 'natural' to these original connections. As we have seen, Hume employs the term 'natural relation' for any 'quality, by which two ideas are connected together in the imagination, and the one naturally introduces the other' (T.13). Such a connection can depend upon a repetition in our experience *or* an intrinsic relation of our ideas (as in the case of resemblance). Relations which are produced by custom or habit are as *natural* as those which are based upon an original and natural instinct.

When he claimed that custom or habit is nothing but one of the principles of human nature Hume was stressing that, under natural observational conditions, it would operate as a means by which we learn, at least to some degree, of the real relations of objects. The regular conjunction and succession of objects in our experience lead us to associate them and infer the existence of one from the other. According to Hume the effects of custom under natural circumstances are just like those of an 'instinct'. Indeed the natural reasoning which arises from custom

is nothing but a wonderful . . . instinct in our souls, which carries us along a certain train of ideas, and endows them with particular qualities, according to their particular situations and relations.

Of course this instinct requires 'past experience and observation' in order to operate. But according to Hume, there is nothing less mysterious about it than about any of our other instinctual beliefs. Hume asks rhetorically: 'Can any one give the ultimate reason, why past experience and observation produces such an effect, any more than why nature alone shou'd produce it?' (T.179). The connection of ideas produced by our observation of regularity in nature is as much a product of human nature as any of the original connections of the Cartesians.

It is important to stress that the notion of custom or habit as expounded by Hume is a principle of human nature in the fundamental Cartesian sense. We have seen that, for Descartes, the human organism is so constituted that, under normal conditions, when it is stimulated by external objects, it will produce a response which directs us toward what is true and useful. This response depends upon certain natural relations between different ideas and between ideas and passions. In arguing that habit is a principle of human nature, Hume is arguing that under appropriate conditions it too will lead to an appropriate connection of ideas.

Certainly, Hume is forced to recognise that custom or habit is the source of pathological as well as healthy reasonings. In his *Enquiry* he admits that 'like other instincts' custom 'may be fallacious and deceitful' (E.159). In his *Treatise* he notes that

one, who is tormented he knows not why, with the apprehension of spectres in the dark, may, perhaps, be said to reason, and to reason naturally too: But then it must be in the same sense, that a malady is said to be natural. (T.225–6)

On Hume's view, as well as that of Locke, these reasonings result from an artificial stimulus – namely, education and indoctrination. Hume appears to consider such pathological reasonings to be 'natural' in the sense that they result from the mechanical processes of the mind. Similarly, in his sixth Meditation, Descartes himself had to admit that 'the nature of man, inasmuch as it is composed of mind and body, cannot be otherwise than sometimes a source of deception' (H.R. I, 198). He discussed cases where, because of unusual circumstances in either the external environment or internal bodily state, a natural connection of ideas will lead to a harmful result (H.R. I, 194–5). In such cases we may also form a false judgement about the nature of the stimulus-object.

But like Descartes, Hume appears to prefer a sense of the word 'natural' which requires that what is natural to man be both beneficial and truth-preserving. He claims that the pathological reasonings of the man who infers that there are ghosts in the dark is 'contrary to health, the most agreeable and most *natural* situation of man' (T.226; italics mine). 'Natural reasoning' in

Hume's most favoured sense arises from *a natural cause* (T.117); that is, an *observed* constant conjunction of events. It results in relations of ideas which make us operate in adaptive ways in our environment:

> A person, who stops short in his journey upon meeting a river in his way, foresees the consequences of his proceeding forward; and his knowledge of these consequences is convey'd to him by past experience, which informs him of such certain conjunctions of causes and effects. . . . The idea of sinking is so closely connected with that of water, and the idea of suffocating with that of sinking. (T.103–4)

Hume believes that such relations give us some notion of causal connections as they exist in reality. For he accepts the view that human nature is constituted in such a way that it produces a psychological response which is appropriate for its own survival. And as Descartes pointed out, in whatever nature teaches us in this sense 'there is some truth contained'.

Thus we see that when he attempted to found the other sciences on 'human nature' Hume drew on a seminal doctrine of *nature as teacher* which he found in Cartesian writings. Hume sought to show that the sciences have their foundation in certain adaptive principles of the imagination. These principles are 'the foundation of all our thoughts and actions, so that upon their removal human nature must immediately perish and go to ruin' (T.225). The survival value of such principles is connected with his doctrine that the natural judgements which they cause have a *prima facie* validity (see pp. 74ff. above). At the same time, like the Cartesians, Hume believed that the primary function of these responses is self-preservation and not truth.[76] Unlike his own critics of the Scottish 'common-sense' school, Hume did not believe that our instinctual beliefs are self-evident.[77] While he rejected the Cartesian view that reason alone can serve as a foundation for the sciences, he did give reason a role in the correction of natural judgements and inferences.[78] As we have seen throughout this study, reason (or the comparison of ideas) plays a fundamental role for Hume in determining which aspects of our natural judgements are valid.

§21   Conclusion

At the beginning of §19 I noted that in his book *The Philosophy of David Hume* Norman Kemp Smith claimed that adaptive rather than mechanical analogies play the decisive role in Hume's conception of human psychological processes. But we have seen that, in Book I of the *Treatise*, Hume gives equal weight to the mechanical and adaptive aspects of those processes which underlie our conception of the physical world and our scientific inferences. Certainly the fact that such processes do provide a foundation for the sciences is related to their adaptive role. But at the same time Hume is concerned to show that these processes are formed in us mechanically. To disregard this aspect of his thought is to disregard a major aim of his philosophy and ignore the tradition in which his psychological concepts make sense. Moreover, in his account of the origins of political society in Book III of the *Treatise*, Hume comes to deny that our natural psychological processes are adaptive; the mechanisms of the imagination come to play a crucial role in Hume's analysis. This is the opposite of what Kemp Smith's interpretation would have led us to expect. I shall conclude with a few remarks contrasting Hume's account of the origins of political society with his account of the origins of science.

In a letter to Francis Hutcheson, written as he was preparing the final manuscript of Book III of the *Treatise*, Hume repudiated the sense of the word 'natural' which has seemed to me to be important in his account of natural judgements. Hume wrote: 'I cannot agree to your Sense of *Natural*. Tis founded on final Causes; which is a Consideration, that appears to me pretty uncertain & unphilosophical.'[79] It appears that Hutcheson had objected to Hume's claim that justice is not a natural virtue. For Hume himself was willing to admit that the respect for the property of others and the keeping of contracts were 'absolutely necessary' for the well-being of mankind.[80] Yet he clearly denied that such teleological considerations were relevant to his distinction between artificial virtues (like justice) and natural ones (like benevolence). In his original discussion Hume had denied that justice was natural because it was based on 'thought or reflexion' (T.484). He argued that our *natural* acquisitive tendencies are 'directly destructive of society' (T.492). Hence it is clear that in Book III of the *Treatise* Hume withheld the term 'natural' from a mental process which leads to adaptive behaviour because it requires the use of reason. He applied the term to a spontaneous psychological process which, by itself, leads to harmful results. Like Hobbes,[81] Hume believed that the natural processes of the passions destroy civil society.

Hume's claim that our natural psychological processes lead us into conflict with our fellows is based on his analysis of the mechanisms of *sympathy*. In order to see this, it is helpful to remind ourselves of the central role which this principle plays in Hume's moral and political thought. Unlike Hobbes, Hume believes that our sense of morality is based on a direct interest which we take in the feelings of others.[82] Such feelings are conveyed to us by sympathy. We approve of actions, characters, and political and legal arrangements because of a general sympathy for all creatures which resemble ourselves:

the good of society, where our own interest is not concern'd, or that of our friends, pleases only by sympathy: It follows, that sympathy is the source of the esteem, which we pay to all the artificial virtues. (T.577)

However, it is the nature of sympathy itself which also accounts for the fact that we need to invent an artificial virtue like justice. For, as we have seen (p. 208 above), the degree of transfer of feelings by sympathy depends on *the closeness of our relation* to the other person: 'sympathy with persons remote from us [is] much fainter than that with persons near and contiguous' (E.229). As soon as our own interests *or* those of anyone close to us are involved, the very mechanisms of sympathy cause us to disregard the general interest of mankind. Hume thinks that these mechanisms contribute to that 'partiality of our affections' which needs to be remedied by 'judgment and understanding' (T.489). Hume's analysis depends on his general thesis about the control which imagination – or the relations of ideas – exercises over the transference of feeling.

It seems appropriate that we should close this study by suggesting one final way in which a comparison with the writings of the Cartesians can help us to understand Hume's own doctrines. Both Descartes and Malebranche stressed that the passions are beneficial to man. According to Malebranche, the passions 'incline us to love our body and everything which can be useful to its conservation'.[83] He extended this analysis to an account of *sympathy*. He gave a mechanical account of the way in which the cries and facial expressions of a man in terror will agitate in other people 'the same passion with which he is affected' (R. II, 145). The process of sympathy occurs entirely without the will of the person in whom it originates (R. I, 208) and without reason on the part of the person to whom the passion is transferred (R. II, 242). Initially Malebranche used the word 'sympathy' to represent a purely physiological connection between the nerves of the face and certain others which correspond to other places in the body' – a physiological connection with important effects on human behaviour (R. I, 208). At the same time, he claims to be more interested in the effects of this mechanism than in the actual 'springs and relations' of the brain. Malebranche stresses that God has put these invisible connections in men's brains 'in order to maintain the harmony and union *necessary for their conservation*' (R. II, 116–17; my italics). He describes how sympathy brings men spontaneously to the aid of others, or generally allows them to share each other's feelings. In general, the adaptive role of sympathy is in the forefront of all Malebranche's discussions.

While concerns of biological adaptation played an important role in Hume's discussions of the foundations of scientific reasoning in Book I of the *Treatise*, they play little or no role in his discussions of the passions and morals in Books II and III. Hume nowhere stresses the adaptive role of the passions; yet like the Cartesians he wanted to show that they operate in a purely mechanical manner (see p. 211 above). Moreover, he holds that moral sense has no influence on our actions when it conflicts with our own interests. Sympathy does not operate in a way that contributes to social harmony. Hume, unlike Malebranche, argues that sympathy is controlled by the imagination – that is, by the relations of ideas. In contrast to the Cartesians, Hume's major aim is to connect his account of the natural mechanisms of the imagination with the actual behaviour of men in society. When he applies the experimental method to a study of men's social and political behaviour he dispenses with any assumptions concerning the survival value of their natural psychological processes.

Notes

1 T.xvi; see especially the first sentence of the last paragraph on this page, which marks the change in Hume's discussion. For a typical confusion of his concerns see N. Capaldi, *David Hume: the Newtonian Philosopher*, p. 72: 'The method by which Hume plans to achieve his end is the Newtonian experimental method. This, of course, is the science of man.'

2 See, for example, J. Noxon, *Hume's Philosophical Development*, pp. 190–1; and J. Passmore, *Hume's Intentions*, pp. 157–8.

3 The most definitive study of Hume on imagination is still Jan Wilbanks' *Hume's Theory of Imagination*. Wilbanks surveys the main literature on this topic. None of these studies, including that of Wilbanks, considers the sense of the word 'imagination' which was current in Hume's own day. I believe that the main contribution of Wilbanks' study lies in the claim that there is a 'special supposal sense of "imagination" ' (p. 82): 'what is noteworthy about such imaginative acts . . . is that no idea (in Hume's sense of the term) of the entity supposed or imagined to exist is possible' (p. 81). Wilbanks attacks the commonplace that Hume 'ignored the possibility of our imagining (supposing) anything without an accompanying image' (Annis Flew, 'Images, supposing and imagining', cited by Wilbanks, p. 82). As we have seen in Chapters 2 and 3 of the present study, this 'supposal' sense of 'imagination' actually plays a central role in Hume's philosophy. I do not believe that Wilbanks sufficiently recognised the importance of this employment of the imagination.

What one may call, rather loosely, the physiological sense of 'imagination' has been recognised by some writers who take into account the importance of this faculty in eighteenth-century medicine. See, for example, G. S. Rousseau, 'Science and the discovery of the imagination in enlightened England', *Eighteenth Century Studies*, 3 (1969). There is interesting material presented in this article, but Rousseau fails to distinguish the different theories he discusses. Like other writers, he fails to understand the Cartesian roots of many of the accounts of imagination prevalent in England in the early eighteenth century. His conclusion that 'Association and madness were now wedded' (p. 125) seems to be a more accurate description of the manner than the matter of the paragraph in which it occurs! A philosophically more sophisticated account of imagination in seventeenth- and eighteenth-century medicine is given in Lester King, *The Philosophy of Medicine*, Chapter Seven. Hume shared the view of his contemporaries that "tis certain we may feel sickness and pain from the mere force of imagination, and make a malady real by often thinking of it' (T.319).

4 Chambers, *op. cit.* (1728), vol. 2, p. 375. This article, with slight variations, appeared in all editions of the *Cyclopaedia* during Hume's lifetime. In John Harris' *Lexicon Technicum* (1704) the following article appears under 'Imagination': 'Imagination, is an Application of the Mind to the Phantasm or Image of some *Corporeal Thing*, impressed in the Brain.' In the article 'Imagination' in Robert James, *A Medicinal Dictionary* (vol. 2 (1745)) there is no stress on the material nature of the image – only upon the pathological consequences of strong imagination. A general reaction to mechanism in physiology and medicine set in during the 1740s. See Robert Schofield, *Mechanism and Materialism*, esp. pp. 191ff. and the Epilogue to Theodore Brown, *The Mechanical Philosophy and the 'Animal Oeconomy'*, pp. 354ff. At the same time one must recognise that at the end of the decade Hartley and La Mettrie published their most famous books.

5 See esp. §19(*a*) and §19(*c*).

6 The essence of the Cartesian 'imagination' – what clearly distinguishes it from earlier accounts – lies in the claim that it *'is a genuine part of the body*, of sufficient size to allow its different parts to assume various figures in distinctness from each other' (*Regulae* XII, H.R. I, 38; my italics). Descartes' theory of imagination should be contrasted with the scholastic theory where the 'species' communicated to and created by the imagination are immaterial. See L. J. Rather, 'Thomas Fienus' (1567–1631) dialectical investigation of the imagination as cause and cure of bodily disease', *Bulletin of the History of Medicine*, 41 (1967), esp. p. 352. Descartes' own seminal ideas on the corporeal imagination were clearly set out in the *Treatise of Man*, first published posthumously (in Latin) in 1662, but written prior to 1637. A useful English translation was published by T. S. Hall in 1972. For the account of imagination in Descartes see pp. 86ff. of Hall's translation, A.T. XI, pp. 176ff., and my later discussion in §19(*c*).

Malebranche's own philosophical inspiration came in 1664 with his reading of Descartes' *Treatise of Man* (F. Alquié, *Le Cartésianisme de Malebranche*, pp. 24ff.). His own account of imagination is much more elaborate than that of Descartes, but builds on Descartes' scattered remarks in various works. Even more than Descartes, Malebranche provided a vivid mechanical account of the formation of ideas and of their interrelation with the passions.

The significance which eighteenth-century writers found in Malebranche's psychophysiology needs to be studied. La Mettrie says of Malebranche that 'quoiqu'il admette dans l'homme deux substances distinctes, il explique les facultés de l'ame par celles de la matière' (quoted by Aram Vartanian, *La Mettrie's L'Homme Machine*, p. 60); Vartanian also cites an early eighteenth-century manuscript, *L'Ame materielle*, which describes Malebranche's *Recherche* as the best current treatise in physiological psychology (p. 73). It may be more difficult to determine the significance which *English* authors found in the physiological psychology of the *Recherche*: as we have seen, its doctrines are repeated by writers such as Isaac Watts and Bernard de Mandeville, who have entirely different philosophical loyalties.

7   See Henry Pemberton's Introduction to William Cowper's *Myotomia Reformata* (1724), pp. lxxi ff.; and George Cheyne, *The English Malady* (1733), pp. 79ff. The theory was originally suggested in the final 'General Scholium' which Newton appended to the 1713 edition of his *Principia*. The theory is also developed in the Queries to the *Opticks*. Cheyne's rejection of the animal spirit theory is given strong support by Robert James, *A Medicinal Dictionary*, vol. 3 (1745), article entitled 'Spiritus'.

8   *First Lines of Physiology* (Edinburgh, 1786), p. 223, §383. This edition is prepared from an earlier one published by Hume's physician and friend, William Cullen.

9   In the Cartesian theory, the animal spirits were purely physical; they operated in a purely mechanical way. See my 'Hysteria and mechanical man', p. 240. Descartes' modification of the older Galenic theory of 'spirits' is discussed in footnote 128 to T. S. Hall's translation of the *Treatise of Man*. However, from an eighteenth-century point of view *Malebranche* was 'le premier des Philosophes, qui ait mis fort en vogue les esprits animaux' (J. O. La Mettrie, cited by A. Vartanian, *La Mettrie's L'Homme Machine*, p. 60).

10 See Hume's letter to an unknown physican, H.L. I, 14, lines 1 and 12; compare Hume's expression 'Want of Spirits', on p. 13. Hume draws a parallel between his own mental condition and that which he has read about in 'the French Mysticks' whose 'kind of Devotion depends entirely on the Force of Passion, & consequently of the Animal Spirits' (p. 17). Hume attributes his loss of spirits to intense reflections – especially Stoic 'Reflections against Death, & Poverty, & Shame, & Pain, & all the other Calamities of Life'. Hume also reports that another physician has told him he 'had fairly got the *Disease of the Learned*' (p. 14; my italics). Hume's explanation of his condition indicates that he was acquainted with Mandeville's book. Mandeville attributes hypochondria to 'the Waste of Spirits' (p. 212) and stresses that excessive reflection is the most common cause of the disease (pp. 216ff.). Mandeville (who explicitly identifies himself with the physician of his dialogue) tells his patient: 'there is not a Symptom you have labour'd under, that might not with great Ease be accounted for from the Deficiency of the Spirits' (p. 215). I have studied a number of works on hypochondria and hysteria written at this time and find that Mandeville's causal account of the disease is unique. It was Mandeville who used the phrase 'the Disease of the Learned': persons who suffer from the symptoms he discusses 'are oftner Men of Learning, than not insomuch, that the *Passio Hypochondriaca* in High Dutch is call'd *Der Gelahrten Krankheydt*, the Disease of the Learned' (p. 106).

It is not clear that Hume's letter was ever sent, though it was *intended* for a fellow Scotsman, 'a skilful Physician, a man of Letters, of Wit, of Good Sense, & of great Humanity' (H.L. I, 12). The leading candidates have been George Cheyne (see Greig's footnote *ad loc.*) and John Arbuthnot (see E. C. Mossner, 'Hume's epistle to Dr Arbuthnot, 1734: the biographical significance', *Huntington Library Quarterly*, 7 (1944)). However, neither of these physicians would have subscribed to the explanation which Hume gives of his own symptoms. It seems to me far more· important to understand the origins and nature of Hume's own analysis of his ailment than to identify the intended recipient of the letter.

11 *A Treatise of the Hypochondriack and Hysterick Passions* (1711), pp. 125–6 et seq. Of course, Mandeville denies that he is putting forward any hypothesis (see p. 118, for example).

12 *Ibid.*, p. 140. Mandeville had defended a thesis in Leyden in 1689 on the (Cartesian) theory of animal automatism. In the 1711 edition of his *Treatise of the Hypochondriack and Hysterick Passions* Mandeville cites Descartes' principle *'Cogito ergo sum'* in support of the principle that 'matter it self can never think' (p. 124). But he goes on, quite inconsequentially, to say that it 'would be contradictory to human Reason, that when the Body is dead Thought should remain, if from Principles of Religion we were not assured of the Soul's Immortality' (p. 129). In the 1730 edition Mandeville does not draw the consequence from Descartes' first principle that he drew earlier (p. 154) and concludes unequivocally that when we consider 'how absolutely necessary the Brain is, in the Act of Thinking, to such Creatures as we are, it must be . . . contradictory to human Reason, that any Part of Man should continue to think, when his Body is dead and motionless' (p. 159). He can 'as easily conceive the Stars without a Sky, as Memory without a Brain' (p. 160).

13 'The Second Dialogue' consists largely of an attempt of the physician to convince the patient of his explanation *by experience*. Toward the end of the dialogue the patient finally concludes: 'A little while ago I disputed with you, and denied the Existence of animal Spirits; but now again, when I come to reason *a Posteriori*, I think it impossible that there should be none' (1730 ed., p. 215).

14 The importance of models in theoretical explanation in science has been widely recognised by philosophers of science. See, for example, Stephen Toulmin, *The Philosophy of Science, an Introduction*, esp. chapter two; also, Mary B. Hesse, *Models and Analogies in Science*, esp. pp. 157ff. A central thesis of both these authors is that theoretical explanation leads to metaphorical redescription of the phenomena. There is what Hesse calls an 'interaction' between the *explanans* and the *explanandum* which results in a new way of seeing the latter.

15 *Hume's Intentions*, p. 92. Compare James Noxon, *Hume's Philosophical Development*, p. 121: 'His mental psychology has to do with phenomena which are inherently private.' Hume thought

moral science superior to natural science *only* in the sense that its basic concepts do not involve contradictions like those involved in the concept of 'matter': 'What is known' concerning the intellectual world 'agrees with itself', and 'what is unknown, we must be contented to leave so' (T.232).

16   *Hume's Intentions*, p. 43.

17   Hume appears to have drawn upon Aquinas' commentary on Aristotle's *De Memoria et Reminiscentia* in developing his own list of the principles of association at T.10ff.: see J. K. Ryan, 'Aquinas and Hume on the laws of association', *New Scholasticism*, 12 (1938). S. T. Coleridge claimed to have found Hume's copy of Aquinas' work: see *Biographia Literaria*, p. 60.

18   T.xviii. Hume's strongest statement against hypotheses is in the *Abstract* where he claims to talk 'with contempt of hypotheses' (A.646). I have not found any place in the *Treatise* where Hume claims to reject hypotheses *per se*. There is nothing which approaches Newton's *'Hypotheses non fingo'*. But see below, p. 198.

19   James Noxon has put together a partial list of places in the *Treatise* where Hume discusses his 'hypothesis' (*Hume's Philosophical Development*, p. 91).

20   Cf. pp. 103–4 above.

21   T.60. The distinction between 'general causes' and the 'particular explication of them' is made at E.30.

22   Alexandre Koyré, *Newtonian Studies*, pp. 42–3 et seq. Koyré's analysis is based largely on a passage from Newton's 'Theory about Light and Colors', *Philosophical Transactions* No. 80, 19 February 1671/2, which he quotes. According to Koyré (p. 37n.), 'Newton actually includes under the designation "phenomena" not only the data of observation, but also the Keplerian laws of planetary motion'. Hume's passing reference to the theory of light at T.444 appears to capture the essence of the Newtonian theory.

23   J. Passmore, *Hume's Intentions*, p. 43; J. Laird, *Hume's Philosophy of Human Nature*, p. 20; cf. N. Kemp Smith, *The Philosophy of David Hume*, pp. 53ff.

24   Cf. J. Noxon, *Hume's Philosophical Development*, p. 68.

25   'Newton and the method of analysis', *Dictionary of the History of Ideas*, vol. 3, p. 387.

26   *Sir Isaac Newton's Mathematical Principles of Natural Philosophy*, p. xx. Cotes added, of course, that experimental philosophers 'assume nothing as principle, that is not proved by phenomena'.

27   Elie Halévy, *The Growth of Philosophic Radicalism*, p. 6. Halévy's book was originally published in French, 1901–4.

28   E.M.204. However in the same work, Hume claims that the attempt to derive all moral principles from self-love (as in Hobbes and Mandeville) proceeds 'from that love of *simplicity* which has been the source of much false reasoning in philosophy' (E.M.298). This statement against simplicity seems to be at odds with the general tenor of Hume's philosophy, certainly that of the *Treatise*. Of course,

Hume always opposed the selfish hypothesis.

29 *Franklin and Newton*, pp. 106–7.

30 Robert Schofield, *Mechanism and Materialism*, p. 206.

31 Reid thought that Hume had drawn out the inevitable sceptical consequences which result from admitting his 'hypothesis'. See the passage from the Dedication to his *An Inquiry into the Human Mind* quoted Chapter 2, n. 16 above; compare his letter to Hume of 18 March 1763 in *The Works of Thomas Reid, D.D.*, vol. 1, pp. 91–2. Also, chapter 1 of the *Inquiry* itself which was published separately in the *Annual Register* in 1764 under the title 'Essays on the importance of an inquiry into the human mind'.

32 *On the Intellectual Powers of Man*, in *The Works of Thomas Reid, D.D.*, vol. 1, p. 470. Reid thinks that the theory of ideas arises from the belief that, in perception, body must act on mind, or mind on body. This action, he thinks, is conceived on analogy with the transference of motion by impact. He himself claims that 'an object, in being perceived, does not act at all' (p. 301). In his earlier *An Inquiry into the Human Mind*, Reid speaks of the 'picture upon the *retina*' as a '*mean* or *occasion* of my seeing an external object of the same figure and colour in a contrary position, and in a certain direction from the eye' (p. 157; my italics). He stresses that causation is no more that law-like succession. It appears from this passage that Reid holds an occasionalist view of the connection between mind and body – and indeed *all* causal connections (cf. Chapter 4, n. 35 above).

33 'Thomas Reid and the Newtonian turn of British methodological thought', in R. E. Butts and J. W. Davis (eds.), *The Methodological Heritage of Newton*, pp. 103ff.

34 *On the Intellectual Powers of Man*, p. 471.

35 *On the Intellectual Powers of Man*, pp. 250ff.; cf. n. 7 above. In this discussion Reid appears to reject any principle which cannot be verified by direct observation. In *Philosophy, Science, and Sense Perception*, M. Mandelbaum has argued convincingly that Newton did not accept any such methodological rule (pp. 61ff.).

36 To understand Hume's use of this term see §20(*c*).

37 This interpretation is, I think, somewhat surprising in the light of the bulk of the discussion of association in Book I of the *Treatise*; but a careful reading of Hume's original section on association should have prepared us. There, discussing causation, he writes: 'Cousins in the fourth degree are connected by *causation* . . . ; but not so closely as brothers, much less as child and parent' (T.11). See also his discussion of 'power' at T.12. It is very difficult to connect Hume's discussion of these natural relations of causation with his account of the *origin* of that idea in Book I of the *Treatise*. Do we derive the idea of the causal power of the father or the master in the same way as we derive the idea of the causal power of the billiard ball which strikes another?

38 Compare here Locke's use of the word 'conceive' at the end of *Essay* 2, 33, 6, quoted below.

39   In following the posthumous (1777) edition of the *Enquiry*
     Selby-Bigge and Nidditch omit without comment Hume's long
     discussion of critical theory which appeared in the earlier editions.
     My quotation is from G.G. IV, 23n. (see also the editors' note to
     p. 19 and the List of Editions in G.G. III, 85–6). Cf. M. Kallich, *The
     Association of Ideas and Critical Theory in Eighteenth-Century England*,
     especially pp. 74–95.

40   'Of Tragedy', G.G. III, 258ff. The essence of Hume's theory lies in
     his claim about the 'conversion' of painful passions to pleasurable
     ones via the force of the imagination. The theory appears to be
     directly related to that put forward in the Section VI of the
     Dissertation of the Passions (G.G. IV, 162–6). But the conversion of
     passions in 'Of Tragedy' depends on 'the movements of the
     imagination' (p. 264). However, I am not sure I understand how the
     mechanism of association of ideas is supposed to operate here. For
     an enlightening account of Hume's theory see Ralph Cohen, 'The
     transformation of passion: a study of Hume's theories of tragedy',
     Philological Quarterly, 41 (1962).

41   T.284; the passage is from *The Spectator*, No. 412, vol. 3, p. 544. The
     phrase 'the Pleasures of the Imagination' is first used by Addison in
     The Spectator, No. 411, vol. 3, p. 536.

42   In *Spectator* No. 417, vol. 3, pp. 562–3, Addison claims that
     pleasurable scenes 'appear more so upon Reflection, and that the
     Memory heightens the Delightfulness of the Original'. He
     continues: 'A *Cartesian* would account for both these instances in
     the following Manner. The Sett of Ideas, which we received . . .
     having entered the Mind at the same time, have a Sett of Traces
     belonging to them in the Brain, bordering very near upon one
     another; when, therefore, any one of these Ideas arises in the
     Imagination, and consequently dispatches a flow of Animal Spirits
     to its proper Trace, these Spirits, in the violence of their Motion, run
     not only into the Trace to which they were more particularly
     directed, but into several of those that lie about it.' And so on. It is
     curious to find that, in his discussion of this passage in his book *The
     Association of Ideas and Critical Theory in Eighteenth-Century England*,
     M. Kallich goes to such a great deal of trouble to dissociate Addison
     from the Cartesian tradition. At first, 'Addison steps momentarily
     out of the native English tradition when he assigns a "Natural
     Cause" for the successions of ideas'; then Kallich argues that
     Addison could have derived his physiological account from Locke
     anyway (pp. 48–9). I believe Kallich is right, however, in pointing
     out that Addison's account has no direct parallel in Descartes'
     writings. Of course, the important question is not about the origins
     of the theory of the imagination, but about the general
     understanding of that faculty in early eighteenth-century Britain;
     on this point I entirely disagree with Kallich.

43   T.415. The account given in this paragraph is a summary of pp. 8–14
     of Kemp Smith's book.

44 It was Hartley, not Hume, who attempted to apply Newtonian mechanistic conceptions to the study of man. In Chapter 4 n. 41, above, I have suggested one way in which the difference between the models employed by these two philosophers might be crucial.

45 'Il y a presque tousjours deux sortes de mouvemens que procedent de chaque action: sçavoir les exterieurs, qui servent à poursuivre les choses desirables, ou à eviter les nuisibles; & les interieurs, qu'on nomme . . . *les passions.*' Descartes also speaks of the mechanism operating in response to external stimuli in such a way as to produce 'mouvemens convenables' (*Treatise of Man,* A.T. XI, 193; cf. Hall translation, pp. 105–6). Compare *The Passions of the Soul,* Art. 13, (H.R. I, 337–8). Descartes' general position on final causes is expressed in his *Principles of Philosophy* I, 28 (H.R. I, 230).

46 Herbert Butterfield in his book *The Whig Interpretation of History* described 'the tendency in many historians . . . to praise revolutions provided they have been successful, to emphasise certain principles of progress in the past and to produce a story which is the ratification if not the glorification of the present' (p. v). Hume, of course, was among the first – in his history of Charles I – to try to debunk the Whig manner of doing history. There is incredible irony in the fact that his philosophy has so universally been employed to justify this or that twentieth-century philosophy. I have quoted one of Hume's best maxims against Whig historiography on p. 10 above. Kemp Smith, of course, is far less guilty of the vice described here than are most twentieth-century commentators on Hume.

47 It seems to me that there is a continuity between the ideas expressed in Kemp Smith's *Prolegomena to an Idealist Theory of Knowledge* (1924) and those given expression by A. N. Whitehead (for example) in *Modes of Thought* (1938). In his book Kemp Smith claimed that 'in endowing man with those instinctive emotional needs which finally develop into intellectual curiosity [Nature] also contrived to provide him with the necessary driving power that enables her . . . to make her revelation of herself to him more and more complete' (p. 232). In his later book Whitehead argued that seventeenth-century physics had mistakenly sought to found its conception of reality on passive sensa and that modern physics is now in a position to recognise that nature itself is most directly apprehended in our inner active feelings of value and worth (*op. cit.,* pp. 153–9). My suspicion is that Kemp Smith may have seen Hume as an early opponent of the mechanistic passive view of nature, and a forerunner of the sort of idealism embraced by himself and Whitehead.

48 G.G. IV, 166; my italics. J. Noxon states that Hume concludes the *Dissertation* by saying that its purpose 'is simply to show that the *experimental method* can be applied to the psychology of the emotions' (*Hume's Philosophical Development,* p. 189; my italics)! This is a complete fabrication. Noxon also claims that Hume has lost interest in the psychology of the emotions in 1757: the

Dissertation is 'a sparse, dry abstract of Book II of the *Treatise*'. In fact, Hume took a great interest in the psychology of the emotions during this period, particularly in relation to critical theory. The *Dissertation* is closely related to two papers published along with it – 'Of Tragedy' and 'Of the Standard of Taste'. The work in which they appeared – *Four Dissertations* – was prefaced by a dedication 'To the Reverend Mr. Hume, Author of "Douglas," a Tragedy' (G.G. IV, 439). At this time, Hume was involved in the controversies surrounding his friend John Home's play (Hume intentionally misspells his name in the dedication). As Cohen has shown (see n. 40 above), Hume's contemporaries and successors took some interest in the theory of the emotions which underlay his explanation of the pleasure of tragedy.

The only *explicit* references to the animal spirit physiology which I have found in the *Dissertation of the Passions* are in §VI, though the mechanisms described are essentially the same as those in the *Treatise*. On p. 165 Hume clearly employs the Cartesian theory of memory. Hume refers to the 'principles or internal mechanism, which we here explain' (p. 155): he certainly leaves his reader in no doubt about the *general* nature of the principles which he is describing.

49 *Essay* 2, 1, 23. After quoting this passage and one from Malebranche, John Laird claims that Hume 'officially . . . renounced all the physical implications of "impressions" ' though sometimes (for example, when one reads the *first page* of the *Treatise*!) 'it is hard to acquit him of an unconscious betrayal of pure phenomenalism' (*Hume's Philosophy of Human Nature*, p. 27). Laird presents very good evidence *against* his own interpretation of Hume as a phenomenalist.

Some commentators have seen evidence that Hume does not identify impressions with neural motions in his claim that we have no argument to decide between competing theories concerning the origin of impressions – including Descartes' theory that they arise immediately from the creative power of the mind or Malebranche's theory that they arise from God himself (T.84; E.153). But, of course, this claim must be understood in the light of Hume's general doctrine that fundamental beliefs cannot be based solely on reason and argument. In these discussions Hume is concerned with the question of whether external objects can be said to be the source of our sensible perceptions; it is not clear how that discussion relates to the one we are concerned with here.

50 Article on 'Imagination' (*Cyclopaedia*, vol. 1, p. 375; my italics). In his article on 'Impressions' Chambers also discusses the Peripatetic theory that 'Bodies emit Species resembling them' and that these '*Impressions*, or impress'd Species, being material and sensible, are render'd intelligible by the active Intellect' (p. 378).

51 T.1, cf. E.18: 'Let us . . . call [our lively perceptions] *Impressions*; employing that word in a sense somewhat different from the usual.

By the term *impression*, then, I mean all our more lively perceptions, when we hear, or see, or feel, or love, or hate, or desire, or will.'

52 In Article 27 of *The Passions of the Soul*, Descartes actually *defined* the passions as perceptions 'which are caused, maintained and fortified by some movement of the spirits' (H.R. I, 344). At the beginning of Book V of the *Recherche* Malebranche writes: 'Here I call *passions* all the emotions which the soul naturally feels on the occasion of extraordinary movements of the animal spirits' (R. II, 127). In both cases the cause is clearly considered part of the meaning of the term 'passion', though the actual relation between the cause and the passion may be different.

The close link which Hume conceived between the passions and agitation of the animal spirits is vividly portrayed in his letter to a physician, where, as we have seen in note 10 of this chapter, he spoke of dependence 'on the Force of Passion, & consequently of the Animal Spirits'. See also p. 214 above.

53 'Every one of himself will readily perceive the difference betwixt feeling and thinking. The common *degrees* of these are easily distinguished; tho' it is not impossible . . . they may very nearly approach to each other' (T.1–2, my italics). Compare: 'We may divide all the perceptions of the mind into two classes . . . which are distinguished by their different *degrees* of force and vivacity' (E.18; my italics).

54 'Les sens & l'imagination ne différent que du plus & du moins' (R. I, 192). I here follow the translation given by Chambers in his article on 'Imagination'. But in their recent English translation of the *Recherche* Lennon and Olscamp translate this passage using the same word employed by Hume in the passages cited in n. 53: 'the senses and imagination differ only in degree' (p. 88).

55 R. I, 191–2. In a general comparison of Hume and Malebranche on sensation it is important to bear in mind that Hume *criticised* Malebranche's criterion of forcefulness: he argued that it was not a *sufficient* criterion for belief in external existence (see pp. 60ff. above). But this difference is not relevant in the context of the present discussion.

56 The title of Part III of Book II is 'Of the contagious communication of strong imaginations' (R. I, 320).

57 R. I, 275. Compare here Descartes' *Treatise of Man*: The spirits 'trace figures [in a certain part of the brain] which correspond to those of the objects; not, however, as easily nor as perfectly as the first blow on the gland . . . , but little by little, more and more according as their action is stronger or lasts longer or *it is repeated many times*' (A.T. XI, 177–8; my italics).

58 William Porterfield, 'An Essay concerning the motions of our eyes', in *Medical Essays and Observations*, second edition (1737), vol. 4, p. 213–14. Porterfield's theory was discussed by his contemporaries, including Robert Whytt and Richard Mead. I plan to discuss Porterfield's theory and its significance for his

contemporaries in a future publication. These essays, which were published by the Philosophical Society of Edinburgh, were already in their third edition (1747) when Hume first published his *Enquiry*.

59　But compare Descartes' *Treatise of Man*, A.T. XI, 178–9. Coleridge must have recognised the origin of accounts of association such as that of Locke: he writes of the theory of 'nervous or animal spirits, where . . . fluids . . . *etch and re-etch* engravings on the brain (as [in] *the followers of Des Cartes* and the humoral pathologists in general)' (*Biographia Literaria*, pp. 58–9; my italics). Nineteenth-century historians of association like Coleridge and Sir William Hamilton (see *The Works of Thomas Reid, D.D.*, vol. 2, pp. 893ff.) self-consciously attempted to undermine earlier mechanistic conceptions of this principle. It is astonishing to see the way their propaganda is continued in twentieth-century historical accounts of association.

60　A.T. XI, 177.

61　*Treatise of Man*, trans. Hall, p. 92, n. 140; cf. Descartes' definition of idea on p. 87 (A.T. XI, 177); cf. also my 'Hysteria and mechanical man', p. 245, n. 73.

62　A.T. XI, 178.

63　There is surely something very odd about Hume's identification of the impression as a 'propensity'. In an important sense his original conception of 'impression' breaks down here: the 'impression' which causes the idea is not in itself forceful. The forcefulness which is the source of the idea is the result of constant repetition. In his *Enquiry* Hume identifies the impression with the 'customary transition of the imagination'. An impression is not a single event with a property of 'forcefulness'; rather it is composed of a series of events which have the same result as such a single event.

64　H.R. I, 144; cf. *Discourse on Method*, H.R. I, 87ff.

65　Descartes' explicit use of the phrase 'la nature de l'homme, en tant qu'il est composé de l'esprit et du corps' is toward the end of Meditation VI (A.T. IX, 70; cf. H.R. I, 198). However it is implicit from the point in the Meditation where he distinguishes 'la nature, considerée en general' from 'ma nature en particulier' (A.T. IX, 64; cf. H.R. I, 192). The discussion in the second half of Meditation VI is about the sense in which one can rely on 'my nature' as a teacher of what is true.

66　See G. Rodis-Lewis, 'Le domaine propre de l'homme chez les Cartésiens', *Journal of the History of Philosophy*, 2 (1964), pp. 158–9: 'il nous semble que l'union de l'âme et du corps, malgré les difficultés pour la conceptualiser, et les divergences des successeurs de Descartes pour en rendre compte, délimite dans le Cartésianisme la sphère originale d'une "anthropologie," en tant que celle-ci vise "l'étude du composé humain considéré dans son unité".'

67　A.T. IX, 69–70; cf. H.R. I, 197.

68　Art. 50, H.R. I, 355; cf. Arts. 34–5, H.R. I, 347.

69　*La Dioptrique*, A.T. VI, 141.

70　H.R. I, 193. Descartes attempts an account of how such habits are formed in *Principles of Philosophy* I, 71 (H.R. I, 249–50).

71 See p. 75 above.

72 It is curious that the connection between the doctrines of natural judgement in Hume and Malebranche was never discussed by Kemp Smith, who clearly knew Malebranche's theory well (see chapter 2, n. 35 above). However, the connection was made by C. W. Doxsee in 'Hume's relation to Malebranche', *Philosophical Review*, 25 (1916), pp. 706–10: Doxsee adopted Kemp Smith's view about the importance of 'natural belief' in Hume's writings.

73 The development of Malebranche's view is discussed by G. Rodis-Lewis in 'Le domaine propre de l'homme chez les Cartésiens', pp. 174–7. Compare F. Alquié, *Le Cartésianisme de Malebranche*, pp. 167ff. and E. Brehier, 'Les "jugements naturels" chez Malebranche' in *Malebranche: recueil publiée par la Revue Philosophique* (1938).

74 T.96–7n.; cf. R. I, 49–50. Malebranche summarised his view by saying that 'the *operations* of the understanding are *only pure perceptions*' (R. I, 50). His doctrine was strongly supported in Chambers' *Cyclopaedia*: see, for example, the article 'Reasoning'.

75 See Art. 136 (H.R. I, 391). Also my 'Hysteria and mechanical man', pp. 241, 244–5.

76 Cf. Malebranche's claim that 'ces jugemens sont tres-faux en eux-mêmes, quoique fort utiles à la conservation de la vie. Car nos sens ne nous instruisent que pour nôtre corps, & tous les jugemens libres qui sont conformes aux jugemens des sens, sont tres-éloignez de la verité' (R. I, 158–9).

77 Beattie defines common sense as 'that power of the mind which perceives truth . . . by an instantaneous and instinctive impulse; derived neither from education nor from habit, but from nature; acting independently on our will' (*Essay on the Nature and Immutability of Truth, in Opposition to Sophistry and Scepticism*, p. 26). In an important article David Norton has argued that, unlike his Scottish critics, Hume 'does not . . . go so far as to say that what we must naturally *believe* must naturally be *true*'. Norton points out that the epistemological conceptions of writers like Beattie and Reid are based on a theological doctrine: on their view 'our natural faculties . . . are God-given, are part of the overall design of a *providential* nature, and can be trusted implicitly. What we *naturally* believe is in fact *supernaturally* guaranteed' ('Hume and his Scottish critics', in D. F. Norton *et al.* (eds.), *McGill Hume Studies*, pp. 317–18).

78 Contrast Reid's view of the relation between reason and natural instinct: 'It is absurd to conceive that there can be any opposition between reason and common sense' (*On the Intellectual Powers of Man*, p. 425). Reid rejects Descartes' view that we can set up reason as a separate faculty which can judge the veracity of our other faculties (see p. 319, n. 23 of Norton's article and L. Marcil-Lacoste, 'Dieu, garant de véracité ou Reid critique de Descartes', *Dialogue*, 14 (1975)).

As we saw in Chapter 1, Hume opposed Descartes' view that

reason itself can establish any truths. However he never undermined what we may call the 'critical role of reason'. Indeed, it is reason – the 'comparison, and discovery of those relations . . . which two objects bear to each other' (T.73) – which is the source of scepticism. The same faculty serves as a corrective to natural belief.

79 H.L. I, 33.
80 T.484; cf. E.304. The passage at T.484 may, in fact, have been written in response to Hutcheson's letter. Hume acknowledges that there is a sense of the word 'natural' – not the sense on which he based his distinction between natural and artificial virtues – in which justice is natural. The *other sense* of the word which Hume talks about here may well be the sense that Hutcheson proposed. But it is important to recognise that that is *not* the sense which Hume employs when he claims to found the sciences on *natural* principles. Compare Hume's discussion at T.474–5 and E.307–8, n. 2. The discussion is further complicated by the fact that Hume appears to consider a society which promotes private property to be one which is most in accord with *natural principles*. For example, he claims that Rome and other ancient republics were supported on principles somewhat more 'natural' than those of Sparta ('Of Commerce', G.G. III, 291). We need a systematic study of the uses of the word 'natural' in Hume's philosophy. I certainly cannot claim to have exhausted the topic here, but I hope that I have made a useful beginning.
81 *Leviathan*, Part 1, esp. Chapter 13.
82 *Leviathan*, pp. 215ff. For Hobbes the laws of morality are conclusions which men arrive at by reason: they are 'Conclusions . . . concerning what conduceth to the conservation and defence of themselves' (p. 217).
83 R. II, 128; compare Art. 52 of Descartes' *Passions of the Soul*.

List of works cited

Addison, Joseph. *The Spectator*, numbers 411, 412, and 417, in *The Spectator*, volume 3, edited by Donald F. Bond. Oxford: Clarendon Press, 1965.

Alexander, H. G. (editor). *The Leibniz–Clarke Correspondence, together with extracts from Newton's 'Principia' and 'Opticks'*. Manchester: Manchester University Press, 1956.

Alquié, Ferdinand. *Le Cartésianisme de Malebranche*. Paris: Vrin, 1974.

Anderson, Robert Fendel. *Hume's First Principles*. Lincoln: University of Nebraska Press, 1966.

—'The location, extension, shape, and size of Hume's perceptions', in *Hume: a Re-evaluation*, edited by D. W. Livingston and James T. King, pp. 153–71. New York: Fordham University Press, 1976.

Anderson, Wallace E. 'Cartesian motion', in *Motion and Time, Space and Matter*, edited by Peter K. Machamer and Robert G. Turnbull, pp. 200–23. Columbus: Ohio State University Press, 1976.

Armstrong, David M. *Perception and the Physical World*. London: Routledge & Kegan Paul, 1961.

Arnauld, Antoine. *Des Vraies et des Fausses Idées* (1683), in *Oeuvres de Messire Antoine Arnauld*, volume 38. Paris: Sigismond D'Ainay, 1780; reprinted Brussels: Culture et Civilization, 1967.

—et Nicole, Pierre. *La Logique ou L'Art de Penser*, introduction de Louis Marin. Paris: Flammarion, 1970.

—*The Art of Thinking*, translated by James Dickoff and Patricia James. Indianapolis: Bobbs-Merrill, 1964.

Ayer, Alfred J. *The Problem of Knowledge*. London: Macmillan, 1956.

Ayers, Michael. 'Analytical philosophy and the history of philosophy', in Jonathan Rée, Michael Ayers, and Adam Westoby, *Philosophy and its Past*, pp. 41–66. Hassocks, Sussex: Harvester Press, 1978.

Barrow, Isaac. *The Usefulness of Mathematical Learning Explained and Demonstrated: Being Mathematical Lectures Read in the Publick Schools at the University of Cambridge*, translated by John Kirkby. London: Stephen Austen, 1734; reprinted London: Cass, 1970.

Bayle, Pierre. *Oeuvres Diverses*. 4 volumes. The Hague: P. Husson, 1727–31; reprinted Hildesheim: Georg Olms, 1966.

—*The Dictionary Historical and Critical of Mr. Peter Bayle*, translated and edited by Pierre Des Maizeaux, 2nd edition. 5 volumes, London: J. J. and P. Knapton et al., 1734–8.

—*Historical and Critical Dictionary: Selections*, translated and edited by Richard H. Popkin and Craig Brush. Indianapolis: Bobbs-Merrill, 1965.

✓ Beattie, James. *Essay on the Nature and Immutability of Truth, in Opposition to Sophistry and Scepticism*, in *Essays*. Edinburgh: Wm. Creech, 1776.

✓ Beck, Lewis White. 'A Prussian Hume and a Scottish Kant', in *McGill Hume Studies*, edited by David Fate Norton, Nicholas Capaldi, and Wade L. Robison, pp. 63–78. San Diego: Austin Hill Press, 1979.

Berkeley, George. *The Works*, edited by A. A. Luce and T. E. Jessop. 9 volumes. Edinburgh: Nelson, 1948–57.

Berman, David. 'An early essay concerning Berkeley's immaterialism', *Hermathena*, 109 (1969), pp. 37–43.

Boerhaave, Hermann. *Dr. Boerhaave's Academical Lectures on the Theory of Physic, Being a Genuine Translation of his Institutes, and Explanatory Commentary*, Volume 5. London: J. Rivington *et al.*, 1757.

Boyer, Carl B. *The History of the Calculus and Its Conceptual Development* (formerly *The Concepts of the Calculus: a Critical and Historical Discussion of the Derivative and the Integral*, 1939). Reissued under the new title, New York: Dover, 1959.

Brehier, E. 'Les "jugements naturels" chez Malebranche', in *Malebranche: Recueil Publié par la 'Revue Philosophique'*, pp. 14–22. Paris: Librairie Félix Alcan, 1938.

Brown, Theodore. *The Mechanical Philosophy and the 'Animal Oeconomy'*. New York: Arno Press, 1981.

Buchdahl, Gerd. *Metaphysics and the Philosophy of Science*. Oxford: Blackwell, 1959.

Butterfield, Herbert. *The Whig Interpretation of History*. London: G. Bell, 1931.

Capaldi, Nicholas. *David Hume: The Newtonian Philosopher*. Boston: Twayne, 1975.

Carnap, Rudolf. *Philosophy and Logical Syntax*. London: Kegan Paul, 1935.

Chambers, Ephraim. *Cyclopaedia: or, an Universal Dictionary of Arts and Sciences*. 2 volumes. London: James and John Knapton *et al.*, 1728.

—*Cyclopaedia: or, an Universal Dictionary of Arts and Sciences*, 2nd edition, corrected and amended, with some additions. 2 volumes. London: D. Midwinter *et al.*, 1738.

Cheyne, George. *The English Malady: or, a Treatise of Nervous Diseases of all Kinds*. London: G. Strahan and J. Leake, 1733; reprinted New York: Scholars' Facsimiles and Reprints, 1976.

—*An Essay on Regimen, together with Five Discourses, Medical, Moral, and Philosophical*, 2nd edition. London: C. Rivington and J. Leake, 1740.

Chisholm, Roderick M. *Theory of Knowledge*, second edition. Englewood Cliffs, New Jersey: Prentice-Hall, 1977.

Church, Ralph Withington. 'Malebranche and Hume', *Revue Internationale de Philosophie*, 1 (1938), 143–61.

—*A Study in the Philosophy of Malebranche*. London: G. Allen & Unwin, 1931.

Cohen, I. Bernard. *Franklin and Newton*. Cambridge, Mass.: Harvard University Press, 1966.

Cohen, Ralph. 'The transformation of passion: a study of Hume's theories of tragedy', *Philological Quarterly*, 41 (1962), 450–64.

Coleridge, Samuel Taylor. *Biographia Literaria: or Biographical Sketches of my Literary Life and Opinions*, edited by George Watson. London: Dent, 1956; reprinted with additions and corrections, 1965.

Collier, Arthur. *Clavis Universalis: or, a New Inquiry after Truth. Being a Demonstration of the Non-Existence, or Impossibility, of an External World*. London: Robert Gosling, 1713.

Collins, Antony. *A Philosophical Inquiry Concerning Human Liberty*. 2nd edn. London: R. Robinson, 1717. Reprinted in *Determinism and Free Will: Anthony Collins' 'A Philosophical Inquiry Concerning Human Liberty'*, edited by J. O'Higgins. The Hague: Nijhoff, 1976.

Cordemoy, Gerauld de. *Oeuvres Philosophiques*, edited by Pierre Clair and François Girbal. Paris: Presses Universitaires de France, 1968.

Cotes, Roger. 'Preface to the Second Edition', *Sir Isaac Newton's Mathematical Principles of Natural Philosophy and his System of the World*, translated by Andrew Motte, translation revised and edited by Florian Cajori. 2 volumes. Berkeley: University of California Press, 1934; reprinted New York: Greenwood Press, 1969.

Cowper, William. *Myotomia Reformata: or, an Anatomical Treatise on the Muscles of the Human Body . . . to which is prefix'd an introduction concerning muscular motion*, edited by Richard Mead, assisted by Joseph Tanner, James Jurin and Henry Pemberton. London: R. Knaplock *et al.*, 1724.

Cudworth, Ralph. *The True Intellectual System of the Universe*. London: Richard Royston, 1678; reprinted Stuttgart-Bad Cannstatt: Friedrich Frommann, 1964.

Descartes, René. *Oeuvres*, edited by Charles Adam and Paul Tannery. New edition, C.N.R.S. 12 volumes. Paris: Vrin, 1973.

—*Philosophical Letters*, translated and edited by Anthony Kenny. Oxford: Clarendon Press, 1970.

—*The Philosophical Works*, translated by Elizabeth S. Haldane and G. R. T. Ross. 2 volumes. Cambridge: Cambridge University Press, 1911; reprinted with corrections, 1931.

—*Treatise of Man*, translated by Thomas Steele Hall. Cambridge, Mass.: Harvard University Press, 1972.

Diderot, Denis. *Lettre sur les Aveugles*, in *Oeuvres Philosophiques de Diderot*, edited by Paul Vernière. Paris: Garnier, 1964.

Dobbs, Betty Jo Teeter. *The Foundations of Newton's Alchemy, or 'The*

Hunting of the Green Lyon'. Cambridge: Cambridge University Press, 1975.

Donovan, A. L. *Philosophical Chemistry in the Scottish Englightenment*. Edinburgh: Edinburgh University Press, 1975.

Doxsee, C. W. 'Hume's relation to Malebranche', *Philosophical Review*, 25 (1916), 692–710.

Ellenberger, François. 'La thèse de doctorat de James Hutton et la renovation perpetuelle du monde', *Annales Guebhard*, 49 (1973), 497–533.

Emerson, Roger L. 'The Philosophical Society of Edinburgh, 1737–1747', *British Journal for the History of Science*, 12 (1979), 154–91.

—'The Philosophical Society of Edinburgh, 1748–1768', *British Journal for the History of Science*, 14 (1981), 133–76.

Ferguson, James P. *Dr. Samuel Clarke: an Eighteenth Century Heretic*. Kineton: Roundwood Press, 1976.

Flew, Antony. *Hume's Philosophy of Belief*. London: Routledge & Kegan Paul, 1961.

Fontenelle, Bernard de. *Doutes sur la Système Physique des Causes Occasionelles*, in *Fontenelle: Oeuvres Complètes*, volume 1, edited by G. B. Depping. Paris, 1818; reprinted Geneva: Slatkine, 1968.

Gay, John, Pope, Alexander, and Arbuthnot, John. *Three Hours After Marriage: a Comedy*, in *A Supplement to the Works of Alexander Pope, Esq*. Dublin: W. Whitestone, 1758; reprinted by the Augustan Reprint Society, with an introduction by John H. Smith. Los Angeles: Wm. Andrews Clark Memorial Library, 1961.

Guerlac, Henry. 'Newton and the method of analysis', in *Dictionary of the History of Ideas*, edited by Philip P. Wiener, volume 3, pp. 378–91. New York: Scribner's, 1973.

Halévy, Elie. *The Growth of Philosophic Radicalism*, translated by Mary Morris, new edition. London: Faber & Faber, 1934.

Hall, Roland. 'Hume's actual use of Berkeley's *Principles*', *Philosophy*, 43 (1968), 278–80.

Haller, Albrecht von (Albertus). *First Lines of Physiology*, translated from the correct Latin edition printed under the inspection of William Cullen. 2 volumes. Edinburgh, 1786; reprinted New York: Johnson, 1966.

Hamilton, Sir William. 'Contribution towards a history of the doctrine of mental suggestion or association', Note D to Volume 2, *The Works of Thomas Reid, D.D.*, 8th edition. Edinburgh: Maclachlan & Stewart, 1880.

Hare, R. M. 'Theology and falsification: a symposium', with A. Flew and B. Mitchell, in *New Essays in Philosophical Theology*, edited by Antony Flew and Alasdair MacIntyre. London: SCM Press, 1955.

Harris, John. *Lexicon Technicum: or, a Universal English Dictionary of Arts and Sciences*. London, 1704; reprinted London: Cass, 1971.

Hartley, David. *Observations on Man, his Frame, his Duty, and his Expectations*. 2 volumes. London: S. Richardson, 1749.

Hatfield, Gary. 'Force (God) in Descartes' physics', *Studies in the History and Philosophy of Science*, 10 (1979), 113–40.

Heimann, Peter M. ' "Nature is a perpetual worker": Newton's aether and eighteenth-century natural philosophy', *Ambix*, 20 (1973), 1–25.

—'Voluntarism and immanence: conceptions of nature in eighteenth-century thought', *Journal of the History of Ideas*, 39 (1978), 271–83.

Hearne, Thomas K. ' "General rules" in Hume's *Treatise*', *Journal of the History of Philosophy*, 8 (1970), 405–22.

Hendel, Charles W. *Studies in the Philosophy of David Hume*. Princeton: Princeton University Press, 1925.

Hesse, Mary B. *Models and Analogies in Science*. Notre Dame: University of Notre Dame Press, 1966.

Hobbes, Thomas. *Leviathan*, edited by C. B. Macpherson. Harmondsworth: Penguin, 1968.

Home, Henry (Lord Kames). *Essays on the Principles of Morality and Natural Religion*, second edition. London: C. Hitch *et al.*, 1758; reprinted Hildesheim: Georg Olms, 1976.

—'Of the laws of motion', in *Essays and Observations, Physical and Literary*, edited by David Hume and Alexander Munro, pp. 1–69. Edinburgh: G. Hamilton and J. Balfour, 1754.

Hume, David. *An Abstract of a Book Lately Published, Entituled, a Treatise of Human Nature, &c.: Wherein the Chief Argument of that Book is farther Illustrated and Explained*, reprinted in *A Treatise of Human Nature*, edited by L. A. Selby-Bigge, 2nd edition, revised by P. H. Nidditch. Oxford: Clarendon Press, 1978.

—*Dialogues Concerning Natural Religion*, edited by Norman Kemp Smith. 2nd edition. Edinburgh: Nelson, 1947.

—*Enquiries Concerning Human Understanding and Concerning the Principles of Morals*, edited by L. A. Selby-Bigge. 3rd edition, revised by P. H. Nidditch. Oxford: Clarendon Press, 1975.

—*Essais Philosophiques sur l'Entendement Humain*, in *Oeuvres Philosophiques de Mr. D. Hume*, volume 1. Amsterdam: J. H. Schneider, 1758.

—*A Letter from a Gentleman to his Friend in Edinburgh*, Edinburgh, 1745; reprinted with an introduction by Ernest C. Mossner and John V. Price. Edinburgh: Edinburgh University Press, 1967.

—*The History of England from the Invasion of Julius Caesar to the Revolution in 1688*, abridged by Rodney W. Kilcup. Chicago: University of Chicago Press, 1975.

—*The Letters of David Hume*, edited by J. Y. T. Greig. 2 volumes. Oxford: Clarendon Press, 1932.

—*Philosophical Essays Concerning Human Understanding*, 2nd edition. London: A. Millar, 175.

—*Philosophical Essays Concerning Human Understanding*, 2nd edition. Volume 2 of *Essays and Treatises on Several Subjects*. London: A. Millar, 1753.

—*Philosophical Essays Concerning Human Understanding*, 3rd edition. Volume 2 of *Essays and Treatises on Several Subjects*. London: A. Millar, 1756.

—*The Philosophical Works*, edited by Thomas H. Green and Thomas H. Grose. 4 volumes. London: 1882–6; reprinted Aalen: Scientia Verlag, 1964.

—*A Treatise of Human Nature*, edited by L. A. Selby-Bigge, 2nd edition, revised by P. H. Nidditch. Oxford: Clarendon Press, 1978.

—and Munro, Alexander (editors). *Essays and Observations, Physical and Literary, Read before a Society in Edinburgh, and published by them*, volume 1. Edinburgh: G. Hamilton & J. Balfour, 1754.

Hurlbutt, Robert H. *Hume, Newton, and the Design Argument*. Lincoln: University of Nebraska Press, 1965.

Huxley, Thomas H. *Hume*, new edition. London: Macmillan, 1887.

James, Robert. *A Medicinal Dictionary*. 3 volumes. London: T. Osborne, 1743–5.

Kallich, Martin. *The Association of Ideas and Critical Theory in Eighteenth-Century England*. The Hague: Mouton, 1970.

Kant, Immanuel. *Groundwork of the Metaphysic of Morals*, in *The Moral Law*, translated and edited by H. J. Paton, 3rd edition. London: Hutchinson, 1956.

—*Prolegomena to any Future Metaphysics*, translated by P. Carus, translation revised and edited by Lewis White Beck. Indianapolis: Bobbs-Merrill, 1950.

—*Critique of Pure Reason*, translated by Norman Kemp Smith. London: Macmillan, 1929.

Kemp Smith, Norman. *A Commentary to Kant's Critique of Pure Reason*. London: Macmillan, 1923.

—'Malebranche's theory of the perception of distance and magnitude', *British Journal of Psychology*, 1 (1905), 191–204.

—'The naturalism of Hume', *Mind*, 14 (1905), 149–73 and 335–47.

—*New Studies in the Philosophy of Descartes*. London: Macmillan, 1953.

—*The Philosophy of David Hume: a Critical Study of its Origins and Central Doctrines*. London: Macmillan, 1941.

—*Prolegomena to an Idealist Theory of Knowledge*. London: Macmillan, 1924.

King, Lester. *The Philosophy of Medicine: the Early Eighteenth Century*. Cambridge, Mass.: Harvard University Press, 1978.

Koyré, Alexandre. *Newtonian Studies*. Chicago: University of Chicago Press, 1968.

Kozanecki, Tadeusz. 'Dawida Hume'a Nieznane Listy W Zbiorach Muzeum Czartoryskich (Polska)', *Archiwum Historii Filozofii I Mysli Spolecznej*, 9 (1963), 127–39.

La Mettrie, Julien Offray de. *La Mettrie's 'L'Homme machine': a Study in the Origins of an Idea*, edited with an introductory monograph by Aram

Vartanian. Princeton: Princeton University Press, 1960.

Laird, John. *Hume's Philosophy of Human Nature*. London: Methuen, 1932.

Laudan, L. L. 'Thomas Reid and the Newtonian turn of British methodological thought', in *The Methodological Heritage of Newton*, edited by Robert E. Butts and John W. Davis, pp. 103–31. Oxford: Blackwell, 1970.

Leland, John. *A View of the Principal Deistical Writers that have appeared in England in the Last and Present Century*, 2nd edition. 2 volumes. London: B. Dod, 1755.

Lennon, Thomas M. 'Occasionalism and the Cartesian metaphysic of motion', *Canadian Journal of Philosophy*, supplementary volume 1, part 1 (1974), pp. 29–40.

—'Philosophical Commentary', in N. Malebranche, *The Search after Truth*, translated by Thomas M. Lennon and Paul J. Olscamp, pp. 755–848. Columbus: Ohio State University Press, 1980.

Livingston, Donald W. 'Hume on ultimate causation', *American Philosophical Quarterly*, 8 (1971), 63–70.

—and King, James T. (editors). *Hume: a Re-evaluation*. New York: Fordham University Press, 1976.

Locke, John. *An Essay Concerning Human Understanding*, edited by Peter H. Nidditch. Oxford: Clarendon Press, 1975; reprinted with corrections, 1979.

Luce, A. A. *Berkeley and Malebranche: a Study in the Origins of Berkeley's Thought*. Oxford: Clarendon Press, 1934.

Mach, Ernst. *The Science of Mechanics*, translated by Thomas J. McCormack, 6th edition. La Salle, Ill.: Open Court, 1960.

Machamer, Peter K. and Turnbull, Robert G. (editors). *Motion and Time, Space and Matter*. Columbus: Ohio State University Press, 1976.

Maclaurin, Colin. *An Account of Sir Isaac Newton's Philosophical Discoveries*. London: A. Millar *et al.*, 1748.

Macnabb, D. G. C. *David Hume: his Theory of Knowledge and Morality*, 2nd edition. Oxford: Blackwell, 1966.

Malebranche, Nicolas. *Entretiens sur la Métaphysique et sur la Religion*, edited by André Robinet. *Oeuvres de Malebranche*, edited by André Robinet, volume 12, 2nd edition. Paris: Vrin, 1976.

—*Oeuvres Complètes*, edited by André Robinet. 20 volumes in 18. Paris: Vrin, 1958–68.

—*The Search after Truth*, translated by Thomas M. Lennon and Paul J. Olscamp. Columbus: Ohio State University Press, 1980.

Mandelbaum, Maurice. *Philosophy, Science, and Sense Perception*. Baltimore: Johns Hopkins Press, 1964.

Mandeville, Bernard de. *A Treatise of the Hypochondriack and Hysterick Passions . . . in Three Dialogues*. London: D. Leach & W. Taylor, 1711.

—*A Treatise of the Hypochondriack and Hysterick Diseases . . . in Three Dialogues*, 2nd edition, corrected and enlarged by the author. London:

J. Tonson, 1730; reprinted New York: Scholars' Facsimiles and Reprints, 1976.

Marcil-Lacoste, Louise. 'Dieu garant de véracité ou Reid critique de Descartes', *Dialogue*, 14 (1975), 584–605.

Martin, C. B., and Armstrong, D. M. (editors). *Locke and Berkeley*. New York: Doubleday, 1968.

[Martine, George]. *An Examination of the Newtonian Argument for the Emptiness of Space and of the Resistance of Subtile Fluids*. London: T. Cooper, 1740.

Mattern, R. M. 'Locke on active power and the obscure idea of active power from bodies', *Studies in the History and Philosophy of Science*, 11 (1980), 39–77.

McGuire, J. E. 'Force, active principles, and Newton's invisible realm', *Ambix*, 15 (1968), 154–208.

—'Neoplatonism and active principles: Newton and the *Corpus Hermeticum*', in Robert S. Westman and J. E. McGuire, *Hermeticism and the Scientific Revolution*. Los Angeles: University of California Press, 1977.

McMullin, Ernan. *Newton on Matter and Activity*. Notre Dame: University of Notre Dame Press, 1978.

McRae, Robert F. *The Problem of the Unity of the Sciences: Bacon to Kant*. Toronto: University of Toronto Press, 1961.

Mossner, Ernest Campbell, 'Hume's Early Memoranda, 1729–1740: the Complete Text', *Journal of the History of Ideas*, 9 (1948), 492–518.

—'Hume's Epistle to Dr. Arbuthnot, 1734: the biographical significance', *Huntington Library Quarterly*, 7 (1944), 135–52.

—*The Life of David Hume*. Edinburgh: Nelson, 1954.

Mouy, Paul. *Le Développement de la Physique Cartésienne*. Paris: Vrin, 1934.

Newton, Sir Isaac. *Opticks or a Treatise of the Reflections, Refractions, Inflections and Colours of Light*. London: G. Bell, 1931; reprinted New York: Dover, 1952.

—*Sir Isaac Newton's Mathematical Principles of Natural Philosophy and his System of the World*, translated by A. Motte (1729), revised and edited by Florian Cajori. 2 volumes. Berkeley: University of California Press, 1934; reprinted New York: Greenwood Press, 1969.

Nidditch, Peter H. *An Apparatus of Variant Readings for Hume's Treatise of Human Nature*. Sheffield: University of Sheffield, 1976.

Norton, David Fate. 'Hume and his Scottish critics', in *McGill Hume Studies*, edited by David F. Norton, Nicholas Capaldi, Wade L. Robison, pp. 309–24. San Diego: Austin Hill Press, 1979.

Noxon, James. *Hume's Philosophical Development*. Oxford: Clarendon Press, 1973.

Pap, Arthur. *Semantics and Necessary Truth: an Inquiry into the Foundations of Analytic Philosophy*. New Haven, Conn.: Yale University Press, 1958.

Pappas, George S., and Swain, Marshall (editors). *Essays on Knowledge and Justification*. Ithaca: Cornell University Press, 1978.

Passmore, John. *Hume's Intentions*, revised edition. London: Duckworth, 1968.

Pemberton, Henry. 'Introduction concerning muscular motion', in William Cowper, *Myotomia Reformata*. London: R. Knaplock *et al.*, 1724.

Penelhum, Terence. *Hume*. London: Macmillan, 1975.

—'Hume's skepticism and the *Dialogues*'. *McGill Hume Studies*, edited by David F. Norton, Nicholas Capaldi, and Wade L. Robison, pp. 253–78. San Diego: Austin Hill Press, 1976.

Popkin, Richard H. 'David Hume: his Pyrrhonism and his critique of Pyrrhonism', *Philosophical Quarterly* 1 (1951); reprinted in V. C. Chappell (editor), *Hume: a Collection of Critical Essays*, pp. 53–98. New York: Doubleday, 1966.

—'So Hume did read Berkeley', *Journal of Philosophy*, 61 (1964), 773–8.

Popper, Karl. 'A note on Berkeley as precursor of Mach and Einstein', *British Journal for the Philosophy of Science,* 4 (1953). Reprinted in *Locke and Berkeley,* edited by C. B. Martin and D. M. Armstrong. New York: Doubleday, 1968.

Porterfield, William. 'An essay concerning the motions of our eyes', *Medical Essays and Observations, revised and published by a Society in Edinburgh*, volume 3, pp. 160–263; volume 4, pp. 124–294, 2nd edition. Edinburgh: T. & W. Ruddimans, 1737.

Price, H. H. *Hume's Theory of the External World*. Oxford: Clarendon Press, 1940.

—'The permanent significance of Hume's philosophy', *Philosophy* 15 (1940), 10–36; reprinted in *Human Understanding: Studies in the Philosophy of David Hume,* edited by Alexander Sesonske and Noel Fleming, pp. 5–33. Belmont, California: Wadsworth, 1965.

Prichard, Harold A. *Knowledge and Perception*. Oxford: Clarendon Press, 1950.

Radner, Daisie. *Malebranche: a Study of a Cartesian System*. Assen: Van Gorcum, 1978.

Rather, L. J. 'Thomas Fienus' (1567–1631) dialectical investigation of the imagination as cause and cure of bodily disease', *Bulletin of the History of Medicine*, 41 (1967), 349–67.

Reichenbach, H. *The Rise of Scientific Philosophy*. Berkeley: University of California Press, 1951.

Reid, Thomas. *The Works of Thomas Reid, D.D.*, edited by Sir William Hamilton, 8th edition. 2 volumes. Edinburgh: Maclachlan & Stewart, 1880.

Rodis-Lewis, Geneviève. 'Le domaine propre de l'homme chez les Cartésiens', *Journal of the History of Philosophy,* 2 (1964), 157–88.

Rousseau, George S. 'Science and the discovery of the imagination in enlightened England', *Eighteenth Century Studies*, 3 (1969), 108–35.

Ryan, John K. 'Aquinas and Hume on the laws of association', *New Scholasticism*, 12 (1938), 366–77.

Schofield, Robert E. *Mechanism and Materialism: British Natural Philosophy in an Age of Reason.* Princeton: Princeton University Press, 1970.

Sextus Empiricus. *Outlines of Pyrrhonism,* in *Sextus Empiricus,* volume 1, translated by R. G. Bury. London: Heinemann, 1933.

Smith, Norman Kemp. *See* Kemp Smith, Norman.

Stewart, John. 'Some remarks on the laws of motion, and the inertia of matter', in *Essays and Observations, Physical and Literary,* edited by David Hume and Alexander Munro, pp. 70–140. Edinburgh: G. Hamilton & J. Balfour, 1754.

Stove, David C. *Probability and Hume's Inductive Scepticism.* Oxford: Clarendon Press, 1973.

Stroud, Barry. *Hume.* London: Routledge & Kegan Paul, 1977.

Thackray, Arnold. *Atoms and Powers.* Oxford: Clarendon Press, 1970.

—'The industrial revolution and the image of science', in *Science and Values: Patterns of Tradition and Change,* edited by Arnold Thackray and Everett Mendelsohn, pp. 3–18. New York: Humanities Press, 1974.

—and Everett Mendelsohn (editors). *Science and Values: Patterns of Tradition and Change.* New York: Humanities Press, 1974.

Theau, Jean. 'La critique de la causalité chez Malebranche et chez Hume', *Dialogue* 15 (1976), 549–64.

Toulmin, Stephen. *The Philosophy of Science: an Introduction.* London: Hutchinson, 1953.

Van Fraassen, Bastiann. *The Scientific Image.* Oxford: Clarendon Press, 1980.

Vartanian, Aram. *Diderot and Descartes: a Study of Scientific Naturalism in the Enlightenment.* Princeton: Princeton University Press, 1953.

—(editor). *La Mettrie's 'L'Homme machine': a Study in the Origins of an Idea,* with an introductory monograph. Princeton: Princeton University Press, 1960.

Watts, Isaac. *Philosophical Essays on Various Subjects.* London, 1733.

Whitehead, Alfred North. *Modes of Thought.* London: Macmillan, 1938.

Wilbanks, Jan. *Hume's Theory of Imagination.* The Hague: Nijhoff, 1968.

Wittgenstein, Ludwig. *On Certainty,* edited by G. E. M. Anscombe and G. H. von Wright, translated by Denis Paul and G. E. M. Anscombe. Oxford: Blackwell, 1969.

—*Philosophical Investigations,* translated by G. E. M. Anscombe, third edition. Oxford: Blackwell, 1968.

Wright, John P. 'Hysteria and mechanical man', *Journal of the History of Ideas,* 41 (1980), 233–47.

Yolton, John W. 'Ideas and knowledge in seventeenth-century philosophy', *Journal of the History of Philosophy,* 13 (1975), 145–65.

—*Perceptual Aquaintance from Descartes to Reid,* forthcoming.

—'Perceptual acquaintance in eighteenth-century Britain', *Journal of the History of Ideas,* 40 (1979), 207–34.

Zabeeh, Farhang. *Hume, Precursor of Modern Empiricism,* 2nd edition. The Hague: Nijhoff, 1973.

Index

abstraction 91–3, 100–2, 106, 108. *See also* distinctions: of reason

activity **163**–4, 166, **168**; of external objects in sensation 47–9, 61, 79n.11, 80n.14; and volition 48, 62, 82n.26, 163–4, **164**–7. *See also* matter; power or force

adaptation 187, 192, 210, 223, 225–6, **229**–**34**, 241n.45, 246n.82. *See also* cause(s): final

Addison, Joseph 84n.41, 207, 240n.41 & n.42

aesthetics *see* critical theory

aether 15, 145–6, 162–3, 173, 180–1n.33 & n.34, 184n.51, 190, 200. *See also* gravity

Alexander, H. G. 120n.24

Alquié, Ferdinand 83n.35, 121n.29, 235n.6, 245n.73

analysis of ideas: and knowledge **89**–**90**, 97–9, **100**; and geometry 96–100; and ontology 100–101, 105–8, 111–12, 124–5, 141–2, 144–5, 222; opposes natural and scientific belief 3–4, 97, 104, 113–14, 222; leads to Pyrrhonism 108–10, 126. *See also* conceivability; metaphysical reasoning(s); reason

Anderson, Robert F. 8n.14, 34n.10, 34n.15, 78n.7, 182n.36

Anderson, Wallace E. 179n.22

animal spirits 15–16, 104, 189, 218; smooth and easy movement of 69–71, 73, 204, 215, 218; and imagination 190, 212ff., 240n.42; evidence for 190–91, 237n.13; Cartesian theory of 190, 236n.9; and psychosomatic illness 190, 236n.10; mechanical nature of 190; excitation of 204, 216; forceful motion of 213, 219; and passions 213, 242n.48, 242n.52; and feelings 213; motions accompanying impressions and ideas 214; and repeated stimuli 215; and the causes of belief 204, 216; and formation of ideas 189, 219–20; in Malebranche 236n.9; in Mandeville 236n.10. *See also* psychophysiology

appearance(s) 41–2, 60, 66, 71–3; as basis for axioms of geometry 96–7. *See also* phenomenalism

Aquinas, St Thomas 194, 238n.17

Arbuthnot, John 5, 9n.24, 237n.10

Aristotle 238n.17

Armstrong, David M. 78n.5

Arnauld, Antoine 28, 30, 36n.30, 79n.10, 93. *See also* Port-Royal Logic

association of ideas 128, 198, 209–10, 244n.59; mechanical model of 16, **68**–**70**, 83n.41, 182n.41, 195, 200, 204–6, 218–19, 244n.59; productive principles of 24, 25, 68–70, 194, **203**, 206, 208, 216–18, 221, 226–8; and notion of self-identity 71; relation to passions and feelings 195, 200, **203**–**10**, 216–17; and criticism 207; original vs. acquired 227–9. *See also* relation(s): natural

association of impressions 203

atheism: Stratonician 168–71; kinds of 185n.60

atoms 93–4, 179n.23. *See also* divisibility

222; sense of, given through feeling 211, 213–15; natural judgement of 217; system of 217

reason, or comparison of ideas 6, 29, 245n.78; and scepticism 4, 7, 28–30, 124–6, 135–50, **150**, **153–5**, **161**, 246n.78; and morality 5; standards of 10, 21; in experimental philosophy 13, 26–7, 58, 202; limits of 19, 21–3, 29, 144; and belief in external existence 19, 40, 48–59; corrects natural principles 39, **155**, 210, **230**, 246n.78; and correspondence 35n.25; and knowledge **89**; opposed to belief in empty space 104; opposed to senses 110; and distinctions of ideas **136–7**, 140–1, 150, 161, 178n.17; opposed to instinctive belief 153, 245n.78; subservient to the passions 209; cannot undermine natural belief 219; as foundation for civil society 231, 246n.82. *See also* analysis of ideas; metaphysical reasoning(s); reflection

reasoning(s), natural 22, 66, 79n.10, 83n.32, 106, 125, 154, 225, 229–30. *See also* imagination; natural judgement(s); relations, natural

reasoning(s), pathological 154, 182n.39, 227–8, **229**, 245n.75

reflection 13, 18–19, 27, 193, 231

Reichenbach, H. 118n.15

Reid, Thomas 8n.15, **9n.18**, 80n.16, 81n.20, 182n.35, 199–200, 239n.31 & n.35, 245n.77 & n.78

relation(s): natural 74, 182n.38, 187, **203–6**, 208, **216–17**, 223, 226–8, 232, 239n.37, 274 (*see also* association of ideas); of ideas 88–9, 115, 127 (*see also* analysis of ideas; reason); philosophical **25**, 35n.25, **56**, **91**, 115, 126, 130, 182n.38

relativism 20–1

representation: and resemblance 57, 109; and adequacy of ideas 88, 92–3, 98, 113; and knowledge **88–9**; representative or objective reality 91–2, 105–6; Hume's conception of, contrasted with Arnauld's 79n.10; proportional, of parts of extension 96; and truth 115. *See also* ideas; indirect or representative realism

resemblance: and representation 57, 81n.19, 109; of distinct perceptions

64–6; of actions of the mind 69; and confusions of ideas 68, 70

Rodis-Lewis, Geneviève 244n.66, 245n.73

Rousseau, G. S. 234n.3

rules for the determination of causes 13, 25, **26–7**, 35n.29, 161, 181n.33

Ryan, J. K. 238n.17

scepticism, in Hume's philosophy: and the theory of ideas 4, 9n.18, 31; and justification 11–**19**, **39**, **75**; and knowledge 17, **19**, 31, **88**; and truth 20–7; and belief 27–30, 36n.31, 88; and reason 28–30; and Descartes' first Meditation 28–9, 36n.33, 41; and Berkeley's 'scepticism' 29, 88, 109–10; philosophical 29–30, **32**, **38–9**; and the foundations of science 31–2; with regard to the senses 34–84; dependence on Cartesian maxim of metaphysics 98; 'modest scepticism' 103. *See also next entries*

scepticism, mitigated (Academical philosophy): and inadequacy of ideas 4, 126, 144–5; double aspect, explained **126**, 155; and natural instinct 126–7, 151; cure for Pyrrhonian doubt 126–7, 135; and causality **144–5**, **155**

scepticism, objective: explained **89–90**, **106**; contrasted with material (existential) scepticism 90; of Sextus Empiricus 90; and inadequacy of ideas 105; concerning space and time 105–6; source of 105, 107; and irregular reasoning 106–7; and 'modern' philosophy 111–12; an aspect of mitigated scepticism 126; concerning causality 143–4; and Cartesianism 143–5

scepticism or doubt, Pyrrhonian 124; and Hume's philosophy **8n.12**, 28, 36n.31 & n.34; and analysis of ideas 1–2, **126–7**, 174–5; a state of mind 27–8; Bayle on 28, 36n.32; and reason 28–30; of external existence 28, 75; and 'modest scepticism' 103; as balance between reason and natural instinct 104; cured by mitigated scepticism 123, **126**, **135**, 151; causal, based on the senses 128–34; and Hume's principle of idea derivation **133–4**